Anna Jones

The Modern Cook's Year

Over 250 vibrant vegetable recipes
to see you through the seasons

Photographs by Ana Cuba

4th Estate | London

For Mum and Dad
Your kindness and love are limitless.
Parents and humans don't come better.

And in memory of Laura Plane,
a shining beacon to how life should be lived.
Your unstoppable kindness, grace and sense
of fun sparkle on.

4th Estate
An imprint of HarperCollinsPublishers
1 London Bridge Street
London SE1 9GF
www.4thEstate.co.uk

First published in Great Britain in 2017 by 4th Estate

1

Copyright text © Anna Jones 2017

Copyright photography © Ana Cuba 2017

Design by Jonathan Pelham

Art direction by Rachel Vere

Anna Jones asserts the moral right to be identified as the author
of this work in accordance with the Copyright, Designs and
Patents Act 1988

A catalogue record for this book is available from the
British Library

ISBN 978-0-00-817245-9

MIX
Paper from
responsible sources
FSC
www.fsc.org
FSC™ C007454

This book is produced from independently certified FSC™ paper
to ensure responsible forest management.

For more information visit: www.harpercollins.co.uk/green

Typeset by GS Typesetting
Printed and bound in Germany by Mohn Media Mohndruck GMBH

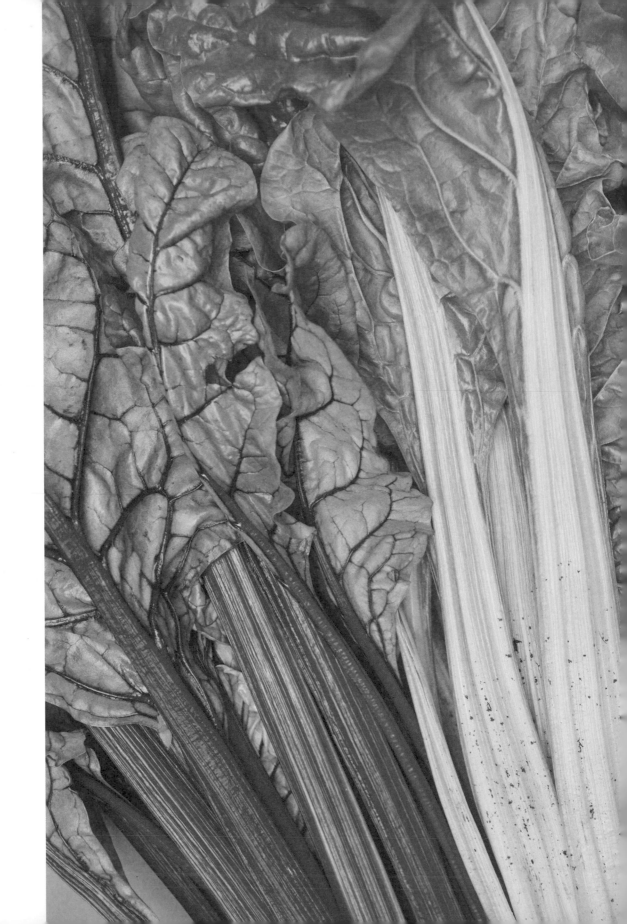

Introduction

There is something so joyful about eating food at its very best. Damsons as the nights draw in, apricots when the nights are at their longest, watermelon on a searing hot day, squash at Halloween. It is about an ingredient at its peak, the apex of its flavour, but more than that it's about a time, a place and the memories of summers, Christmases and days past that are wrapped up in every bite of food we eat.

In London, where I live, the ebb and flow of the year is so apparent, the seasons come and go with force and how we eat changes dramatically. As a young chef, learning to cook with the seasons was truly the most miraculous discovery. Every Saturday would start with strong coffee alongside almost every London chef at Borough market. Then I'd walk over to Tony Booth's veg stall, smell peaches, squeeze tomatoes, bite sharp little apples. It reconnected me with nature, with what was growing.

For me a year divided into four seasons feels too vague. Anyone who has stepped into a greengrocer on the winter side of spring and then again at the summer end will tell you that the two are very different. There are so many more subtleties to what's growing than spring, summer, autumn and winter. It's this rhythm, this relationship with nature, which I encourage you to foster. No June is the same, wild garlic will fill the hedgerows up at different times each year, the French apricots will arrive a few weeks later. The seasons are a useful tool but our eyes and taste buds should be our guide. This book is written in six chapters, which roughly knit together two months at a time, but let your senses, and the fruits and vegetables you find at your market, lead you. As each year comes and goes I am led to cook dishes at slightly different times and find the very best day for an ingredient does vary. With this in mind I encourage you not to think too rigidly about the seasons and the chapters of this book, use the produce on your doorstep to make the food that you feel like eating. If that's macaroni cheese in July, so be it. The pages of this book are intended as a guide; you are the cook and the eater.

As much as the ripeness and readiness of an ingredient, and how it is cooked are important, the feeling at a certain time of year can inform how I cook too. A cool green salad eaten outside with little fuss suits the hot impatience of summer, a bowl of soup eaten with a spoon from a cushion balanced on a lap is homely, comforting and grounding like autumn. A just warm salad of freshly podded peas, broad beans and the first asparagus, echoes the promise, the smell of new-mown grass, the verdant green of spring. It's my desire as a cook to feel and allow others to share these emotions, to punctuate the year with the memorable meals I have loved again and again, to nourish those I love with more than the flavour of food.

With that in mind I have included milestones and things I do at different times of year here too, from antique shopping at Christmas to resetting my culinary clock in spring. I hope they help to weave a picture of the year.

The techniques I lean on in the kitchen change too as the year unfolds. In winter my heavy cast-iron pots never leave the hob, always full of soup, or a vegetable braise. In spring vegetables which are tender and fresh need only a lick of heat from a hot frying pan. In summer, I use my mandoline most, to finely slice fennel and courgettes, for grilling and for raw salads. The dishes, the way I cook and the time I want to spend doing it change as dramatically as the contents of my fruit bowl and fridge.

While summer cooking tends to be the quickest I am somewhat of an impatient cook all year round. There are odd days when I linger in the kitchen but most often I cook dinner for the three of us in under an hour and those are the kind of recipes you will find in this book. A few use quite a few ingredients, for layering flavour and texture, which I feel is such an important part of cooking vegetables. I work with a palette of ingredients throughout the recipes in this book, so I hope that if you do invest in something new you will find lots of ideas for cooking with it in these pages.

Eating with the seasons naturally leads us to putting vegetables at the centre of our tables. This is how I eat every day and increasingly how many of us are eating. In the five years since I started writing my first book, the food landscape of how we eat has changed dramatically for the better. Vegetable-focused meals a few nights a week have become the norm for many and for that I am deeply grateful. We have damaged this planet, there have been decades of misuse and eating mostly vegetables, and shopping and eating in season and locally, are huge personal steps we can take in a better direction.

I have wherever possible tried to include vegan alternatives in lots of recipes; my brother and sister are both vegan so I cook this way often. For me it's also important not to rely too heavily on dairy and eggs; while I do include good organic versions in my diet, I make sure a few meals each week are completely egg- and dairy- free, helping further reduce our load on the world around us.

The UK is a small country so when I think about seasonal eating I include Amalfi lemons, apricots from Provence, rice from Puglia. While I shop as locally as possible and my focus is on British produce, where I need to I lean on our European friends and their incredible offerings. Never has it been more important to foster the links that food creates, the trade it encourages and the barriers it breaks down.

A note on shopping

I long for a vegetable garden and to grow what I eat, but that's not the reality just now; I shop for all my food (with the exception of a little foraging). The bulk of what I buy is from local shops and our excellent farmers' market, topped up with the odd supermarket delivery for bulky things and dry goods.

My weekly trip to the market is my connection with nature, with food at its source. Seeing the first courgettes appear or the array of apples in autumn is my connection with the earth. Of course, I walk in the parks and trees and escape to the sea often but in the city it's this trip that connects me with nature, with a place in time. I don't need to be told when asparagus is in season any more; having cooked for years I know when it will arrive but I still go, I still walk the stalls, even if there is very little to buy and even if my fridge is full. It grounds me, reminds me of the wonder of food and the weeks I can't make it I miss it.

I know the reality for many is that their shopping is done at a supermarket or online, and for a few months when my son was small so was mine (and our local shops are less than a five-minute walk away). Supermarkets are getting better at stocking and championing seasonal, local produce so it is absolutely possible to eat seasonally and shop at supermarkets. If you aren't in tune with the season then perhaps remind yourself of what's growing and good to eat now before you shop, look at labels, buy local food if you can. Even if sometimes it does cost a little more it will without doubt taste superior. The more we buy ethical, local and seasonal produce from our supermarkets the more they will stock, so with each purchase you are making a change.

Start of the year

Best of the season
    Kale
    Leeks
    Swede
    Purple sprouting broccoli
    Savoy cabbage
    Brussels sprouts
    Winter tomatoes
    Cavolo nero
    Radicchio
    Winter citrus
    Pomegranate
    Forced pink rhubarb

Flowers
    Mimosa
    Hellebores
    Magnolia
    Anemone

Grapefruit with honey and coriander seed toasted oats

I eat fruit for breakfast every day but at the start of the year I find my fruit bowl a little empty. We eat pears, apples, pomegranates and, when they arrive, blood oranges, but it's not the offering of spring or summer and I get a bit bored. That's when I turn back to grapefruit. I ate them growing up, an inch of sugar as a roof, with a special serrated spoon to scoop out each segment. This is now a breakfast we eat on repeat. It feels grown-up and delicate but requires little more than a few minutes at the stove.

Coriander seeds find their way into as many sweet things as savoury in my kitchen these days, their lemony character a perfect pep to a bright bit of winter citrus. This is as good at the end of a meal as for breakfast.

Peel and segment or slice your grapefruit, taking care to get rid of any big bits of bitter pith. If you have any pieces of grapefruit peel with juicy flesh attached, keep them to use in the syrup. Bash the coriander seeds in a pestle and mortar until they have broken down a little and smell fragrant.

Put a small pan on a medium heat, add the coriander seeds and toast them for a minute until they smell toasty and more fragrant. Take the pan off the heat and add 2 tablespoons of cold water and the honey then squeeze in the juice from any of the bits of grapefruit you have saved. Put the pan back on the heat and simmer for a minute or so until the liquid all bubbles down into a thick syrup.

In another pan melt the butter until it's foamy, then add the oats and toast, stirring them all the time until they are buttery brown and smelling great. Add the vanilla paste and stir for another minute or so.

Put the grapefruit slices on to two plates, pour over the warm syrup and top with the yoghurt and oats and a little more honey if you like things sweet.

SERVES 2

2 grapefruit

½ teaspoon coriander seeds

2 tablespoons honey or agave nectar, plus more to finish

1 teaspoon butter

4 tablespoons rolled oats

1 teaspoon vanilla paste

100g yoghurt (I use coconut yoghurt)

Saffron breakfast kheer

Kheer is an Indian rice pudding eaten on high days and at feasts. It is a calming mix of gentle spice, milk and rice, which I find especially good to eat at breakfast time. There is nothing more nourishing to my mind than milk and rice together – easy to eat and cleansing in the best possible sense of the word. We make a double batch of this and reheat it with a little extra milk on the following days; sometimes it's dessert too. *Kheer* is used in the Ayurvedic tradition to balance the system during the winter; the sweet cinnamon helps digestion and the warmth of the rice and milk protects against any wintery cold.

I use brown rice here but white rice would be just as delicious. I suggest soaking the rice overnight – it is a 2-minute job and will vastly speed up the cooking process. If you don't remember to do it overnight, then soaking it as long as you have will be okay. If saffron is a bridge too far for breakfast, then you can just leave it out, the other spices will hold up.

SERVES 4

150g long-grain brown rice

100g cashew nuts

50g blanched almonds

1 litre almond milk (I use unsweetened)

6 cardamom pods

100g raisins (I use golden ones)

¼ teaspoon ground ginger

a pinch of saffron threads, soaked in 50ml boiling water

1 small cinnamon stick

2 tablespoons runny honey

TO SERVE

the zest of 1 unwaxed lime

a small handful of toasted coconut flakes

Soak the rice in one bowl and the cashews and almonds in another in cold water for at least 30 minutes but ideally overnight.

In the morning drain the rice and put it into a saucepan with the milk and 500ml of cold water and bring to a simmer. Cook for 20 minutes at a gentle bubble until the rice has puffed up and the liquid is beginning to thicken.

Meanwhile drain the nuts and finely chop them – you can do this in a food processor if you like. Bash the cardamom pods using a pestle and mortar and remove the fragrant seeds, then discard the pods and grind the seeds until you have a powder.

After 20 minutes add the nuts, raisins, spices and honey to the rice and cook for another 15 minutes until thick and creamy, somewhere between rice pudding and porridge. You want to reach the sweet spot where the rice is soft, with very little bite, and the kheer is creamy but not too thick. If it looks like it is thickening too fast, turn the heat down and top up with a little boiling water from the kettle. Serve spooned into bowls with the lime zest and coconut flakes on top; if you have a sweet tooth you could add a little extra honey on top.

Baked apple porridge with maple butter

The snap of cold that comes at the start of the year is perfect porridge weather. I've never understood those who eat it like clockwork, regardless of the temperature. I love the warmth of it on a cold day, a bowl in my hands like a morning hot-water bottle, the quick but nourishing time spent stirring at the stove a welcome interruption to the busy rush of the morning and a few minutes to let my mind wander at the start of the day.

This porridge is a bit different in that it is baked so the edges crisp and the starry apple slices on top soften and burnish. I top it with a maple cream so good it's hard not to spoon it all straight from the dish before the porridge is ready. It takes a little longer to make than a regular porridge – it's a weekend one.

I make it to feed a crowd, or on a Sunday with intentional leftovers so that I know we have a good breakfast in the fridge to start the week. This keeps well in the fridge for a few days and any extra can be reheated with a little extra milk in a small pan. I make a big batch of spice mix, which I keep in a jar and add to my stovetop porridge through the week too, hence this making more than you'll need for the baked porridge, but if you prefer you could add a pinch of each spice to the recipe rather than making a large batch. I make this without dairy, using almond milk and coconut oil, as that's how I like to eat it, but regular milk and butter work just as well.

SERVES 6

FOR THE SPICE MIX

2 tablespoons ground cardamom

2 tablespoons ground ginger

½ teaspoon ground nutmeg

½ teaspoon ground cloves

½ teaspoon ground cinnamon

coconut oil or butter

3 large apples

1 unwaxed lemon

200g rolled oats

1½ teaspoons baking powder

¼ teaspoon fine sea salt

100g nuts, toasted and chopped (I use pecans and hazelnuts)

750ml almond milk

125ml pure maple syrup, plus extra for drizzling

FOR THE MAPLE CREAM

2 tablespoons nut butter (I use cashew)

2 tablespoons maple syrup

4 tablespoons almond milk

a tiny pinch of fine sea salt

a drop of vanilla extract or paste

Make the spice mix first by stirring the spices together in a small jar, then set aside.

Preheat the oven to 210°C/190°C fan/gas 6. Grease a deep ovenproof dish, about 20 x 20cm, with coconut oil.

Grate two of the apples. Turn the last apple on to its side and slice it very thinly, so that you get a lovely star pattern. Grate the zest from half the lemon to use later, then cut the lemon in half and squeeze the juice from one half over the sliced apple to stop it browning. →

In a large bowl, combine the oats, baking powder, salt, 1 teaspoon of the spice mix, the grated apple and most of the chopped nuts (saving a small handful for the topping). Stir to combine. In a jug or separate bowl, mix the milk with the maple syrup, the juice of the remaining half lemon and the reserved zest.

Tip the oat and apple mixture into the greased dish, pour over the milk and maple syrup mixture, arrange the sliced apples on top and drizzle over a little maple syrup. Dot the top of the oats with little pieces of coconut oil or butter. Bake for 25–30 minutes, or until the top of the porridge is golden brown and all the liquid has been absorbed.

While the porridge bakes, make the maple cream. In a medium bowl, whisk together the nut butter, maple syrup, milk, salt and vanilla. You are looking for something totally smooth and pourable. If the mixture seems too thick, add a little more milk.

Serve the baked porridge hot, spooned into bowls with the maple cream for pouring over.

Lentils on toast

We all, even chefs and cooks, sometimes sit down to a dinner of beans on toast. I am sure the childhood comfort of it is as nourishing as the actual food on the plate. These yoghurt-spiked lentils are something I have taken to making as an alternative to beans when we want something quick without a trip to the shops, but that feels a bit more put together. The lentils are warming and filling and have a depth of flavour which would make you think they'd taken much longer than five minutes.

This recipe is intended to be made from fridge and store-cupboard staples, so the herbs are optional – if you have some in the fridge or on the window sill all the better. The same goes for the cheese; I always have a piece of Parmesan in the top of my fridge, but pretty much any hard cheese would work here.

First, toast your nuts in in a dry pan over a medium heat until they smell toasty and are beginning to brown. Once toasted, tumble them into a bowl and when they are cool enough to handle, chop or crumble them.

Meanwhile, put the pan back on a medium heat and add a good glug of oil and the garlic. Sizzle until the edges of the garlic are beginning to brown, then add the lentils and their liquid (if you are using home-cooked lentils you'll need about 150ml of their cooking liquid) along with the vinegar and honey. Cook for about 5 minutes until all the liquid has been absorbed.

Now add a pinch of salt and a good grind of pepper to the lentils along with a good drizzle of olive oil. Taste and add more salt, honey, pepper or vinegar if needed. Once they taste great, take them off the heat and stir in the yoghurt.

Drizzle olive oil over hot toast and serve the lentils piled on top with the herbs, nuts and a good grating of cheese. Any leftover lentils can be eaten hot or cold and will keep for 3–4 days in the fridge.

SERVES 2

50g nuts (I like walnuts or almonds)

olive oil

1 clove of garlic, thinly sliced

1 x 400g tin of green lentils (or 250g home-cooked, see page 461)

1 tablespoon red wine vinegar

a squeeze of runny honey

4 tablespoons thick Greek yoghurt

TO SERVE

a few slices of good toast

a small bunch of soft herbs (basil, parsley, dill, tarragon), leaves picked and roughly chopped

a little grated cheese (I use a vegetarian one)

Cooking with grace

I have spent time in ashrams and been to more yoga classes than I can remember. When I was pregnant I became really interested in the power of the mind and hypnotherapy. All of these things – meditation, yoga and positive thinking – are tools I use in my life to make it happier and better. And the more I have delved into how to keep my life as happy, free of stress and joyful as possible the more I know that my kitchen is where I find my calm space. Not every night. Some nights I clatter around, throwing things in a pan with very little grace, and the end result, while usually edible, is never repeated. But I know that the kitchen can be a transformative place, and that goes for anyone – you don't need to consider yourself a cook.

When I centre myself and take in every little nuance of what's going on, cooking becomes my solace, my meditation. Whether it's the pleasing glide of my favourite potato peeler, taking in the intoxicating perfume of a bunch of mint or basil, or the searing splattering of juice that sprays up when I cut into a lemon, noticing these moments connects me with my food and reminds me of the wonder of where it has come from. Cooking is an offering: to me, to my body and to those I love – the people I cook for. And it is healing, not just through the nourishment it provides but in the very act and process of doing something physical and practical. It calms my mind and allows me to focus on just one thing.

A big part of this grounding, nourishing practice has been lost in cooking. Sure, we all know that making a loaf of bread, or jarring up some jam from heavy-laden fruit trees will give us a deep sense of satisfaction. But I think that our everyday cooking can be as much an act of meditation, escape and dare I say it,

mindfulness. This may be nothing new, and it is by no means groundbreaking information but if, like me, you tend to get caught up in the day-to-day of life let this be my encouragement to you to remember that even the simplest of tasks in the kitchen can be something to embrace and delight in.

I truly believe that when we cook the emotions, thoughts and feelings of the cook get translated into the food. That may sound a little far out, but having cooked thousands of dishes, I know that when I'm paying close attention to what I am doing, giving each task and ingredient the reverence it deserves, the food tastes infinitely better. Equally sometimes I throw everything in a pan with a million other things going on as that's all I can manage, and when I do I don't give myself a hard time.

For me, focusing on how I cook means turning off other things like TV or music, following each task with dedication, taking as much care as I have time to do. To appreciate and even, if I don't sound like too much of a hippy, marvel at my ingredients, our natural treasures. Make sure you take time to smell, taste and immerse yourself in the amazing process of cooking, and then finish it by putting the food on each plate with care if you can. When I cook like this I find it soothing, rewarding and everything I cook tastes better.

Our state of mind as we eat has a huge effect on how we digest our food and how we take in the nutrients and energy from it. Stress and anxiety around food and eating is something I try to avoid in my recipes and in my kitchen. I truly believe that a pizza and a beer enjoyed in good spirits, slowly and calmly with friends, can be as nourishing as endless green smoothies, which are inhaled on the run or sipped while reading emails at our desks with no real thought about the true meaning of nourishment. We've lost the connection with how we eat our food, the emotions going on around eating and the sense of offering that comes with feeding ourselves. I don't manage it every time I eat but a couple of seconds to slow down and be thankful for the food on my plate before diving in seems to set a good tone for the meal and often allows me to appreciate the flavours, textures and sensations a little more.

A few observations on cooking and eating mindfully and with grace

— Turn off music, radio and phones, if you can, so that you can focus on all the sensations of cooking.

— Try to notice the little things – the colour change in the skin of a peach, the tiny pores on the skin of an orange, the condensation on the lid of a pan.

— Notice the sounds – the sizzle of frying, the bubbling of a pot. These tell you as much about what you are cooking and where you are in the process as anything you can see.

— Follow the process with all your senses, smell the changes as ingredients are added, feel how a mixture firms up as you stir it, notice the change in colour as you fry or blanch. And notice how you feel, whether ingredients or smells bring up memories or emotions.

— Try and keep your attention totally focused on your food and if your mind wanders, don't worry, just bring it back to the food.

— Tune in to even the most mundane parts of the job – peeling carrots, picking herbs – immersing yourself totally in the detail of each task will allow you to switch off from other pressures.

Broken eggs with cavolo nero, ricotta and chickpeas

Broken eggs are somewhere between scrambled and poached eggs. They cook gently in the pan with a couple of turns of the spoon, then finish their cooking at the table. A heavy or cast-iron frying pan is great here, as it holds on to the heat better.

I first ate eggs like this at Raw Duck, a favourite breakfast spot near where I live. Cooking eggs this way means the last bit of cooking is controlled at the table, which means no overcooked, rubbery eggs, and that you can spoon them out when they are cooked just as you like, leaving some in the pan for people who like their eggs less runny.

You can use kale or any greens you have, and any other beans would work in place of the chickpeas – if they are home-cooked so much the better. A scattering of toasted almonds or hazelnuts or even dukkah would be welcome here too.

SERVES 4

1 head of cavolo nero (about 300g)

olive oil

1 x 400g tin of chickpeas, drained (or about 250g home-cooked – see page 461)

1 clove of garlic, thinly sliced

1 red chilli, finely chopped

the juice of 1 unwaxed lemon and the zest from half

a good grating of nutmeg

6 medium organic eggs

4 rounds of toast or toasted flatbreads, to serve

100g ricotta or thick Greek yoghurt

Strip the leaves from the cavolo nero, shredding any larger ones. Finely chop the stalks, discarding any really thick sinewy ones.

Heat a heavy, ideally cast-iron, medium frying pan (about 28cm) on a medium heat. Add a little olive oil, then the chickpeas, cook for a couple of minutes to crisp a little, then add the chopped cavolo nero stalks, garlic and chilli. Cook for another few minutes until the stalks are tender and the garlic has started to brown, then add the leaves. Add the lemon juice, zest, a good pinch of salt and pepper and the nutmeg, then cook for 4–5 minutes until the cavolo nero leaves have softened.

Next break each egg into a bowl and get your flatbreads or toast ready. Spoon the ricotta into the pan, dotting it around, then pour the eggs one by one gently on top of the cavolo nero mixture. Keep the pan on the heat and gently stir the eggs a couple of times, just to break them a little. You want the whites and yolks to stay separate, not to mix them together as you would with scrambled eggs. Quickly take the pan off the heat and carry it to the table along with a wooden spoon; the residual heat of the pan will continue to cook the eggs. Use the wooden spoon and continue to stir until the eggs are set to your liking, I like mine to be soft and curdy. Serve right away with charred flatbreads or hot toast.

Twice-baked potato skins with crispy buffalo chickpeas

These double-baked potato skins bring back childhood memories of American diners but, rather than the inch-deep cheese, these are piled high with spicy baked chickpeas, which pick up a pleasing crunch in the oven, and a grown-up 'sour cream' dip. I make the dip using cashews, which I blitz to a cream, but you can use yoghurt instead of the cashews if you'd prefer. I serve these with a salad for dinner but they would be great as a party snack if you used smaller potatoes. Kids love them if you go easy on the spice.

Preheat the oven to 200°C/180°C fan/gas 6. Set up two oven racks in the middle of the oven. Wash and dry the potatoes, prick with a fork and rub with a little olive oil, then sprinkle over some salt and rub in with your hands. Place the potatoes directly on the top oven rack. Bake them until they feel tender and the skin is crisp, about 1–1½ hours.

While the potatoes are baking, get on with the chickpeas. Heat a pan on a medium heat. Pour in a little olive oil, add the onion and cook for 10 minutes, until soft, then add the celery, paprika, cumin and garlic and cook for another 10–15 minutes until soft and sticky.

Add the chickpeas, passata and chilli and stir again. Season with a little salt and pepper and cook for another 10 minutes, until the passata has thickened and it has all come together nicely. While the chickpeas are cooking, make the dip. If you are using the cashews, drain them and put them into a blender with 5 tablespoons of cold water and blitz until very smooth, then mix with the other ingredients. If using yoghurt, simply mix everything together.

Once the potatoes are baked and cool enough for you to handle them, cut them in half lengthwise. Lay the halves on a baking tray. Scoop out a couple of tablespoons of potato from each half, season the inside of the potato with salt and drizzle with olive oil.

Save the scooped out potato for another meal. Divide the chickpeas between the potatoes and bake in the oven for another 10 minutes so that the chickpeas crisp a little. Serve each potato topped with the parsley and celery leaves and the dip.

SERVES 4

- 4 medium baking potatoes
- olive oil
- 1 red onion, finely chopped
- 1 stick of celery, finely chopped (reserving the inner leaves)
- 1 teaspoon smoked sweet paprika
- 1 teaspoon cumin seeds
- 1 clove of garlic, finely chopped
- 2 x 400g tins of chickpeas or other white beans, drained (or 500g home-cooked chickpeas, see page 461)
- 200ml passata or blitzed tinned tomatoes
- a pinch of dried chilli flakes (I use a generous pinch of a mild Turkish variety called pul biber)
- a small bunch of flat-leaf parsley, leaves picked

FOR THE DIP

- 100g cashew nuts, soaked in cold water for about an hour or 150ml thick Greek yoghurt
- the zest and juice of 1 unwaxed lemon
- a small bunch of chives, chopped

Caper, herb and egg flatbreads

This recipe is really quick to make and is one of the most flavourful fast lunches I know. Corn tortillas crisped and filled with egg, herbs and some punch from capers and cornichons; it's a recipe that crosses continents, but that's often how I cook. It's as quick as making a sandwich, and while we eat this all year round it's something I make most often in the winter, when I want food from the stovetop and warmth. It is loosely based on a much-cooked recipe from my friend Heidi Swanson.

This recipe serves two as a lunch or light dinner, but scale it up as you need. For the herbs I use dill and basil, but mint, tarragon, parsley and chives would all work too. I buy large corn tortillas online from a good Mexican supplier (the Cool Chile company: coolchile. co.uk); the standard ones in the shops just aren't the same. Flour tortillas will work well here too.

First, in a bowl mix the yoghurt with the grated zest and juice of half the lemon, a pinch of sea salt and a good grind of black pepper.

Cut the avocados into quarters and remove the stones, then cut each one down to the skin in thin slices. Squeeze over the juice from the remaining lemon half and set aside. Beat the eggs in a little cup with a pinch of salt.

It's best to cook the tortillas one by one. Heat a frying pan big enough to fit your tortilla over a medium heat. Add a tiny splash of olive oil, then add half the egg and let it set into a kind of pancake for 10–15 seconds. Working quickly, place a tortilla on top of the egg; you want the egg still to be a bit runny so that it will attach itself to the tortilla as it sets. When the egg has set, use a spatula to turn the whole thing over, sprinkle over half the herbs, half the capers and cornichons and half the cheese. Cook until the cheese has melted. Repeat this process for the second tortilla.

To serve, fold the tortillas in half and top with the yoghurt and slices of the avocado. To make a meal of them, serve with a little lemon-dressed green salad.

SERVES 2 AS A LIGHT MEAL

- 200g thick Greek yoghurt
- 1 unwaxed lemon
- 2 avocados
- 2 organic eggs
- olive oil
- 2 medium corn or flour tortillas or wraps (about 12cm)
- a few sprigs of soft herbs (see note above), chopped
- 2 tablespoons small capers
- a few cornichons, roughly chopped
- 25g freshly grated Parmesan (I use a vegetarian one)

Beetroot and mustard seed fritters with cardamom yoghurt

This time of year gets a tough write-up; grey, dark and rainy, and yes, sometimes it is. But my kitchen is filled with arguably the most colourful produce of the year: blood oranges, pink radicchio and creamy Castelfranco, splattered with pink like a Jackson Pollock painting. There is so much deep red, orange, pink and scarlet.

Beetroots too, in all their colours: neon yellow, bright burnt orange, candy-cane stripes and of course the deep magenta of the red beets. You can use any beetroot you like for these spiced fritters; I often make them with ready-cooked ones.

Vegans can add some extra flour and a tablespoon of chia seeds mixed with 3 tablespoons of water in place of the egg, and use coconut yoghurt.

SERVES 4

1 x 400g tin or jar of chickpeas, drained (or 250g home-cooked, see page 461)

coconut or groundnut oil

2 teaspoons mustard seeds

2 teaspoons cumin seeds

250g cooked beetroot, peeled

2 tablespoons chopped coriander

2 spring onions, chopped

the zest and juice of ½ an unwaxed lemon

1 organic egg

FOR THE YOGHURT SAUCE

2 cardamom pods

150g thick Greek yoghurt

the zest and juice of ½ an unwaxed lemon

TO SERVE (OPTIONAL)

chapatis or flatbreads

a few handfuls of green salad leaves

First, put two thirds of the chickpeas into a food processor and pulse until you have a rough paste, Roughly squash the remainder with a fork so they break into smaller pieces.

Next, make the yoghurt sauce. Bash the cardamom pods to remove the seeds, then lightly toast the seeds in a dry frying pan over a medium heat. Grind in a pestle and mortar until you have a fine powder. Transfer this to a bowl, add the yoghurt, lemon zest and juice and a good pinch of salt to taste. Stir well and put to one side.

Put the frying pan back on the heat, add a splash of oil, then add the mustard and cumin seeds. When the mustard seeds begin to pop and start to smell more fragrant, tip them into a mixing bowl.

Grate the beetroot using a coarse grater, then squeeze the beetroot to remove excess liquid and transfer to a mixing bowl with the seeds. Add the other fritter ingredients, season with salt and pepper and mix well. Using the palms of your hands, take heaped tablespoons of the mixture and shape into small fritters (about 12). Put a little oil into a large frying pan and place it on a medium heat. Fry some of the fritters for 2–3 minutes on each side, until golden brown. Transfer to a plate lined with kitchen paper and repeat with the rest.

Serve warm with the cardamom yoghurt, some green leaves and chapatis or flatbreads.

Gentle potato chowder with toasted chilli oil

This soup is like yin and yang: a very gentle, warming potato chowder, cooked in milk, with lentils for sustenance, that I top with a searing chilli and toasted almond oil. The oil sits on top of the white soup like lava, a serious punch of toasty fire. It's one of the most comforting soups and warms you right down to your toes.

I use ancho chilli flakes. Ancho is a lot milder and has a more rounded, complex, dried fruit flavour than the supermarket dried chilli flakes, which can just add heat, so if you are using those I would suggest a teaspoon, unless you like things very hot. The chilli oil makes more oil than you need but keeps for months. It can be made in the time it takes to simmer the soup, but shop-bought chilli oil will stand in.

SERVES 4

25g unsalted butter or 2 tablespoons coconut oil

2 leeks, washed, trimmed and cut into 1cm-thick rounds

2 tablespoons flour (I use spelt)

1 tablespoon vegetable stock powder or 1 stock cube

800g floury potatoes, peeled and cut into rough chunks

300ml whole milk or soy milk

1 x 400g tin of green lentils, drained (or 250g home-cooked, see page 461)

FOR THE CHILLI OIL

2 red chillies

1 teaspoon to 1 tablespoon dried chilli flakes (see note above)

2 cloves of garlic

1 heaped tablespoon almonds

200ml mild-flavoured oil (light olive or rapeseed)

Fill and boil a kettle. In a medium-large pot, melt the butter over a medium heat. Add the leeks with a pinch of salt, lower the heat and cook, stirring occasionally, until they are soft and sweet; this should take about 10 minutes.

Stir in the flour and allow to cook for another minute or so to get rid of the raw flour flavour. Gradually add 600ml of hot water from the kettle, a bit at a time, then add the stock powder or cube. Add the potatoes and bring the mixture to a simmer. Cook until the potatoes are cooked through, which should take about 25 minutes, making sure you stir the soup from time to time to stop it sticking.

Meanwhile, make the chilli oil. Put the fresh and dried chilli and garlic into a food processor and pulse until fine, then add the almonds, a good pinch of salt and a generous amount of black pepper. Pulse again, put the lot into a small saucepan with the oil and cook slowly for 10 minutes or so, until everything is toasted and golden, then remove from the heat and set aside. The oil can be used warm (not hot) on your soup. The leftovers should be left to cool completely, then stored in a jar in the fridge for up to 3 months.

Back to the soup. Add the milk to the pot, stir in the lentils, and heat until the milk is just simmering. Serve the soup ladled into deep bowls, topped with a slick of the chilli oil.

Kimchi and miso noodle soup

I make kimchi purely so that I can make this soup. It is clean-tasting and enlivening, nicely sharp with spice and the mellow vinegary punch of the kimchi. I don't care much for kimchi on its own (John eats it by the jar), but I do think that it is an incredible ingredient to use as a flavourful base for stews, in dressings, and in wraps and sandwiches. The amount of kimchi that you use is quite dependent on how strong it is. My home-made one (on page 68) is quite mellow but shop-bought ones can be much more potent, so taste it first and use your tastebuds as a guide, adding more if you need.

I cook with miso a lot and it happens to be really good for you too. I learned recently that if you heat it too much it loses a lot of its goodness, so now, when I can, I mix it with a little of the liquid I am adding it to, then stir it in at the end like a seasoning and don't cook it for ages.

I have used gochujang paste here, which is a fermented chilli paste from Korea with complex flavours. It's getting easier to find and it does add an extra edge to the soup. If you can't get the paste, dried chilli works just fine. Do be careful to check the paste's ingredients list, as some varieties contain ingredients I'd rather not eat!

SERVES 4

200g Asian mushrooms (enoki, shimeji, shiitake, oyster)

1 tablespoon tamari or soy sauce, plus a little extra to season and serve

juice of ½ a lemon

2 tablespoons runny honey or agave nectar

250g soba noodles (I use 100 per cent buckwheat ones)

3 tablespoons sesame oil

6 spring onions, trimmed and finely chopped

a small thumb-sized piece of ginger, peeled and grated

1 teaspoon gochujang paste or dried chilli flakes

4 cloves of garlic, thinly sliced

100–150g cabbage kimchi, (see page 68) drained

250g purple sprouting broccoli, woody ends removed and cut into thumb-length pieces

3 tablespoons miso paste (I use a brown rice one)

250g extra-firm tofu

TO SERVE

sesame seeds

squeeze of lemon or lime

some coriander or shiso leaves (optional)

First, put your mushrooms into a bowl with the tamari, lemon juice and 1 tablespoon of the honey, and put to one side to marinate for at least 15 minutes.

Cook the soba noodles according to the packet instructions. Drain and run under cold water then toss in the sesame oil.

Heat the oil in a large soup pan over a medium to high heat. Once the mushrooms have had their marinating time, drain them but keep the marinade. Add the mushrooms to the pan in a single layer with a pinch of salt (you can do this in batches if you need to). Cook until the mushrooms are golden where they meet the pan, then toss and keep cooking until the mushrooms are deeply browned all over – this should take 5 minutes or so. Remove from the pan and set aside. →

Fill and boil the kettle. Put the empty pan back on a medium heat, add the spring onions and sauté for a few minutes before adding the ginger and gochujang paste. After another minute or so, add the garlic and the drained kimchi. Sizzle until the garlic is starting to brown around the edges. Add 1¼ litres of water from the kettle along with the remaining tablespoon of honey and bring to the boil. Now, add the broccoli and simmer for 1 minute, or just until the broccoli becomes bright green.

Remove the soup from heat. Place the miso in a small bowl and whisk it with a splash of the broth to thin it out. Stir the thinned miso into the soup. Taste your soup; you really need to get the balance right here. If the broth tastes a bit flat, you might need more salt or miso, or a splash of soy sauce.

Just before serving, cut the tofu into little 2cm pieces and drizzle it with the reserved marinade from the mushrooms.

To serve, divide the noodles between four bowls and ladle over the soup. Top with the tofu, mushrooms and a sprinkle of sesame seeds. Finish with more soy if you like, a squeeze of lemon or lime and the shiso or coriander leaves if using.

Green peppercorn and lemongrass coconut broth

This is what we eat when we feel like the cold has got the better of us. It's packed with immune-system-boosting turmeric, ginger and garlic to fight off colds, and some fiery green chilli to blow away cobwebs. I use green peppercorns too, as I love the grassy punch they give; seek out the fresh ones on tiny branches if you can, but if not the brined ones in jars will do just fine. The paste can be made in advance or in a double batch and the leftovers will keep in the fridge for a few days and in the freezer for a couple of months.

Gently melt the coconut oil in a pan over a low heat – you don't want to heat it, just melt it. Put the ginger, garlic and chilli (the amount you use and whether you keep the seeds in depends on how hot you like things) into your food processor with the spring onions, almost all of the coriander and the mint leaves (keep a few leaves back for serving). Add the coconut oil, then blitz for 30 seconds or until you have a smooth, deep green paste.

Place a deep, medium-sized pan over a medium heat and add the herb paste, stirring it for a minute while it warms. Stir in the turmeric, peppercorns, both tins of coconut milk, the juice of one of the limes, the stock powder and the tamari. Fill one of the tins one and a half times with hot water from the kettle and add the water to the pan.

Using a rolling pin or pestle, smash the lemongrass so that it splinters but remains together, then tuck it into the pan. Bring the liquid to the boil, then lower the heat and leave to simmer, bubbling gently.

Fill and boil a kettle. Meanwhile, slice the squash as thinly as you can and add this to the pan too. Place the noodles in a heatproof bowl and pour over enough of the boiling water from the kettle to cover them.

Once the squash is cooked through, add the greens to the soup and allow the liquid to come to a simmer again. Check the seasoning of the soup, adding the coconut sugar if it needs some sweetness and more lime and salt as needed. Drain the noodles, then divide them between four deep soup bowls. Ladle over the soup and vegetables, adding a generous squeeze of lime juice and, if you like, a few of the reserved coriander and mint leaves.

SERVES 4

4 tablespoons coconut oil

a thumb-sized piece of ginger (about 50g), peeled and roughly chopped

2 cloves of garlic, peeled

1–2 small green chillies, stalk removed

4 spring onions, trimmed and roughly chopped

a small bunch of coriander (leaves and stalks)

a few sprigs of mint, leaves only

1 heaped teaspoon ground turmeric or a small thumb of fresh, grated

15 fresh or brined green peppercorns (see note above)

2 x 400ml tins of coconut milk

2 limes

1 tablespoon vegetable stock powder or ½ a stock cube

1 tablespoon tamari or soy sauce

1 stalk of lemongrass

½ a medium butternut squash, deseeded and peeled

100g thin vermicelli brown rice noodles

100g spinach or winter greens, shredded

1 tablespoon coconut sugar or honey

Not-chicken soup

This is a soup for the soul; chicken soup without the chicken and with no apology. It's the get-well soup I have been searching for, to cure whatever ails you, whether that's a cold or a broken heart. As gentle and as nourishing as they come, the soup has a base of slow-cooked sweet fennel and leek, layered with old friends celery and carrot, with a pep of ginger and lemon and a warmth from a generous amount of white pepper. Crisp little pieces of tofu top the broth, sticky from a minute or two in a pan, with some soy and a sprinkling of seasoning.

The seasoning, nutritional yeast, adds depth and umami and tastes much more complex and gentle than its ungenerous name suggests (though it is a great source of elusive B vitamins for vegetarians and vegans). If you don't have it the soup will still be delicious without. Be sure to save the fronds from your fennel and leaves from your celery for finishing it prettily.

SERVES 4

olive oil

1 onion, finely sliced

1 leek, finely sliced

3 bulbs of fennel, trimmed and finely sliced, fronds reserved

3 sticks of celery, chopped into 1cm pieces, leaves reserved

1 carrot, peeled and chopped into rough 1cm pieces

8 cloves of garlic, very thinly sliced

a small thumb-sized piece of ginger, peeled and grated

1 lemon

1 teaspoon whole white peppercorns, plus more to taste

50g small pasta or broken up spaghetti pieces

extra virgin olive oil, to serve

FOR THE TOFU

200g firm tofu, sliced roughly into 1cm sticks

3 tablespoons soy sauce

1 heaped teaspoon nutritional yeast

Pour a little olive oil into a large soup pot and place over a medium heat. Add the onion, leek, fennel, celery and carrot, turn the heat down low and cook gently for 20–30 minutes, until everything is very soft and sweet, without browning too much. Add a splash of water if it looks like anything is going to stick.

Add the garlic and ginger, cook for another couple of minutes, then squeeze in the lemon and add the peppercorns. Add 2 litres of cold water (or you can use vegetable stock) and a good pinch of sea salt. Bring to the boil and simmer for 20–30 minutes.

Once the soup is nearly ready, toss the tofu in 2 tablespoons of the soy sauce. Heat a pan with a little olive oil, fry the tofu over a medium to high heat until crisp then add the final tablespoon of soy sauce and toss quickly – the soy should stick to the tofu and give it a rich stickiness. Remove from the heat, add the nutritional yeast and toss again.

Roughly break or bash your pasta into bite-sized pieces or lengths, add to the soup and cook for another 8 minutes (or as long as your pasta takes). Taste and add more salt or water or even a squeeze more lemon. Ladle into shallow bowls, top with the tofu, some fennel fronds and celery leaves and a good drizzle of olive oil.

Soups – a flavour map

1	2	3	4
Create the base layer	**Choose a herb**	**Choose a spice**	**Choose the main body of your soup**
1 onion or leek, finely chopped	a few sprigs of thyme	cumin seeds	butternut squash
+	a couple of sprigs of rosemary	coriander seeds	sweet potato
2 sticks of celery, trimmed and finely chopped	10 sage leaves	3 cardamom pods (remember to take the seeds out before you blend)	peas
+	3 bay leaves	½ cinnamon stick	celeriac
2 carrots, roughly chopped	a few sprigs of oregano	mustard seeds	parsnips
	the stalks from a bunch of basil	smoked paprika	tomatoes
	the stalks from a bunch of coriander	black pepper	carrots
		dried chilli flakes	broccoli
			cauliflower
Sweat all three in a little olive oil over a medium heat until soft and sweet.	Add the herb and sizzle for a couple of minutes to release its flavour.	Add 1 tablespoon, or the quantity suggested, and sizzle for a minute or two.	Add your main vegetable (about 800g–1kg), peeled and chopped if needed, and enough hot stock to cover. Simmer for 40 minutes.

5	6	7
Choose a back-up flavour	**How to make it more substantial**	**Finish your soup**

Choose a back-up flavour	How to make it more substantial	Finish your soup
broccoli	cooked quinoa	roasted seeds
peas	drained tinned beans	yoghurt
broad beans	cooked amaranth	tahini
artichokes	cooked brown rice	toasted nuts
asparagus	torn-up bread	quick croutons
spinach (add at the end)	broken-up noodles	chopped soft herbs
	small or smashed pasta	herb oil

Add a couple of handfuls of washed, podded or chopped veg and simmer for 5 more minutes.	This is optional. If using, add a couple of handfuls just before your soup is ready, warm through (make sure it's cooked if it's noodles or pasta) and blitz if you like.	Top with 1 or 2 of these options and a drizzle of olive oil.

Pomelo and peanut winter noodles with carrot and coconut dressing

Cheerful and layered with flavour, this is a bright bowl that makes the most of January citrus. I use pomelo, but you can use another citrus if pomelo is hard to come by; clementines and blood oranges are both great. The carrot and coconut milk dressing makes more than you will need, which is intentional, as it's easier to make in a big batch and I love having it in the fridge to use through the week. I have made suggestions on how else to use it opposite but if you'd prefer not to have extra, halve the ingredients.

I use 100 per cent buckwheat soba noodles, as I love their super savoury note, but any noodles you like would work here. If you are using soba, be careful not to overcook them and be quick to refresh them in cold water so that they don't stick together.

SERVES 2 AS A MAIN MEAL, 4 AS PART OF A MEAL

200g soba noodles

200g shelled edamame (fresh or frozen)

½ a medium pomelo

2 big handfuls of watercress or other peppery leaves

100g unsalted peanuts, toasted

a small bunch of coriander, leaves picked

FOR THE DRESSING

50ml full-fat coconut milk

a generous pinch of ground turmeric

a large thumb-sized piece of ginger, peeled and grated

1 carrot, peeled

1 green chilli

2 tablespoons extra virgin olive oil

1 tablespoon toasted sesame oil

1 tablespoon maple syrup

2 tablespoons brown rice vinegar

1 shallot, peeled and roughly chopped

Bring a large pot of well-salted water to a boil and cook the noodles according to the packet instructions. When the noodles are nearly cooked, add the edamame to the pot for a quick swim. Remove from the heat, drain, rinse with cold water to stop the cooking and shake off as much water as possible.

Meanwhile, make your dressing. Put the coconut milk, turmeric, ginger, carrot, chilli, olive oil, sesame oil, maple syrup, brown rice vinegar, shallot and some salt into a blender and blend until very smooth. Taste and adjust, if needed, with more salt or vinegar, or any other ingredient you think might need a little boost.

Cut the peel from the pomelo and use your knife to slice between the membrane to cut it into segments, removing as much of the pith as you can.

Transfer the noodles and edamame to a large serving bowl, add a few tablespoons of the dressing and toss well. The noodles really absorb the sauce, so start by adding a couple of tablespoons at a time, then mix and add more if needed as you don't want to drown them. Finish with the watercress, peanuts, pomelo and coriander and toss everything together gently.

How to use your dressing

- Add to grated winter roots with rounds of citrus and some toasted seeds

- Use it to finish a bowl of simple steamed rice and green veg and top with a few toasted nuts

- Use it to finish some flash-fried tofu and serve with rice noodles and some greens

- Toss a packet of feta cheese in a little of the dressing, then roast for 25 minutes until golden and toss through a salad of leaves or grains

Winter tomatoes with whipped feta

In the last few years I have been buying my favourite tomatoes of the year in the winter. January, February and March see a few winter tomato varieties make their way to UK shores from Spain and Italy: the salty Ibérico tomato; the pert and pleasingly green-flavoured Marinda and the deeply red, sometimes almost black Camone. They are an entirely different affair from the ripe summer fruits we think of when we talk about tomatoes. For me these have more interesting and individual flavours; you can taste the saltiness of the sea where some of them grow and the green scent of their vines comes through.

—————————————

Preheat your oven to 220°C/200°C fan/gas 7. Roughly tear the sourdough into pieces and pulse in a food processor until you have rough breadcrumbs. A bit of texture is good here, so try not to go too far, otherwise your crumb will be too fine and sandy.

Toss the breadcrumbs in a roasting tray with a drizzle of olive oil, a pinch of salt and some black pepper. Place in the centre of the warmed oven for 4–5 minutes, or until the breadcrumbs have turned toasty and golden.

SERVES 2

50g stale sourdough bread

800g winter tomatoes (I like the Camone, Marinda and Ibérico varieties)

1 tablespoon of the best quality extra virgin olive oil you can find, plus a little extra

½ tablespoon sherry vinegar

the zest and juice of 1 unwaxed lemon

200g feta cheese

2 tablespoons thick Greek yoghurt

1 teaspoon nigella seeds

4 sprigs of marjoram or oregano, leaves picked

Meanwhile, cut the tomatoes into slices and wedges, keeping them quite irregular and making the most of the shape of each tomato. Place the lot in a bowl with the tablespoon of olive oil, sherry vinegar, lemon zest and a couple of generous pinches of salt and some black pepper. Leave to one side while you get on with the feta.

In a food processor, whip the feta and yoghurt together until the cheese is completely smooth and creamy. Taste and add salt if necessary, pepper and some of the lemon juice. Scoop into a bowl and top with the nigella seeds.

Spoon the tomatoes with their olive oil and vinegar on to plates and dot the whipped feta around the tomatoes to fill in any empty spaces. Sprinkle over the breadcrumbs, scatter over the marjoram and drizzle with a little more oil.

Cauliflower rice with eggs and green chutney

I make this because I love it. It's quick and can be eaten from the bowl. Our weeknight dinners, and even dishes on restaurant menus, have more and more become a collection of elements eaten from a bowl. Often though, when I eat them outside of my kitchen I find they lack a cohesiveness – they need something to bring them together as a whole. That's where a chutney or pesto comes in.

Here I use a quick, zippy chutney of green chilli, coriander and mint, with coconut backing them all up. This is my guess at a chutney made by a friend's mum, a great Gujarati cook, that we enthusiastically pile on everything we eat when we are at their house. I haven't had the nerve to ask for the recipe, as it seems a proud inherited family one; I hope this does it justice.

SERVES 4

FOR THE CHUTNEY

a large bunch of coriander

2 green chillies

a few sprigs of mint

juice of 1 lime

50g coconut cream

½ teaspoon runny honey

1 tablespoon groundnut or mild olive oil

800g–1kg cauliflower

coconut oil

6 spring onions, peeled and finely sliced

a thumb-sized piece of ginger, peeled

1 teaspoon ground turmeric

1 head of chard or other winter greens, stalks finely sliced, leaves roughly shredded

1 lemon

50g coconut cream

4 organic eggs

1 tablespoon nigella seeds

100g roasted unsalted peanuts, roughly chopped

First, make your chutney. Put half the coriander (reserving the rest for later) into a food processor with all the other ingredients and blitz until grassy green and smooth, adding a little water as you go if it looks too dry. You are looking for a spoonable consistency, a little thinner than a pesto.

Take the leaves and gnarly root off your cauliflower and chop it into big pieces, using the stalks too. Put them into the food processor and pulse until you have a rice-like texture. You could also use the coarse side of a box grater.

Put your largest frying pan on a high heat (if you don't have a nice big one, two smaller ones will work). Add a large knob of coconut oil along with the spring onions. Cook for 5 minutes, until soft, stirring from time to time.

Meanwhile, grate the ginger and finely chop the stalks of the remaining coriander, keeping the leaves for later. Once the spring onion is soft, add the ginger and turmeric and cook for a couple of minutes, then season well with salt.

Turn the heat right up. Add the cauliflower rice and cook, stirring every couple of minutes to make sure all the rice gets a little browned on the bottom of the pan; this will take about 10 minutes. →

Meanwhile, heat another pan on a medium heat and add a teaspoon of coconut oil. Add the shredded greens, a little splash of water, a tiny squeeze of lemon juice and a good pinch of salt. Once the water has evaporated and the greens are wilted, take the pan off the heat and cover to keep warm.

Once the edges of the cauliflower rice have nicely browned, squeeze over the rest of the lemon juice and grate in the coconut cream. Cook until it has all been absorbed by the rice and there is a slightly caramelly smell. Push the rice to one side of the pan and spoon the greens into the other.

Put the pan that had the greens in back on the heat and add another teaspoon of coconut oil, then crack in the eggs and cook on a medium to high heat until the edges are crispy and the yolks are just cooked. Sprinkle the eggs with the nigella seeds and take off the heat.

Serve the cauliflower rice in bowls, topped with the greens, chutney, peanuts, crispy eggs and with the rest of the coriander leaves for sprinkling over the top.

Ways to use this chutney

- Next to any curry or dhal.

- To marinate paneer or tofu before frying or baking.

- Diluted with a little oil and used to dress a simple salad of grated carrot and shredded cabbage, topped with toasted cashews.

- On top of scrambled eggs.

- Mashed into some avocado for an Indian riff on guacamole.

- To add some punch to some roasted beetroots.

- Mixed with oil and a little lemon or lime juice as a dressing for any grain or rice salad.

Golden miso potato salad

Potatoes are pretty magical in all their forms: the crispy-edged golden brown crunch of a roastie; cloud-like mash; a little new potato, boiled and tossed with grassy green herbs, good oil and flaky salt… This warm potato salad has become a household staple, a dinner for cold nights and wet homecomings: bolstering, full of flavour and comfort. I bake the potatoes in miso until deeply golden brown, then slather them in a tomato and ginger dressing before mixing them with lentils and toasted almonds. A complete meal.

Although new potatoes aren't around yet, I find this recipe works well with smaller potatoes, so I buy them from the loose bin and pick out the smallest ones I can find. If yours are bigger you might want to cut them in half or quarters.

Preheat the oven to 220°C/200°C fan/gas 7.

Rinse the potatoes, scrubbing off any gnarly bits, and dry well. Mix the miso and olive oil with 1 tablespoon of water. Put the potatoes into a large baking tray or two smaller ones, add the miso mixture and toss well to coat.

Put the garlic cloves into the tray as well. Roast the potatoes until they are fluffy inside and golden outside: this should take 25–35 minutes depending on the size of your potatoes.

Meanwhile, make your dressing. Mix the sun-dried tomatoes and their oil with the lime zest and juice and the ginger, and mix well.

Remove the potatoes from the oven and spoon out the garlic cloves. Squeeze the softened cloves from their papery outsides, mash them and add them to the dressing.

Tumble the potatoes into a large bowl, add the lentils and the dressing and toss together. Top with the almonds and tear over the basil.

SERVES 4

1kg small floury potatoes

2 teaspoons white miso paste

2 tablespoons olive oil

the cloves from 1 head of garlic, skin on

1 x 400g tin of Puy lentils or 250g home-cooked, (see page 461), drained

100g almonds, skin on, toasted and sliced

a handful of basil, leaves picked

FOR THE DRESSING

2 tablespoons sun-dried tomatoes in olive oil, chopped, plus 2 tablespoons of their oil

the zest and juice of 1 unwaxed lime

a thumb-sized piece of ginger, peeled and finely chopped

39

Roasted Savoy squash with Cheddar and rye

In the colder months of the year I find it all too easy to lean on Asian, Indian or Mexican flavours to perk me up and create a bit of excitement when the offerings of the season have become a bit monotonous. But truthfully it's at this time of year I want simple British flavours most, and this salad sings with them. The sometimes forgotten Savoy cabbage is roasted into crisp-edged wedges, more pleasing to me than the now ever-present roasted broccoli or kale, and paired with plump roasted squash, caraway seeds, a rye crumb and a mustard-spiked dressing, all finished with a crumble of sharp Cheddar (though vegans can happily leave this out). This dish is so rooted in time and place, and that's when eating and cooking feels best to me.

SERVES 4

a small Delicata or butternut squash (about 500g)

1 Savoy cabbage (about 400g), tough outer leaves removed

olive oil

1 teaspoon caraway seeds

50g rye bread (about 2 thin slices)

2 tablespoons baby capers, drained

100g good sharp Cheddar, crumbled

FOR THE DRESSING

1 tablespoon wholegrain mustard

1 teaspoon honey

1 tablespoon cider vinegar

3 tablespoons good extra virgin olive or rapeseed oil

Preheat the oven 220°C/200°C fan/gas 7.

Halve and deseed the squash and cut into wedges 2cm thick. Cut your cabbage into eight chunky wedges. Place them both on a large roasting tray and sprinkle with a good amount of salt and pepper. Add a good drizzle of oil and the caraway seeds and roast in the hot oven for 35 minutes until the squash is soft and cooked through and the cabbage is golden and crisp and charred at the edges.

Meanwhile put the rye bread into a food processor and blitz until you have rough breadcrumbs – you still want a good bit of texture here. Put the crumbs on a baking tray with a drizzle of olive oil, a good pinch of salt, a generous grind of black pepper and the capers, and toast in the hot oven for 5 minutes until they smell toasty and have a pleasing crunch, being careful not to burn them – with the dark colour of the rye bread it can be easy to overcook them.

Mix the dressing ingredients, season well and put to one side.

When the cabbage and squash are cooked, take them out of the oven and tumble on to a platter with the Cheddar. Drizzle generously with the dressing, mix well, then scatter over the rye crumbs and take to the table.

Toasted quinoa, roast brassicas and spiced green herb smash

There is something about the burnished edges of a vegetable, especially brassicas, which suit the darker nights and more complex flavours I love. These roasted florets sit next to some lemon-scented toasted quinoa and are topped with a Yemeni herb and spice smash called *skhug*. It's good stirred into hummus, to finish a soup or mixed with oil to dress a salad.

SERVES 4–6

1 small head of broccoli
(about 400g)

1 small cauliflower
(about 400g)

a pinch of dried chilli flakes

1 teaspoon cumin seeds

a good drizzle of olive oil

250g quinoa (see note above)

1 unwaxed lemon

½ a vegetable stock cube or
1 teaspoon of vegetable
stock powder

100g almonds, skin on,
toasted and roughly
chopped

FOR THE HERB SMASH

a large bunch of coriander

the juice of 2 lemons

1 clove of garlic, roughly
chopped

1–2 green chillies (depending
on how hot you like
things), roughly chopped

1 teaspoon cumin seeds

½ teaspoon ground
cardamom (or the crushed
seeds from 5 pods)

a pinch of ground cloves

2 tablespoons extra virgin
olive oil

Preheat your oven to 200°C/180°C fan/gas 6.

Roughly chop your broccoli and cauliflower into small florets, about 2–3cm, and the stalks and root into thin slices. You want to cut your cauliflower a little smaller than the broccoli as it cooks a little slower. Place the lot on a baking tray with the chilli, cumin seeds and a good pinch of salt. Drizzle with the olive oil and roast in the hot oven for 20–25 minutes.

Next, cook the quinoa for a couple of minutes in a large dry saucepan over a medium heat, letting it crackle and toast. This will give it a deep nutty flavour. Once it is beginning to smell fragrant, cut the lemon in half, place both halves in the pan and quickly pour over 600ml of water. Crumble in the stock cube and bring the liquid to the boil, then reduce the heat and simmer for about 15 minutes, until most of the water has been absorbed. Top up with more boiling water, if needed, as you go.

To make the herb smash, put all the coriander, including the stalks, the juice of one of the lemons and the other ingredients into a food processor along with 2 tablespoons of cold water and blend on a high speed to make a smooth grassy-green sauce. Taste and adjust the seasoning as necessary, adding more lemon, garlic or oil as you see fit. (Any leftovers can be stored in the fridge for up to one week.)

Once the brassicas are roasted and the quinoa is cooked, tumble them all into a bowl and pour over one third of the dressing. Scatter over half the almonds, mix well and finish with the rest of the almonds and a good squeeze more lemon.

Little pea and white bean polpette

This recipe is made out of stuff I always have on hand in the store cupboard, freezer and fridge. It's at this time of year that I rely on these staples: frozen peas and preserved lemons add a flash of green and some freshness, an interruption from the roots and grains while we wait for the fresh green march of spring. I make a batch of these and turn them into a few meals: served with a grain and greens for dinner, in a wrap with some pickles or with spaghetti and a spiced tomato sauce (see page 362). I add a little Parmesan to balance the flavour here, but vegans can use nutritional yeast.

Preheat the oven to 200°C/180°C fan/gas 6 (if you are baking your polpette).

To make the salsa, roughly chop together all the ingredients except the oil. Put in to a bowl and add the oil little by little, stirring well. Taste as you go – you may not need all the oil.

Put the onion into your food processor with the garlic, coriander seeds and chilli and pulse until the onion is finely chopped. Heat a frying pan, add 3 tablespoons of olive oil, and fry the onion mixture gently until it's soft and fragrant. Next, add the rest of the polpette ingredients to the food processor with a good grind of black pepper and mix until the beans have been mashed and everything has come together.

Shape the polpette. Wet your hands and roll into balls using roughly a tablespoon of mixture for each one (you should get about 18), then place on a baking sheet. If you are baking them, drizzle the balls with a little olive oil and bake in the oven for 20–25 minutes, or until golden. To cook them in a frying pan, chill them for at least 20 minutes, then simply fry them in a little olive oil on a medium heat for about 10–15 minutes, turning every few minutes. Serve with the salsa verde.

If you are freezing the polpette, cook them for a few minutes less, then let them cool completely (they firm up as they cool down). Transfer to containers or bags and freeze.

SERVES 4

FOR THE STORECUPBOARD SALSA VERDE

a small bunch of flat-leaf parsley

2 tablespoons capers, drained

1 tablespoon cornichons, drained

2 sun-dried tomatoes, drained

the zest of 1 unwaxed lemon

10 tablespoons extra virgin olive oil

FOR THE POLPETTE

1 red onion, peeled and roughly chopped

2 cloves of garlic, peeled

2 teaspoons coriander seeds

a generous pinch of dried chilli flakes

olive oil

300g frozen peas

1 x 400g tin of white beans (or 250g home-cooked, see page 461), drained

50g breadcrumbs or roughly blitzed oats

½ a preserved lemon, flesh removed and discarded, peel finely chopped

1 teaspoon flaky sea salt

the zest of 1 unwaxed lemon

4 sun-dried tomatoes

50g freshly grated Parmesan (I use a vegetarian one) or 1 tablespoon nutritional yeast

Spelt with pickled pears and pink leaves

This warm winter salad has everything going for it. It's the prettiest of salads, with gentle off-white celeriac and caramel-coloured spelt offset by the dusky rose of its pink cousin and the Expressionist pink and cream splatter of Castelfranco. If you haven't guessed already, I love these bitter lettuces; they cheer up my January table and happily, they are now much more widely available, though a few heads of chicory would do fine in their place. Be careful not to use overripe pears; you need them to be a little on the firm side so they hold their shape as they cook.

Put 4 tablespoons of the vinegar, the black peppercorns, caster sugar and salt into a saucepan with 100ml of water and bring to the boil. Meanwhile, peel the pears, halve them and scoop out the cores with a teaspoon. Lower the pears into the pickling liquid, lower the heat and leave to cook until tender (about 10 minutes). Remove from the heat, cover with a lid and leave to rest.

Preheat the oven to 200°C/180°C fan/gas 6. Roast the celeriac in the oven on a baking tray, with a little oil, for 20 minutes. Mix the honey with the miso and mustard. After 20 minutes take the tray out of the oven and add 1 tablespoon of the miso mixture, toss through the celeriac, then return to the oven for a further 5–10 minutes, until crispy and golden.

Meanwhile, cook the spelt. Bring a pan of salted water to the boil, then add the spelt and cook for 20–25 minutes or until cooked through and tender. Mix the remaining miso mixture with the remaining tablespoon of vinegar and the olive oil, drain the spelt and toss in the dressing.

Once everything else is ready, tear all the leaves from your bitter lettuces and lay on plates. Top with the spelt, celeriac and the pickled pears and crumble over the cheese.

SERVES 4

5 tablespoons white wine vinegar

½ teaspoon black peppercorns

2 tablespoons golden caster sugar

a generous pinch of flaky sea salt

4 just-ripe pears

400g celeriac or parsnip, peeled and cut into small 2cm pieces

1 tablespoon runny honey

1 tablespoon white miso paste

2 tablespoons wholegrain mustard

200g pearled spelt

1 tablespoon extra virgin olive oil

2 heads of bitter salad leaves (see note above)

50g blue cheese

Quick carrot dhal

SERVES 4

2 cloves of garlic

1 green chilli

a thumb-sized piece of
  fresh ginger, peeled

1 red onion, peeled

coconut or vegetable oil

1 teaspoon cumin seeds

1 teaspoon coriander seeds

1 teaspoon black mustard
  seeds

1 teaspoon ground turmeric

1 teaspoon ground cinnamon

200g red lentils

1 × 400ml tin of coconut milk

600ml vegetable stock

6 carrots, peeled

2 large handfuls of spinach

juice of 1 lemon

FOR THE PICKLE

a thumb-sized piece of
  fresh ginger, peeled

1 green chilli

1 unwaxed lemon

2 handfuls of radishes

1 tablespoon nigella seeds

1 tablespoon white wine
  vinegar

honey or agave nectar

a bunch of coriander, chopped

TO SERVE

plain yoghurt

cooked brown basmati rice

a few poppadoms

This dhal has its roots in South India. It comes together quickly but has rich layers of flavour which might lead you to think it had spent hours on the hob – curry leaves, pops of mustard seeds, warming cinnamon, all the things I love in a dhal.

The turmeric and carrots make this a vibrant sunny-hued bowl, and on top lies a colour pop of sweet-shop pink radish pickle. I serve it with poppadoms scrunched into shards over the top for a welcome bit of crunch. We have dhal in some form or another at least once a week, and this is one I keep coming back to. If you really wanted to speed things up you could do all your grating in the food processor.

Finely grate the garlic, chilli and ginger (I use a sharp Microplane grater; if your grater isn't quite up to the job, finely chop them), then coarsely grate the red onion. Put a large saucepan on a medium heat, add a little oil and everything you have grated and cook for 10 minutes until soft and sweet.

Pound the cumin and coriander seeds a bit in a pestle and mortar, then add to the pan with the other spices and cook for a couple of minutes to toast and release their oils. Add the lentils, coconut milk and stock to the pan and bring to a simmer, then turn the heat down and bubble for 25–30 minutes. Meanwhile, grate all the carrots and add those too.

While that is cooking make a little pickle to go on top. Finely grate the ginger, chilli and the zest of the lemon into a bowl, then use a coarser grater to grate the radishes into the bowl. Add the nigella seeds, vinegar, a squeeze of honey, half the coriander, a good pinch of salt and mix well.

To finish your dhal, take it off the heat, then stir in the spinach and allow it to wilt a little, stirring in the other half of the coriander and the juice of the lemon too. Pile into bowls and top with the radish pickle, spoonfuls of yoghurt and brown basmati rice. At the table, crumble over your poppadoms.

Beetroot, rhubarb and potato gratin

This might just get the all-time gratin crown. There's gentle comfort from the potatoes and cream, with an unexpected pop of sweet acidity from the rhubarb, a foil for the unrepentant earthiness of the beetroot. The lively warmth of the pink peppercorns tops things off. It's a pretty beautiful-looking dishful too; there are some amazing colours at play: whites, neon pinks, magenta and the dots of fluoro pink peppercorns – you'd struggle to find one pinker.

I tend not to cook with a lot of dairy but here I make an exception, using the best I can get my hands on. Vegans might try this with almond or oat milk, or even some vegetable stock in place of the creams. I make the stock for this with about half the powder or stock cubes that the packet suggests, so the flavour of the stock doesn't overwhelm; if you have homemade stock (see page 460), all the better.

SERVES 4–6

butter, for greasing

1kg potatoes, preferably waxy ones, such as Desiree or Charlotte

500g cooked beetroot (the ones in vacuum packs or home-cooked), peeled

300ml weak vegetable stock (see note above)

300ml double cream

150ml sour cream

2 bay leaves

2 teaspoons pink peppercorns or ½ teaspoon black peppercorns

200g forced rhubarb, thinly sliced

Preheat the oven to 200°C/180°C fan/gas 6. Butter a large gratin dish.

Peel the potatoes and slice them very finely – a mandoline or the fine slicer attachment on a food processor is the best way to do this; just watch your fingers if you're using a mandoline. Cut the beetroot into fine slices as well – they don't have to quite be as thin, so you could cut them with a knife.

Put the stock and both the creams into a large saucepan, along with the bay leaves and 1 teaspoon of the peppercorns. Bring the liquid to just under the boil, then take off the heat and leave to sit for 30 minutes or so. Remove the bay leaves, leaving the peppercorns in, then bring the liquid to just below a simmer. Add the sliced potatoes and cook gently for 5 minutes.

Remove from the heat, season really well with salt and pepper, and spoon half the potatoes into the gratin dish. Put half the beetroot and rhubarb on top, seasoning as you go, then top with the rest of the potatoes and their cream, followed by the rest of the beetroot.

Roughly bash the remaining pink peppercorns in a pestle and mortar and sprinkle on the gratin. Bake for 1 hour, or until the vegetables are completely tender. Cover the top with foil after about 45 minutes if it looks like it is becoming too dark.

Butter bean stew with kale and sticky blood oranges

This is a seriously comforting bowl. Sweet spiced beans, burnished blood oranges and the bright green goodness of kale, all topped off with a hazelnut and sesame seed crunch; full of flavour and texture. It's quick but nourishing, with the satisfying depth of a pot that's been very slowly ticking away on the stove for hours.

SERVES 4

olive oil

3 cloves of garlic, finely sliced

1 x 400g tin of chopped tomatoes

2 bay leaves

a small bunch of thyme (4 or 5 stalks)

1 red onion, finely chopped

2 x 400g jars or tins of butter beans, drained (or 250g home-cooked beans, see page 461)

2 blood oranges, or normal oranges, peeled and sliced

1 tablespoon sherry vinegar

1 teaspoon honey

300g curly kale, leaves pulled away from the stalks and roughly torn

100g hazelnuts

2 tablespoons sesame seeds

the zest of 1 unwaxed lemon

1 tablespoon sumac

feta or goat's cheese, to serve (optional)

Fill and boil the kettle. First put a little olive oil into a pan, add 2 cloves of the garlic and fry for a minute or two, then add the tomatoes, herbs and a good pinch of sea salt and simmer for 10 minutes.

Meanwhile, heat a frying pan on a medium heat, add a little oil, then add the onion and the other garlic clove and cook for 10 minutes until soft and sweet. Add the butter beans to the tomatoes, then half fill the tomato can with hot water from the kettle, add this too and simmer for 10 minutes.

Once the onions are cooked, add the blood oranges, sherry vinegar and honey to the frying pan and cook for 3–4 minutes until the orange slices are starting to caramelise and catch around the edges. Add the kale, put a lid on the pan, turn the heat down and cook until wilted, about 8 minutes. Meanwhile, roughly chop the hazelnuts and mix with the sesame seeds, the lemon zest and 2 tablespoons of olive oil. Fry in a pan on a medium heat for 2–3 minutes until crisp and starting to toast brown.

By now the bean mixture should be nicely reduced. Remove the thyme and the bay leaves, season and add a good drizzle of olive oil.

Serve the beans topped with the kale and oranges and a good sprinkling of the hazelnuts, sumac and sesame seeds. Crumble a bit of feta or goat's cheese over the top if you like too.

One-pan squash, caper and kale pasta

This may not be for traditionalists, but I think this way of cooking pasta is clever – the starch from the pasta water comes together to make a velvety, creamy sauce that you wouldn't get if they were cooked separately. I'm not suggesting all pasta is cooked this way, but when a quick dinner is needed this is where I look.

You can swap in any pasta that cooks in about 8 minutes. I've gone for a wholewheat rigatoni here, but I've had success with normal, quinoa and corn pasta too. I use Delicata squash, but you could use butternut squash instead – the skin is tougher, so it's best to peel it.

Halve the squash and scoop out the seeds, then thinly slice the squash halves into half moons about 5mm thick. Strip the kale leaves from their stalks and roughly tear any big pieces. Finely slice the stalks, discarding any particularly sinewy ones.

Heat a tablespoon of the olive oil in a large shallow pan over a medium heat and add the squash with a generous pinch of flaky sea salt. Cook the squash in the pan for about 10 minutes, stirring every couple of minutes, so that the pieces of squash start to catch and brown at the edges. Fill the kettle and put it on to boil.

Once the squash has had its 10 minutes, add the garlic and kale stalks and stir for a minute or so before adding the pasta, lemon zest, lentils, chilli, stock cube and a litre of water from the kettle. Cover with a lid and cook on a medium heat for 6 minutes.

Next, remove the lid and add the kale leaves and capers. Cover with the lid for a couple more minutes, until the kale is starting to wilt and turn bright green. If your pasta is a little dry you can add a tiny bit more water, about 100ml. Remove the lid and simmer for another 2–3 minutes, until the water has been absorbed, then take the pan off the heat and stir through the remaining tablespoon of olive oil and half the Parmesan. Taste and add a little more salt if needed, then leave to sit for a minute or so before piling into bowls and topping with a good grating of the remaining Parmesan.

SERVES 4

1 small Delicata squash (about 400g)

250g curly kale

2 tablespoons good olive oil

3 cloves of garlic, finely chopped

350g pasta (I use wholewheat rigatoni or penne)

the zest of 2 unwaxed lemons

½ x 400g tin of green lentils, drained

a pinch of dried chilli flakes

½ a vegetable stock cube or 1 teaspoon vegetable stock powder

2 tablespoons baby capers, drained

50g Parmesan (I use a vegetarian one)

Turmeric and coconut baked aloo gobi

There is something grand and celebratory about roasting a vegetable whole. It becomes a centrepiece, which is something I think people look for in vegetable-centred cooking. The food I make most nights celebrates vegetables in some way, but cooking them whole like this takes a cauliflower one step further: golden and crackled, its colour intensified, in all its glory as nature intended.

Whole roasted cauliflower is something that has been finding its way on to restaurant menus the last couple of years, partly due to the cauliflower renaissance spearheaded by vegetable magician Yotam Ottolenghi. Burnished and browned, a whole cauliflower is such a pleasing thing to put in the middle of the table, with a sharp knife for everyone to cut brave wedges for themselves and uncover the buttery clean white inside, a sharp contrast to the crisp and highly flavoured outside.

This is my favourite way to eat cauliflower: the sweet note of coconut milk, the punch of ginger and green chilli, the earthiness of mustard seeds and the clean spiced note of turmeric are perfect sidekicks to the neutral-flavoured, buttery roasted cauliflower. I add some halved potatoes to the pan to absorb the coconut and lemon goodness. There are few things which are as friendly in the way they soak up flavour as a cauliflower.

SERVES 4

1 large cauliflower or
  2 small ones

600g potatoes

4 tablespoons coconut oil

a thumb-sized piece of
  ginger, peeled

4 green chillies

4 cloves of garlic, crushed

1 tablespoon black mustard
  seeds

2 teaspoons ground turmeric

1 x 400ml tin of coconut milk

1 unwaxed lemon, cut in half

TO SERVE

thick Greek or coconut
  yoghurt

almonds

a small bunch of coriander,
  leaves picked

Preheat the oven to 220°C/200°C fan/gas 7. Fill and boil the kettle.

Using a pair of scissors cut the large leaves and stalks away from the cauliflower. You can leave the little leaves close to the florets – they will go nice and crispy when roasted. Turn the cauliflower upside down and, using a small paring knife, carefully cut a hollow in the middle of the stalk, so that it cooks evenly. Take a pan big enough to hold the cauliflower, half fill it with water from the kettle and bring it to the boil. Season the water with salt, then immerse the cauliflower and simmer for 6 minutes. Drain the water away, put the lid back on and leave the cauliflower to steam in the residual heat for a further 10 minutes. Meanwhile, cut the potatoes into 2cm pieces, leaving the skin on. →

Take an ovenproof dish or pan (that can go on the hob as well) large enough to take the cauliflower. Spoon in the coconut oil, and grate the ginger into the oil. Finely chop the chillies, discarding the seeds if you wish, then add them to the pan. Add the garlic, then place over a medium heat and let the spices and aromatics cook for a few minutes, until fragrant. Stir in the mustard seeds and continue cooking until the garlic has softened, then add the turmeric and a big pinch of salt.

Pour the coconut milk into the spice mixture, stir well and season with a little black pepper. When the milk starts to bubble gently, turn off the heat, place the drained cauliflower in the dish, then baste it with the coconut-spice mixture. Throw the lemon halves into the side of the dish too, then scatter the potatoes around; they will sit in the coconut milk.

Bake the cauliflower, basting it occasionally with the spiced sauce in the dish, for 40–45 minutes. You want it to catch a little on top. To test if the cauliflower is cooked, insert a small sharp knife into the middle – it should be really tender and the potatoes and cauliflower should have soaked up most of the sauce. Once it's perfect, take it out of the oven and transfer to a serving dish, then squeeze over the roasted lemons. Serve in the middle of the table, with little bowls of yoghurt, almonds and coriander for sprinkling on top.

Wholegrain spelt, date and molasses scones

These are not scones to keep in a tin but scones to eat warm, with salted butter and tea. These are everything I want from something baked on a cold day: rounded deep sweetness from molasses, caramel notes from the dates and maltiness from the spelt.

I have intentionally made them in quite a small batch; they are very quick to whip up and taste much more decadent than their ingredients might suggest. You can use whatever black tea you like here – I love the bergamot kick of Earl Grey, brewed strong, but I can imagine a smoky lapsang souchong might be amazing.

Preheat the oven to 200°C/180°C fan/gas 6. Line a baking tray with baking paper.

Soak the dates in the hot tea for 15 minutes, until the tea has cooled a little. Mix together the flour, baking powder, allspice and salt with your fingertips, then add the butter until the mix looks like breadcrumbs. You could also do this by pulsing it in a food processor.

Drain, then roughly chop the dates and add them to the mix, along with the molasses and buttermilk. Mix slowly and lightly until the mixture forms a soft but not too sticky dough. Shape into a rough round ball, place on your prepared tray and use a knife to score across the top to mark out 6 portions, stopping before the knife reaches the tray; it should look a bit like a loaf of soda bread.

Mix the egg and milk for the glaze with a pinch of salt and brush it over the top, then sprinkle with the oats, pressing them into the dough lightly to stick them down.

Bake for 15 minutes, then turn the tray and reduce the heat to 180°C/160°C fan/gas 4 and continue to bake for about 10 more minutes, until the top is a dark golden brown and when you turn the scone over and tap it, it sounds hollow. Serve warm from the oven and break up as required. The scones are very good with the curd on page 66.

MAKES 6

125g pitted dates

150ml freshly brewed strong black or Earl Grey tea

125g wholegrain spelt flour

2 teaspoons baking powder

¼ teaspoon ground allspice

¼ teaspoon flaky sea salt

30g cold unsalted butter, cubed

1 tablespoon molasses

75g buttermilk or thin natural yoghurt

FOR THE GLAZE

1 organic or free-range egg

1 tablespoon milk

a handful of rolled oats

Brewing your own kombucha

We have been drinking kombucha for years, mostly when I have travelled to visit my sister in LA where it seems to be as available as water. When I started drinking it every day I noticed really positive changes in how I was feeling. Back home I have found it harder to get my hands on and it's very expensive so I started brewing it myself. I am sure it has helped us ward off a few winter colds.

Kombucha is a drink that's been around for thousands of years. It's a sweet fermented green or black tea with a bubbly character that I think is totally delicious. Kombucha has been widely praised as being good for you as it contains digestion-supporting probiotic enzymes that lots of us are lacking in our diets. It supports the healthy bacteria in our guts and can help improve our digestion and how we absorb the nutrients from our food. By making kombucha yourself it will be completely raw (some commercial ones are pasteurised) so it has maximum health benefits; you can also control the fizziness and how long it's brewed to your taste.

The first thing I will say is that I'm not an expert; brewing kombucha is a huge topic and there are books and blogs entirely devoted to the subject. The brewing process is pretty simple: all you need is a bit of time, food (sugar) and good bacteria to create the brew (the scoby). Outlined below is how I brew mine and so far it's been very successful. Before I started I was quite daunted by the process but after you've done it once you'll get into the rhythm and it becomes really easy. Before you brew I recommend you read this explanation a couple of times; it may look like a lot of information but if you have a level of understanding it makes the process easier and quicker.

The scoby

The scoby, which stands for Symbiotic Culture of Bacteria and Yeast, is what you will need to ferment your tea. A scoby is a very strange-looking thing that I am weirdly fascinated by; it is like a big rubbery pancake. You can buy scobys online but as they are live they multiply so there are lots out in the world waiting for owners. A kombucha-brewing friend will have one or a quick search on the internet will probably unearth one for free.

The water

Filtered or at the very least boiled water is essential for kombucha brewing as some of the chemicals in tap water can affect the fermentation process.

The tea

You can use black or green tea but I prefer the flavour of my kombucha when it's made with green and it will be lower in caffeine. Flavoured and herbal teas don't work, as I discovered when I tried to make a batch with Earl Grey; it's best to add any flavours after brewing. The caffeine in kombucha contains only about a third of that in brewed tea.

The sugar

The scoby and the fermentation are fed with sugar. It may seem like you are adding a lot of sugar but during the brewing process it will turn from a very sweet tea into something far less so.

The alcohol

Whilst your kombucha is brewing, it will contain a very small amount of alcohol, about 0.5 per cent. It's all part of the fermentation process, but it's something to bear in mind if people are sensitive to alcohol and I certainly wouldn't give kombucha to children.

The equipment

— 1 large or a couple of smaller teapots or jugs to brew your tea

— 1 × 5- or 6-litre jar or kombucha crock (mine has a tap at the bottom)

— a clean piece of tea towel or muslin to cover

— a piece of string or a rubber band

— a funnel

— 4 × 1-litre bottles to store your finished kombucha

The ingredients

— 1 scoby

— 500ml pre-made kombucha tea (shop-bought or from your last batch)

— 250g sugar (I use golden caster sugar)

— 4 litres filtered or boiled water

— 2 heaped tablespoons green or black tea

The method

First brew your tea. Bring your 4 litres of pre-boiled or filtered water to the boil and pour it over the tea leaves of your choice; I do this in a couple of teapots and measuring jugs. Let it steep for 20–30 minutes, so it's good and strong.

Add the sugar, stir to dissolve then allow the tea to cool. This step is important as the scoby will die if it's too hot.

Remove any metal jewellery and from this point on don't use any metal sieves or spoons as they react with the scoby. Get the jar or crock you are using for the brewing and pour in the pre-made kombucha. Add the cooled tea, then carefully place the scoby on top of the mixture. Cover the jar with a piece of fabric and secure it with string or a rubber band. Some kitchen paper would also work; you just want air to be able to pass into the jar. Place the kombucha container in a place where it will not be disturbed, out of direct sunlight. I leave mine on my work surface where I can keep an eye on it.

The fermentation can take anything from 7–14 days, depending on the heat of the room, the scoby and how you like your kombucha. The longer you leave it the more acidic it will become. During the brewing process it's normal to see things happening in the brew: the scoby moving, bubbles of air. After a few days the surface of the tea will start to look opaque, this is your new scoby forming and a very good sign.

How long to brew?

After it's been brewing for about a week I start to taste mine every day (remembering to use a non-metal spoon). If you like a sweeter drink you may want to bottle yours now, if you like things more tart perhaps wait a full 14 days.

Once your kombucha tastes good to you, you can bottle it. Lift the scoby into a bowl or rimmed plate (remembering to keep any metal away). Divide your kombucha between the 1-litre bottles (a funnel is useful here), saving 500ml for your next batch. Once the kombucha is bottled you can start from the beginning on your next batch.

Once bottled you have a few options:

— Store it in the fridge and drink it as it is (it keeps for several months).

— Flavour your kombucha. I find the best way to do this is using freshly-squeezed or juiced fruits (I've found sweeter ones, such as strawberry, mango, peach, plum, pear, guava and watermelon, work best). You'll need about 600ml so about 150ml per bottle, but you can adjust this to your own taste based on the sweetness of the fruit. Sometimes I add spices too: for each bottle I add a teaspoon of grated fresh turmeric or ginger, some bashed cardamom seeds, a few rose petals, or even fennel seeds. Now you can either put this straight into the fridge or do a second fermentation.

— Ferment it a second time in the bottle to make it bubbly. I always do this as I love the Champagne-like bubbles. Seal the bottles and keep them on the work surface. It's really important to open the bottles every day to let the air out so the tops don't pop off (this is called burping). At the same time I taste for fizziness and when it's nicely bubbly (usually 2–3 days) I put the lot into the fridge to store.

Taking time off

You might want to take a break from brewing. To pause the process, take the scoby out of the jar, separate the new scoby (the baby) from the original one (the mother) and put them into separate glass jars with enough of your brewed kombucha to cover. Place in the fridge and seal, remembering that nothing can come into contact with metal. They will keep like this in the fridge for a few months at least. When you are ready to brew again bring the scoby to room temperature and start the process above, adding all the liquid you stored the scoby in too. If you are organised you can plan your second fermentation to finish on the day you go away.

Basic dos and don'ts

— Ideally use filtered but at the very least boiled water to brew.

— Avoid using any metal during the brewing process; take any rings off when you handle the scoby.

— Use real sugar. Honey and other natural sweeteners don't work as well; I've tried.

— Use green or black tea; I use loose-leaf organic. Flavoured and herbal teas don't work.

— Wash your hands before handling the scoby, being sure to wash off any soap residues.

— I wash my equipment every couple of brews using hot water and vinegar (not soap).

— Make sure the brew is covered at all times, to prevent flies getting in.

— If you see mould or anything unsavoury on the scoby, discard everything and start again.

— While I brew with green tea the most, every 5 brews or so I use black tea as it helps the scoby stay healthy; I don't understand why but it works.

— If I have a bad batch I brew the next batch a little sweeter and use black tea; it usually solves the problem.

— As you brew each batch a new scoby will form on the top of your kombucha; this means it's a good healthy brew and it's a good sign. When you go to make another batch you can separate the old scoby (the mother) and the new one (the baby) and make an additional batch. Give the old scoby away or keep it in the fridge; I tend to separate my scobys every few batches. If you have too many to find a use for they can be composted.

Resources

There are some amazing expert resources online; you can get very specific answers to any kombucha problem in great detail. My favourite is culturesforhealth.com.

Super chocolate tiffin bites

These little chocolate bites were born of two childhood obsessions: Terry's Chocolate Orange bars and chocolate tiffin. I love both but the super-sweet versions I lapped up as a kid now make me a bit crazy, so I came up with these. I make them in batches and keep them on hand for that time of day when I need something sweet. Sure, they have a bit of sugar, but I find the nuts and seeds balance out the hit of sweetness. They are spiked with orange zest, salt and vanilla. I'm always a bit happier after one of these.

You can mix up the nuts and fruit you use here. I imagine any citrus zest, sweet spice or even a hit of chilli would work well. I use little silicone moulds which double up for freezing curry pastes, pestos and even baby food. You could also make this mixture into a bark if you prefer by just pouring the chocolate into a tray lined with baking paper and sprinkling over the toppings.

Preheat your oven to 200°C/180°C fan/gas 6.

Break your chocolate into small pieces (this will help it melt evenly) and put into a small heatproof bowl that fits neatly over a saucepan. Put a couple of centimetres of boiling water in the pan, put your chocolate on top and leave to melt.

Roughly chop your almonds and put on a tray with the pumpkin and sesame seeds. Toast in the hot oven for about 4 minutes – you want the almonds to be just toasted but still a little white and buttery within – then remove from the oven and tip into a bowl.

MAKES ABOUT 20

400g dark chocolate (at least 70% cocoa solids)

100g almonds, skin on

75g pumpkin seeds

2 tablespoons sesame seeds

1 tablespoon coconut oil

1 teaspoon vanilla paste

the zest of 2 unwaxed oranges

a good pinch of flaky sea salt

75g raisins

Once the chocolate is melted, add the coconut oil and stir until this has melted and is incorporated, then add the vanilla, orange zest and salt and mix gently. If you don't have moulds and are making the tiffin in a tray, pour it into a baking tray lined with baking paper, then scatter over the toasted nuts and seeds and the raisins. If using moulds, add the toasted nuts and seeds and raisins to the mixture and gently stir again. Pour into moulds and leave to set.

Once set, turn the tiffin bites out of the moulds. Store in a tin or Tupperware box, where they will keep for up to 2 weeks.

Brownie energy bites with maple pumpkin praline

I am something of a snacker. I marvel at people who stop at three meals a day. Since becoming a mum, I have had less time to cook than ever before, but it has been really important that I feed myself well. In the kitchen, this has put the spotlight on traybake dinners prepared during Dylan's nap, meals that can be cooked with one hand, and ready-to-go bites of energy that perk me up when dinner seems a long way away.

Half truffle and half brownie, of all the things I have tried these have been the quickest to leave the jar. Covering these little bites in chocolate takes a little longer and can be skipped, but I welcome any opportunity to pretend I am in a chocolate factory. I use raw cacao powder here as I prefer its deep pure chocolate flavour (its health benefits are well reported too). If you're using standard dates, soak them in boiling water for 10 minutes first.

MAKES ABOUT 30

200g pecans

100g cashew nuts

4 tablespoons raw cacao or cocoa powder

1 teaspoon vanilla paste

½ teaspoon fine sea salt

½ teaspoon ground cinnamon

175g pitted Medjool dates

1 tablespoon coconut oil

FOR THE PUMPKIN AND MAPLE PRALINE

50g pumpkin seeds

a pinch of flaky sea salt

1 tablespoon maple syrup

FOR THE CHOCOLATE COATING

3 tablespoons coconut oil

2 tablespoons raw cacao or cocoa powder

1 teaspoon maple syrup

In the bowl of a food processor, pulse the pecans and cashews until you have a rough powder. Add the cacao, vanilla, sea salt and cinnamon. Pulse to mix evenly. Add the dates and coconut oil and blitz, scraping down the sides of the bowl here and there. The mixture should ball up, appear glossy and come together in your fingers; if it's still a little powdery, add a teaspoon of water and blitz again until it comes together, but is not too sticky and wet.

Scoop out the mixture in heaped teaspoon-sized bites and roughly roll into balls. Put on a tray lined with baking paper and chill in the fridge for at least 20 minutes. Make the praline by toasting the seeds in a frying pan until they start to pop, then add the salt and maple syrup and toss well. Allow to cook for 1 minute, then tip on to a plate. Once cool, roughly chop.

Make the chocolate coating. In a small saucepan, combine all the ingredients and whisk over a low heat until it thickens slightly, taking care it doesn't catch on the bottom. Set aside to cool. Dip the bites into the coating, turning with two forks to cover. Put on a baking tray, top with a little praline and leave to set. Store in the fridge until you're ready to eat them – they will keep for a week or so.

Chocolate and blood orange freezer cake

This is a no-cook cake, raw in fact if you are into that kind of thing; I use the freezer to set the cake instead of the oven. These cakes are sometimes called ice-box cakes, which I think sounds quite magical. It's the kind of dessert I like to eat in January.

I use a raw cashew butter here, which I buy from the supermarket, though if I have time I make it at home, as the flavour is gentler than the toasted nut butters you can buy and it has notes of white chocolate. Any more subtly flavoured nut butter would work here.

SERVES 6–8

FOR THE CRUST

25g cashew nuts

coconut oil, for greasing

120g pitted Medjool dates

1 teaspoon vanilla extract

1 tablespoon raw cacao or cocoa powder

a generous pinch of flaky sea salt

120g nut butter (I use a raw cashew butter, see note above)

125g whole buckwheat

FOR THE FILLING

70g cashew nuts

50g pitted Medjool dates

a good pinch of salt

450g ripe peeled bananas

the seeds from 1 vanilla pod or 1 teaspoon vanilla paste

70g coconut oil, melted

the zest and juice of 1 unwaxed blood orange

3 passion fruits, cut in half

TO FINISH

3 blood oranges

40g dark chocolate (70% cocoa solids)

First, soak both the cashews for the filling and for the crust in separate bowls of cold water for 3–4 hours if you have time, if not then soak them in warm water for 30 minutes. Grease the bottom of a 22cm loose-bottomed tart tin with coconut oil and put to one side.

Next make the crust. In a food processor, blitz the 25g of soaked, drained cashews and the dates until they have broken down into tiny pieces and start to come together in a ball. Add the vanilla, cacao, salt and nut butter and blitz until combined. Then add the buckwheat and blitz until the buckwheat has broken down a bit and the crust dough comes together in your fingers when pinched. Put the crust mixture into the middle of the greased tin and use your fingers to push it out to the edges and up the sides of the tin, then put it into the freezer to set for at least 3 hours.

Next make the filling. Put the soaked, drained cashews into a jug blender with the dates, salt, bananas and vanilla and blitz until completely smooth. Pour in the melted coconut oil, then add the orange zest and blitz again. Pour two-thirds into the chilled crust.

Scrape the seeds from the passion fruits into a sieve resting over a bowl. Use the back of a spoon to push the juice through, add this to the remaining banana mixture in the blender and add the juice of the blood orange, then pour this layer over the banana one. Smooth everything over with a spatula and put the crust back in the freezer for 30 minutes to firm up, though it can happily sit there for much longer.

To finish, take the tart out of the freezer about an hour before you want to eat. Cut the peel off the blood oranges and slice the flesh into thin rounds. Break the chocolate into shards.

Once the cake is thawed enough that the filling is beginning to soften, arrange the blood oranges and chocolate on top prettily and pat yourself on the back. Any leftovers can be stored in the freezer for up to 2 weeks.

Grapefruit and honey curd

I feel sorry for grapefruit. I think it's been pushed to the sidelines in favour of more its more approachable (clementines) or glamorous (blood orange) cousins. I love it – not just the pink ones, I love the straight-up yellow ones I ate as a kid. You could use either here. This curd is exactly what I want to spread on a piece of toast or to top a bowl of yoghurt year round, but, especially when it's still dark, it sings of the sunshine where these sunny fruits were grown, and the ginger and honey add even more cheer.

Making curd is not for anyone impatient, it's a slow meditative stir that makes the best, smoothest curd. You'll feel like it's never going to thicken, but have faith, it will – it always does. If you get overexcited and turn the heat up too much it will become grainy. If it does, you can press it through a sieve to resurrect it, but the joy comes from the slow stirring. Any citrus can be swapped in for the grapefruit here, just adjust the level of honey a little depending on whether the fruits are sweeter or more acidic.

MAKES A DECENT JARFUL

250ml freshly squeezed
    grapefruit juice

a small thumb-sized piece of
    ginger, peeled and grated

75g unsalted butter, at
    room temperature

60ml runny honey

2 large organic egg yolks

2 large organic eggs

a good pinch of flaky sea salt

the juice of ½ a lemon

Put the grapefruit juice and ginger into a small saucepan, bring it to a simmer and leave it to reduce to about 150ml. Let it cool a bit, then strain through a sieve.

Cream the butter in a medium heatproof mixing bowl. Add the honey and beat until fluffy and light. Add the egg yolks, and then the eggs, one at a time, beating well to incorporate each one before you add the next. Stir in the salt, then gradually add the reduced grapefruit and lemon juice.

Rinse out the small saucepan you used earlier and fill it one-third full with water. Bring to a simmer and place your bowl of curd on top of it. Stir constantly and heat the curd slowly. This step usually takes me about 20 minutes. Pull the curd from the heat when it is just thick enough to coat your spoon; it will thicken as it cools.

There's no need to strain the curd, unless it has some lumps. And you can keep it refrigerated for up to 2 weeks, or up to a month in the freezer.

Apple and white miso kimchi

This is a gentle kimchi; the apple, radish and white miso mellow the chilli and sharpness that comes from the fermentation. Fermented foods contain beneficial bacteria, which is important because we need a diverse population of bacteria in our gut for optimal health; I do notice the difference when I include some fermented foods in my diet (see Kombucha on page 56).

Make sure you use a pure sea salt, as iodised sea salt will prevent this fermenting properly. Check the heat of your chillies, as they vary so much. I use one to two, depending on their heat, for a medium-hot kimchi, but if you like things hot you can use a few more. The amount of time it will take for your kimchi to ferment will depend on two things: the air temperature and the humidity. How fermented you like your kimchi is a very personal thing – I like mine fermented for about two weeks in the winter and only a few days in the summer.

Coarsely shred the cabbage into 2cm-thick pieces, finely slice the spring onions, and put them both into your biggest bowl with the salt. Scrunch the lot with your hands for 5 minutes until the cabbage has released a lot of water, then leave it for 2 hours to release all its water, massaging it another couple of times to help this process.

Meanwhile, peel the mooli and cut it into thin 1cm-long matchsticks. Cut the apples into pieces about the same size – you can leave the skin on.

Mix the miso with the garlic, chillies, ginger and 2 tablespoons of cold water. Once the cabbage has had its 2 hours, add the mooli, apple and miso garlic paste to the bowl of cabbage and its water.

Put the kimchi and the liquid it sits in into a large jar or fermenting pot, taking care to pack the vegetables down firmly under the liquid so that no bits of vegetable are poking out, there are no air pockets and there are a few inches of space at the top of the jar for the air to escape.

MAKES 4 JARS

1 Chinese leaf cabbage (about 850g)

4 spring onions

2 tablespoons good sea salt

1 mooli or kohlrabi (about 200g), or 200g radishes

2 firm green apples

2 teaspoons white miso paste

1 clove of garlic, finely sliced

2–4 red chillies, finely chopped (with seeds)

a thumb-sized piece of ginger, peeled and finely chopped

Cover the jar loosely with a lid, or, if you would prefer to close the lid to keep the smell in, make sure you open it up every day to let the air out. Leave the kimchi on your work surface for 2–3 days, checking every day to see how it tastes. This winter I fermented mine in a cool cupboard for about 2 weeks. Once it tastes good to you, put it into the fridge, where it will keep for several months.

Ways to use your kimchi

- In the kimchi soup on page 24

- In a toasted sandwich with a good sharp Cheddar

- In the bao on page 410

- As a pickle on the side of your favourite bowl of noodles

- Wrapped into summer rolls

- To top some sriracha-spiked avocado on toast

- Chopped finely and mixed with oil and lemon for a punchy dressing for a grain

- As a base for a quick fried rice

- Added to the end of a stir-fry

- Fried in a pan before you add some eggs and scramble them

Tonics and teas for cold days

These are the things I make when winter sets in and coughs and colds strike; when we are cold to the bones or feeling a little depleted. I don't intend these recipes to be medicine. I have no proof that they work but they make me and my family feel better. Perhaps it's just the act of making something to nurture us, perhaps it's the ingredients; whatever it is I keep making them.

Turmeric, ginger and black pepper tea to warm

For two cups, grate about a tablespoon of ginger into a teapot. Squeeze in the juice of 1–2 lemons (depending on their size), add half a teaspoon of ground turmeric or about a tablespoon of fresh grated turmeric, a tiny pinch of dried chilli flakes and a good few grinds of black pepper, then pour in 600ml of hot water. Allow it to cool a little before sweetening with a little honey (I use the raw stuff for maximum goodness); this will make sure the amazing properties of the honey aren't killed by the boiling water.

Magic golden turmeric honey paste for colds

Mix 2 tablespoons of ground turmeric, or a small thumb of the freshly grated root, with 1 tablespoon of ground black pepper. Melt then cool 2 tablespoons of coconut oil. Add to the bowl and mix well then stir in 2 tablespoons of honey – raw is best. You can either eat this from the spoon or stir into hot water or warmed milk – I like oat milk.

Carrot, ginger and red chilli juice to lift and enliven

For one glass, peel 6 carrots and a thumb of ginger. Cut the green stalk off 1 chilli and if you like things hot keep the seeds in; if not then remove. Put the whole lot though a juicer and serve over ice. If you like you can gently warm this juice, though don't heat it too much or let it boil.

Kombucha and kefir (page 56)

These are great things to drink when you are feeling under the weather. I mix some turmeric and lemon into my kombucha and stir some of the golden paste above into my morning kefir. Both support healthy bacteria so are particularly great to drink if you are taking antibiotics.

Cinnamon and cardamom for sore throats

Mix 1 tablespoon of ground cinnamon and the bashed seeds of a cardamon pod with 1 tablespoon of runny honey and 1 of melted, cooled coconut oil. Store in a glass jar at room temperature taking a teaspoon whenever you have a tickle in your throat.

Vilcabamba cold cure

A lady made this cold cure for me on a trip to Ecuador and it worked. Juice 6 oranges into a small saucepan, add the juice of 1 lemon and 1 cinnamon stick. Warm to almost boiling then leave for 10 minutes to steep. Once cooled add a little honey if you like.

Lemongrass and three-chilli tea

For 2 cups, roughly chop a good thumb of ginger, bash 2 lemongrass stalks and add to a pan with 1 red chilli, 1 green chilli and a pinch of dried chilli flakes. Add 1 litre of water and bring to the boil, then turn the heat down and simmer for 30 minutes, until it has a deep aromatic flavour. Now you can add a black or green tea bag and steep for 5 minutes before drinking. Sweeten with honey to taste.

Make the ## Not-chicken soup
on page 28.

Ginger shots for the brave

Use your juicer to juice enough ginger to make about 2 tablespoons of juice. Just knock it back and wait 10 minutes before drinking any water.

Garlic shots for the braver

Stick with me here. This doesn't taste great but I am sure it's helped me stave off a cold more than a few times. Finely chop 1 clove of garlic, put it into a small glass with 3 tablespoons of cold water, take a deep breath and knock it back. Don't chew it. It might make you feel a little weird, but don't be tempted to drink water for about 10 minutes.

Herald of spring

Best of the season
  Wild garlic
  Sorrel
  Lovage
  Butterhead lettuce
  Early spring herbs
  Dandelion
  Radishes
  Watercress
  Celeriac
  Morels
  Broccoli
  Kale
  Forced pink rhubarb

Flowers
  Narcissus and daffodils
  Lily of the valley
  Sweet peas
  Ranunculus

Salted maple buckwheat and seed granola

This isn't strictly a seasonal recipe, but I have included it here as the first light mornings and brighter days mark a transition at our breakfast table, from toast and porridge, to breakfasts that are lighter and not necessarily warm (though on cooler days this does work very well on top of porridge or even with a little warm almond milk).

Buckwheat might not be something you have bought before; if not, then I think you should give it a try. It adds a brilliant crunch to this granola and some good morning energy, though if you like you could swap it for the same volume of quinoa flakes or rye flakes.

This recipe allows for some gentle swaps: seeds for nuts, perhaps a little cinnamon and nutmeg as you see fit. I make mine with a little dried fruit – apricots, cherries and dried peaches and pears are all favourites. How I eat this changes with the seasons – with poached rhubarb and yoghurt in spring, strawberries and rosewater in summer, orchard fruits in autumn.

I have added cup measures in this recipe, as I often find it useful when making granola.

MAKES 1 VERY LARGE JAR, 10–15 SERVINGS

220g oats (about 2 cups)

280g buckwheat (about 1 cup)

200g pumpkin seeds (1 cup)

100g sesame seeds (½ cup)

100g sunflower seeds (½ cup)

200ml maple syrup

1 vanilla pod or 1 tablespoon vanilla paste

2 tablespoons mild olive or coconut oil (melted)

a big pinch of flaky sea salt

150g dried fruit (I use golden raisins; ½ a cup)

Preheat your oven to 200°C/180°C fan/gas 6. Put the oats, buckwheat and seeds into a large mixing bowl. Mix the maple syrup, vanilla seeds or paste, oil and salt in a jug, then pour it over the oats and stir to make sure everything is well coated.

Divide the mixture between two baking trays, spreading it out well to make sure that it's even. Put the trays into the oven for 15 minutes. After 15 minutes take the trays out and give everything a good stir, then put them back into the oven, with the one that was on the top shelf on the bottom this time, and cook for another 15 minutes.

Remove the trays again and stir through your dried fruit, then put them back in the oven for 10 minutes (if you add the fruit any sooner it will burn). Take the granola out of the oven. Everything should be deeply golden and crisp by now and your house should smell like a bakery.

Allow the granola to cool completely before storing in an airtight jar or container, where it will keep for up to a month.

Black bean and tofu scramble

I first ate tofu scramble years ago on a trip to California and it's been a weekend staple ever since. This is a brunch dish in our house but it would work for any meal. Tofu has a pleasing bounciness that is suited to cooking this way; it soaks up the flavours – here big, brave notes of smoked paprika, garlic and the deeply savoury, almost inky, black beans.

The tofu I use here is neither the silken stuff nor the firm stuff. It's usually just labelled as tofu in water; it crumbles nicely in your fingers when you break it up. I always try to buy the best tofu I can: most supermarkets stock good organic varieties these days and some small, UK-based producers are cropping up at markets too.

SERVES 4

2 ripe avocados

2 unwaxed limes

250g cherry tomatoes, roughly chopped

2 red chillies, finely chopped

olive oil

6 spring onions, finely sliced

2 cloves of garlic, finely sliced

a small bunch of coriander, leaves picked, stalks finely chopped

1 teaspoon hot smoked paprika

1 x 400g tin of black beans, drained (or 250g home-cooked, see page 461)

400g tofu (see note above), crumbled into bite-sized pieces

4 flour or corn tortillas

First, mash the avocados with the zest of one of the limes and half its juice and a little salt and pepper.

Mix the tomatoes with the chillies, a good pinch of salt and pepper and squeeze over the juice of the other lime half.

Heat a frying pan over a medium heat and add a little oil. Add the spring onions, garlic and chopped coriander stalks. Cook for around 2 minutes, or until the edges of the garlic are beginning to brown. Add the smoked paprika and a little more salt and pepper, then cook for another minute.

Add the black beans to the pan and fry them for around 2 minutes, or until they have dried out a little. Add the crumbled tofu, turn the heat up and cook until the tofu has begun to catch and burnish a little, this will take about 4 minutes. Make sure you keep stirring so that it doesn't stick. Take off the heat and season well with salt and pepper.

Warm or toast the tortillas: I do this by holding them over the gas flame on my hob for 30 seconds or so on each side, turning them with tongs, but you could also warm yours in a dry frying pan. Wrap them in foil and put them into a low oven to keep warm, if you need to.

Pile the tofu mixture on to the toasted tortillas, with a little chilli and the coriander leaves strewn over, and serve with the avocado and tomatoes for spooning on top.

Avocado and cardamom smoothie

This smoothie is driven more by the mood of the season than by the ingredients that are listed. It's what I want for breakfast when the mornings get a bit more cheerful. It's a meeting of two things I love: avocados and cardamom. I often add a handful of kale or other dark leaves to give it an extra punch of green too. If you'd like something even more sustaining, you could add a handful of oats or quinoa flakes and a little more water. I had a smoothie like this in a café in LA and it was topped with a slick of buttery olive oil. I loved the combination; I realise it's not for everyone but do give it a try if you are curious. It's delicious. A high-speed blender works best here; if you don't have one you might want to use some apple juice instead of a whole apple, and ground cardamom instead of the pods.

Bash the cardamom pods to get the seeds out and put them into a dry pan over a medium heat. Toast for a few minutes until they smell fragrant.

Tip the seeds into a blender, add the rest of the ingredients and whizz until you have a silky-smooth pale green smoothie. Pour into two glasses.

MAKES 2

4 cardamom pods

the juice and zest of 1 unwaxed lime

1 green apple

1 ripe avocado, peeled and stoned

250ml milk (I use unsweetened almond)

1 tablespoon runny honey

250ml cold water

8 ice cubes

Sunny egg muffins

If there is a recipe that makes more of an egg, I am yet to find it: a whole egg hidden inside a muffin, the yolk still runny. These are based on a muffin I ate at a brilliant bakery in the Mission District of San Francisco called Craftsman and Wolves. It's the perfect breakfast muffin: a little bite from polenta, a hit of chilli, some brightness from the dill. They also travel well to a picnic, though be sure to eat them straight from the oven if you want a runny yolk, as the yolk will set a little as they sit.

This is a recipe that you will need to follow closely if you are after a runny egg. If you can't get buttermilk easily, yoghurt thinned down with a splash of milk will work too. You will need to use a deep, non-stick large muffin or Yorkshire pudding tin; normal muffin tins are too small.

MAKES 6 LARGE MUFFINS

8 medium organic eggs,
    at room temperature

100g fine polenta

180g white spelt flour

1 teaspoon flaky sea salt

1 tablespoon baking powder

50g sharp Cheddar,
    coarsely grated

4 spring onions, finely sliced

a small bunch of dill,
    finely chopped

¼ teaspoon dried chilli flakes

240ml buttermilk

90ml olive oil, plus a little
    extra for greasing

First, boil your eggs. Have ready a bowl of iced water. Bring a large pan of water to a rapid boil and lower in 6 of the eggs. Boil for exactly 4 minutes, not a second more. Remove from the pan and immerse in the ice-cold water, then chill in the fridge for at least 30 minutes.

Meanwhile, get your muffin mix ready. In one bowl, mix together the polenta, flour, salt, baking powder, cheese, spring onions, dill and chilli flakes and whisk with a balloon whisk to break up any lumps of baking powder.

In a separate jug, mix together the buttermilk, olive oil and remaining 2 eggs.

When you're ready to bake the muffins, preheat the oven to 200°C/190°C fan/gas 6. Grease 6 moulds of a deep muffin tin with a little oil. Get your eggs out of the fridge and peel them really, really carefully, putting them on a couple of sheets of kitchen paper to stop them rolling away.

Tip the buttermilk mixture into the flour and stir gently. Don't overmix, or the muffins will be tough; a few lumps are fine. Spoon a couple of tablespoons of the muffin batter into the bottom of each muffin mould, then very gently put an egg on top. Carefully add the rest of the batter so that you don't squash the egg, and immediately bake for 20 minutes, not a second longer.

Remove the muffins from the oven, take each one carefully out of its mould and place on a cooling rack. Using a sharp knife, cut right through the middle of the muffin and pat yourself on the back for achieving a perfectly soft yolk.

Wild garlic and yoghurt baked eggs

In early spring wild garlic lines our hedgerows, paths and parks. You can smell it a mile off, so it's pretty easy to be sure you have the right stuff. It's a great place to start gathering your own food – there is a satisfaction from picking something from the wild which would have otherwise gone unloved. While the leaves will smell very garlicky in the hedgerows as you pick them, they will mellow as they cook so don't worry.

That said, you don't have to use wild garlic here. If you can get your hands on some, great; if not, you can add a little more rocket and a clove of finely chopped garlic. It won't taste exactly the same but will still be delicious.

Preheat the oven to 170°C/150°C fan/gas 3. Wash the wild garlic and the rocket and place them in a 23cm ovenproof frying pan with a drizzle of oil. Add some salt and cook over a medium heat for about 5 minutes, or until the rocket has wilted and most of the liquid has evaporated. Strain the liquid from the leaves in a sieve set over the sink, pushing down to remove as much of the water as possible, then put them back into the pan. Grate over half of the lemon zest.

Make four deep indentations in the rocket mix, and crack an egg into each little hole. Place in the oven for 7–10 minutes, or until the egg whites set. Meanwhile, mix the yoghurt with the other half of the lemon zest and some salt and pepper.

Heat about 3 tablespoons of oil in a frying pan until it's good and hot but not smoking, line a plate with kitchen paper, then add the sage leaves to the pan. Cook for a few seconds until they are crisp, then scoop out with a slotted spoon and drain on the paper. Using the same pan, add the sesame seeds to the sage oil for 30–45 seconds, until they turn a deep golden colour. Scoop them out on to a separate sheet of kitchen paper.

Once the eggs are done, take them out of the oven and spoon over half the yoghurt mixture (leaving the rest for the table). Top with the fried sage, the toasted sesame seeds and a sprinkling of pul biber, and serve with flatbreads or good sourdough.

SERVES 2

50g wild garlic

150g rocket

olive oil

1 unwaxed lemon

4 organic eggs

100g Greek yoghurt

12 sage leaves

30g sesame seeds

pul biber or a pinch of dried chilli flakes

flatbreads or sourdough, to serve

Breakfast cake

One day I thought if I could make a cake with all the things I usually eat for breakfast, then it would be completely legitimate to eat cake for breakfast on a regular basis. Life has been much better ever since.

This is a shallow cake that is best cooked in a pan, then spooned out into a bowl and topped with more yoghurt and berries, though as it cools it firms up and any leftovers can be sliced and warmed in the oven.

During early spring seasonal fruit is in short supply, so I reach into my freezer for bags of blueberries, blackberries and dark cherries, which see us through until the first French strawberries find their way to us. Rice flour works well here in place of the wholemeal if you want to make it gluten free. Aquafaba (which, if you've not come across it, is the liquid from cooking chickpeas which miraculously whips up like egg whites) works in place of the eggs (I used 135ml of aquafaba made to the instructions on page 459) and coconut or oat yoghurt works well too for vegans.

SERVES 6

100g coconut oil or olive oil, plus extra for greasing

250g plain yoghurt, plus extra to serve

150ml runny honey or maple syrup

2 firm, crisp apples (I use Cox's), roughly grated

the zest of 1 unwaxed lemon

3 organic eggs, separated

100g rolled oats

100g ground almonds

50g wholemeal flour

1 teaspoon baking powder

200g frozen berries, plus extra to serve

Preheat your oven to 190°C/170°C fan/gas 5. If you are using coconut oil, gently melt it and allow it to cool. In a bowl, mix the yoghurt with the honey and add the apples and the lemon zest. Add the cooled coconut oil or olive oil. Add the egg yolks to the yoghurt mixture.

Put the oats into a food processor and blitz until you have a scruffy flour, then tip into a bowl and add the almonds, wholemeal flour and baking powder and whisk to get rid of any lumps of baking powder.

Add the dry ingredients to the yoghurt mixture and mix to combine everything. Whisk the egg whites with a pinch of salt until they form soft peaks, then gently fold them through the batter with a spatula or large spoon. You want to incorporate as much air as you can here to make the cake light and fluffy, so try not to mix more than you need to.

Rub a 23cm ovenproof frying pan with oil and warm it over a medium heat for a minute or two so the base of the cake crisps up nicely. Take it off the heat and pour the cake batter into the pan (I use an ovenproof frying pan here but you could use a similar-sized cake tin instead. If you're using a cake tin, pour the batter in without heating it on the hob).

Scatter your frozen fruit over the top and put the pan into the hot oven for 45–50 minutes, until the cake is golden and a skewer inserted into the cake comes out almost clean. If you are using a cast-iron pan the cake will continue to cook as it sits, so you can afford a few minutes less.

Serve in the middle of the table, with more yoghurt and some more berries if you like.

On juicing

Juices are pure, alive and potent essences. Juicing brings out the purity of an ingredient with unmatched vibrancy. While I do like to juice fruit and vegetables to drink, that usually only happens when I feel like a reset (see page 96) or if I am under the weather. More often than not I will eat my fruit as I like the texture and it feels like more of a meal somehow. But recently I have been looking at juicing as a much wider culinary tool as it can be an interesting way to think about flavour and cooking. I've been using my juicer to juice stray bunches of herbs, ginger, celery, fennel and even nuts and oats into milk, enhancing the use of what can sometimes be quite a bulky piece of kitchen kit.

Juicing is a great way of extending the life of leftover vegetables or the end of a bunch of herbs. While I like to use the juices fresh when I can, they can also be frozen – I use an ice-cube tray. Savoury juices can be added to soups, stews even risottos; those made with fruit can be added to drinks like ice cubes to flavour water or to add a punch to a smoothie.

Some people are put off juicing as they think that cleaning a juicer is a bit of a pain, and that is partially true, though it only takes a few minutes – not much longer than say, a food processor. The amount of juice you get will depend on how powerful your juicer is, so it's worth investing in a decent one.

Herbs and aromatics

Ginger
A 250g hand of ginger makes about 200ml of juice.
Freezes well; good added to dipping sauces, broths and teas (see cold cures on page 70).

Coriander
A large bunch makes about 100ml of juice.
Good juiced with green chilli; add to yoghurt, mashed avocado or salsas.

Dill
A large bunch makes about 60ml of juice.
Stir into yoghurt, whisk with eggs for an omelette, add to cold summer soups.

Parsley/lovage
A large bunch makes about 80ml of juice.
Add to stocks, risotto, dressings or pour over tomato salads (see page 170).

Basil
A very large bunch makes about 80ml of juice.
Add to dressings, cooked pasta, tomato salads, mozzarella, or to finish soups, stews and risotto.

Savoury

Cucumber
1 large cucumber makes about 250ml of juice (no need to peel).
Add to cold soups in summer or drinks; freeze for gin and tonics.

Beetroot
4 large beetroots make about 250ml juice.
Use it in the beetroot pasta on page 200 instead of the grated beetroot.

Carrot
500g of carrots makes about 250ml of juice (no need to peel).
Use as the base for a soup or stew, to finish pasta, add to dressings (see page 32).

Fennel
1 large bulb makes about 250ml of juice.
Add to broths, use in place of stock, add to dressings and juices.

Celery
1 head of celery makes about 400ml of juice.
Add to broths, use in place of stock, add to dressings and juices.

Kale
2 large heads of kale or cavolo nero make about 250ml of juice.
Add to soups, broths and juices.

Fruit

I like citrus in winter and more vibrant juices combined with veg in the summer. Here are a few combinations, listed with the main ingredient first to the smallest amount needed at the end, which is more of an accent.

—Grapefruit, lemon, ginger

—Pear, apple, kale, ginger

—Cucumber, apple, lettuce, flat-leaf parsley

—Carrot, celery, ginger, lemon, cayenne pepper

Nuts and grains

Almonds
Soak 1 cup of raw almonds in water overnight, drain, add 3 cups of water and juice. Add a touch of vanilla and a pinch of salt. Season the leftover meal and use like nut butter.

Pistachios
Soak 1 cup of unsalted shelled pistachios in water overnight, drain, add 3 cups of water and juice. I like this as it is. Season the leftover meal and use like nut butter.

Hazelnuts
Soak 1 cup of raw hazelnuts in water overnight, drain, add 3 cups of water and juice. I add a pinch of salt. Season the leftover meal and use like nut butter.

Oats
Soak 1 cup of rolled oats in water overnight, drain, add 3 cups of water and juice. Great for adding to coffee.

Creamy cannellini and sorrel on toast

This time of year brings one of my favourite things, sorrel. It's the perfect blend of verdant green herb and zesty lemon all in one succulent little leaf. It is such an under-used herb, probably because it can be hard to get hold of. If you can search it out, sorrel's lemony tart liveliness makes your mouth water like no other food I know. And if there were ever a herb to get our palates excited for spring, it's this one.

This is a quick riff on the creamy Italian-style cannellini beans I learned to make under some great Italian cooks as a young chef. As this is a speedy recipe I have suggested you use a tin of beans; better still would be a jar of the buttery Spanish ones; and even better some home-cooked. Whatever you use, the beans will be delicious, scented with bay and good olive oil and topped with a crown of green sorrel.

Blot the cannellini beans dry on a plate lined with kitchen paper.

In a 23cm frying pan, heat half the olive oil over a medium heat and add the bay leaves. Fry them for 1–2 minutes, until the leaves blister and start to release their oils. Turn the heat right down and add the beans along with a pinch of salt and pepper. Leave the beans cooking over a low heat for 10–15 minutes, stirring occasionally.

While the beans are cooking, heat a griddle over a medium–high heat for couple of minutes. When the pan is really hot and nearly smoking, place the bread into it and char for 2–3 minutes on each side, so you end up with smoky black stripes. Remove from the pan and place on warm plates.

Put the sorrel into a bowl with the orange juice and scrunch with your hands to break it down a little and soften the leaves.

Remove the bay leaves from the beans and crush half the beans with the back of a wooden spoon, so you're left with a creamy, but still textured beany mash. Pile the beans on to the warm toast and top with the sorrel, the remaining olive oil and a sprinkle of salt and pepper.

SERVES 2

1 x 400g tin of cannellini beans, drained

4 tablespoons good olive oil

2 bay leaves

2 chunky slices of sourdough or other good bread

50g bunch of sorrel, washed well

the juice of 1 unwaxed orange

Sesame and green olive bars

My new addiction. I was sceptical about a savoury snack bar, but these are as moreish as they are balanced: salty olives and nori (sheets of dried seaweed used to wrap sushi), buttery sesame seeds, toasted oats, crunchy puffed rice and a hint of sweetness. If you are struggling to find brown rice syrup, you could use runny honey, but they won't set quite as firm, so be sure to store the bars in the fridge. This is a recipe from my column in the *Guardian*; I have made them so many times since it was printed I felt I had to include it here.

MAKES ABOUT 16 BARS

2 sheets of nori

150g rolled oats

150g green olives, pitted and roughly chopped

125g walnuts, toasted and finely chopped

4 tablespoons sesame seeds

30g unsweetened puffed rice cereal

2 tablespoons chia seeds

a small pinch of dried chilli flakes (optional)

300g brown rice syrup

100g coconut oil, plus extra for greasing

Preheat the oven to 200°C/180°C fan/gas 6. Put the nori sheets on one baking tray and the oats on another. Bake for 3–5 minutes, or until the nori has darkened a little and crumbles easily in your hand and the oats smell toasty.

Grease a 20 x 30cm baking tray with coconut oil. Mix all the dry ingredients, including the olives, together in a large bowl and set aside.

Combine the rice syrup and coconut oil in a small saucepan over a medium heat. Stir for a minute or two until it melts and thickens a little – this will take about 4 minutes. Pour the coconut oil mixture over the oat mixture and stir until everything is well mixed.

Spread the mixture out in the tin and press down firmly; this will help your bars stick together. Chill for a few hours before cutting into bars – I go for about 16, but you could make them bigger or smaller as you wish. They will keep in the fridge for up to a week.

Green wild garlic and Puy lentil soup

In wild garlic season, I pick loads and make it into this pesto (no extra garlic added), which can be kept under a slick of olive oil in the fridge for weeks or in the freezer for much longer. Wild garlic has a strong taste when it's raw but that mellows when you cook it. If you can't get your hands on it, a finely chopped clove of garlic and some spinach will stand in; there is no need to soak the garlic or spinach.

First soak the lentils in boiling water for 10 minutes; this will help speed up the cooking time and make them softer. Drain the lentils and put them into a large deep saucepan with 750ml of cold water and simmer until they are cooked and soft but not falling apart – this should take between 20 and 25 minutes.

Put another pan over a medium heat, add a little oil and then the shallot, fennel, celery and your root vegetable. Add a good pinch of salt, then cook for 10 minutes, until soft and sweet.

Meanwhile, toast the hazelnuts in a dry pan until golden brown. Once they are nicely toasted, take off the heat. Grate in the lemon zest and add 2 tablespoons of olive oil, then put the pan back on the heat for a minute or so until you hear a sizzle. Transfer the lot to a bowl to cool. Once cool, roughly chop.

Fill and boil the kettle. Once the vegetables and the lentils are both cooked, stir the vegetables into the lentils and add 500ml of hot water from the kettle. Leave to simmer on a very low heat.

Put the wild garlic into a bowl, cover with boiling water and leave for a minute, then scoop out with a slotted spoon. Squeeze out any excess water, then put into a food processor with a tablespoon of oil and enough cold water (about 2 tablespoons) to purée it.

Stir the spinach and wild garlic purée through the soup. Serve with the lemon hazelnuts, a little more olive oil, and garlic flowers if you have them.

SERVES 4

200g dried Puy lentils

good olive oil

1 banana shallot, finely chopped

1 bulb of fennel, finely chopped

2 sticks of celery, finely chopped

50g swede, parsnip or carrot, finely chopped

50g hazelnuts

1 unwaxed lemon

a good bunch of wild garlic (about 50g)

a bunch of young spinach or other greens (about 50g)

Citrus and lemongrass broth

This time of year feels right for eating crisp, clean food. This gentle broth is as much flavoured with lemon and orange as it is with the aromatic lemongrass; the flavour is subtle and delicate and that's the idea.

The soup is restorative and warming as well as lifting and enlivening, making it perfect to see off a cold, a chill in the air from the change of season or just to eat for a brightening lunch or supper. Such is my love for the gentle citrus notes of this broth, I am pretty sure I could eat this soup every day from April to September.

I keep this very simple, with just noodles, clean tofu and broth, but if you like you could add some more veg: shredded greens, sugar snaps and broccoli would all work well.

SERVES 4

4 stalks of lemongrass, bashed

4 lime leaves

a thumb-sized piece of ginger, peeled and grated

2 shallots, peeled and roughly chopped

1 tablespoon coriander seeds

the juice of 2 oranges or mandarins

the juice of 1 lemon

2 tablespoons white miso paste

TO SERVE

200g cooked noodles (I use buckwheat)

a small bunch of basil, leaves picked

a small bunch of coriander, leaves picked

a few chives, chopped, or a pinch of chive cress

200g firm tofu, chopped into small pieces

Put 2 litres of water into a pan and bring it to the boil. Once boiling, add the lemongrass, lime leaves, ginger, shallots and coriander seeds. Bring to the boil again, then turn down to a simmer and cook for 30 minutes. You can cook it for a bit longer if you'd like a really intense flavour.

Strain the soup, using a large sieve over a big mixing bowl and a spoon to push down on the aromatics to get maximum flavour from them, then tip the liquid back into the saucepan.

Next add the juice of the oranges and the lemon, watching out for pips, and stir in the miso and a little salt, to taste. The broth will keep like this for 4–5 days and freezes well.

When you are ready to eat, warm your broth. Pile your noodles into bowls, topping with the herbs and tofu. Ladle the citrus broth over and serve steaming.

Three-day reset

Spring holds promise. To me it feels like the true start of the year, when everything is waking from its winter sleep; when the first green shoots, leaves and vegetables show their heads. It is rebirth, reawakening, resetting. So it's at this time of year that I often feel like it's time for a reset. Let me be very clear here, this is not a detox; on the whole I don't believe in them – they make me hungry and angry and longing for endless slices of bread or corner-shop chocolate bars. But what I do find helpful is resetting my eating clock. In fact my whole journey into eating vegetarian food and in turn writing these books came out of one such reset.

Like anyone else, I get into patterns and habits with food; some good, some bad, driven as much by emotion as nutrition, so I do a reset to help me connect with what I am eating again. It breaks the habits I have fallen into and allows me to reconsider why I am eating, when I am eating and what really feels good for me and my body. When we eat we are voting for how we want to look, think and feel but it's this very simple connection that can be lost in the day-to-day of life. By eating mindfully for a few days I find I can reconnect.

I know it's time for me to reset when I move to viewing food as fuel; when I lose a bit of that magical connection with food; when I slice into a beetroot or a blood orange and I fail to be awed by it; when I feel a bit jaded and can't come up with ideas for dinner; or I can't work out what I want to eat, what it is I fancy.

So every so often, and always at the beginning of spring, I make space over a few days to simplify things, to eat food wholly centred on fruits and vegetables. This doesn't mean 'boring'; it's food that's delicious and filling and that I am still excited about eating: juices, smoothies, soups and stews; if the odd square of chocolate creeps in, that's okay.

Reset advice

— Fill your fridge with seasonal fruits and vegetables.

— Eat only when you are hungry; listen to your body.

— I would suggest a smoothie for breakfast and soup for lunch and dinner (or one of the recipes I've suggested below) with some snacks in between. If you are really hungry add some cooked brown rice or soba noodles.

— I snack on a piece of fruit or some chopped up veg.

— Avoid caffeine (herbal teas are fine).

— Drink lots of water: 2 litres a day at the least.

— On waking: drink hot water with lemon.

— For breakfast: a smoothie or juice, if you are hungry, kheer (see page 8).

— Snack: a piece of fruit or carrot sticks or a cup of miso soup.

— Lunch: a bowl of soup or salad.

— Snack: a herbal tea.

— Dinner: a bowl of soup.

There are a number of recipes in this book that would be suitable for a reset. I try to avoid using too much salt or soy sauce when eating this way so you may want to reduce them a little when cooking them, as well as leave out heavier things like the bread and pasta if I have suggested serving the recipes with these.

Breakfast

Saffron breakfast kheer (page 8).

Avocado and cardamom smoothie (page 79).

Summer morning bowl (page 232).

Cherry and almond breakfast smoothie (page 231; use frozen cherries at this time of year).

On juicing (see page 86).

Lunch and dinner

Kimchi and miso noodle soup (page 24).

Green peppercorn and lemongrass coconut broth (page 27).

Not-chicken soup (page 28; I do this without the tofu).

Ginger-spiked spring herb salad (page 106).

Simple yellow split pea soup with green olives (page 322).

Smacked cucumbers (page 252; go easy on the soy sauce/tamari).

Sweet potato mash with coriander and chilli (page 357; again easy on the soy sauce/tamari).

Drinks

Kombucha (page 56).

Herbal teas and infusions (page 222).

Gently spiced, lemon braised roots

This is a marriage of humble ingredients and a great example of how careful and considered cooking can transform them. I inherited the recipe from my friend Anna Shepherd. It's loosely Turkish in its flavour: the roots are braised in olive oil, spices and lemon juice, which bring a really generous sweetness to the vegetables, and coat the couscous in the most delicious kind of warm dressing.

I make this during the hungry gap – that little bit of time when the spoils of spring haven't yet arrived and the stores of winter are dwindling. The freshness of the lemon and the bright herbs elevate this to something suited to the first days of spring but still warming and hearty.

Pul biber is a milder Turkish chilli flake, somewhere between chilli and red pepper. The shops near where I live are full of it, but if you can't get your hands on it a pinch of regular dried chilli flakes will step in; they are much hotter, so you'll need substantially fewer. I use mograbieh – giant couscous – and choose the wholewheat version, which you can buy in most supermarkets.

SERVES 4

150g wholewheat giant couscous (mograbieh)

1 small swede (about 500g)

4 small carrots (about 300g)

2 small parsnips (about 300g)

6 tablespoons olive oil

½ teaspoon cayenne pepper

2 teaspoons cumin seeds, roughly bashed

2 cloves of garlic, finely chopped

the zest and juice of 2 unwaxed lemons

1 teaspoon pul biber chilli flakes(see note above)

a large bunch of dill

4 tablespoons pumpkin seeds

2 tablespoons plain yoghurt

Place the giant couscous in a bowl, cover with cold water and set aside. Peel the swede and roughly chop into 2cm cubes. Slice the carrots lengthways into quarters and then across the middle into eighths. Do the same with the parsnips, cutting them into smaller pieces if the parsnips are much larger than the carrots.

In a large, deep frying pan with a lid, gently heat 4 tablespoons of the olive oil, and add all the root veg. Turn the heat up to medium–high and stir for about 5 minutes, or until you can see the oil bubbling at the sides and the edges of the vegetables crisping at the bottom of the pan.

Turn the heat down to medium and add the cayenne pepper and half the cumin, the garlic, lemon juice and 100ml of water. Stir to make sure the spices are lending their flavours evenly through the pan. Cover with a lid, turn the heat down again and leave to braise for 30–35 minutes, until the vegetables are soft all the way through.

While the roots are gently cooking, make the pul biber oil by mixing the remaining 2 tablespoons of olive oil with the pul biber and a generous pinch of salt. Pick the leaves from the bunch of dill. Fill and boil your kettle and drain the giant couscous.

Next, remove the lid from the pan of roots and stir the couscous through. Add 150ml of water from the kettle, or just enough to cover the vegetables and couscous. Cook for a further 8 minutes, or until the couscous is pillowy soft. Stir through the dill.

Meanwhile, heat a glug of oil in a small frying pan and add the pumpkin seeds and remaining cumin. Toast the seeds, stirring frequently until they begin to pop and split a little. Stir through the lemon zest and take off the heat.

Spoon the vegetables and couscous into deep bowls and top with the yoghurt, pul biber oil and toasted pumpkin seeds.

Early spring stew with baked ricotta

This is what I make when I feel like eating something green and vibrant, but the green tide of spring hasn't yet arrived. I use frozen peas and broad beans (I double-pod mine, which I know takes ages, so there is no need to if you are in a hurry. To double-pod the frozen ones you'll need to leave them in a bowl of boiling water for a few minutes before you can pop them out of their little pods). In early spring some fresh Spanish broad beans start arriving, so those would be a great thing to use here if you can get them. When the first fresh British peas and broad beans arrive I'd be sure to use them.

Use whatever soft green herbs you can get your hands on: I like a combination of something heady, like mint or basil, something fragrant like tarragon, and something more neutral like parsley. But you could really use any soft herb you have and this is a great way of using up the end of a few bunches. I use a generous amount of oil here, as it adds a butteriness and a peppery kick to the final dish; you can add it bit by bit and stop when it tastes good to you.

Preheat the oven to 200°C/180°C fan/gas 6. Halve or quarter any larger potatoes and place them on a baking tray. Make a space in the middle for the ricotta, then upturn the tub of ricotta on to the tray so that it sits in a little mound in the middle.

Season everything with salt and pepper and drizzle with a tablespoon of olive oil. Use a spoon to turn the potatoes over to make sure they are coated in the oil and seasonings, then grate over the zest of the lemons, making sure there is plenty of zest on top of the ricotta. Scatter over half the basil leaves. Put the tray into the hot oven to cook for 20 minutes. →

SERVES 4–6

500g baby new potatoes

1 x 250g tub of ricotta

100ml extra virgin olive oil, plus more for cooking

2 unwaxed lemons

a large bunch of basil, leaves picked

2 heads of small lettuce, such as baby Cos or Little Gem

½ teaspoon Dijon mustard

¼ teaspoon runny honey

a bunch of spring onions, finely chopped

1 litre good vegetable stock

300g frozen broad beans or 900g fresh, unpodded weight

200g frozen peas (600g fresh (unpodded weight)

a couple of bunches of soft herbs, leaves only, roughly chopped

Meanwhile, cut your lettuces into 4 wedges and put them on another tray. In a small bowl, mix together the juice of half a lemon, 2 tablespoons of the olive oil, the mustard, honey and a good pinch of salt and grind of pepper. Pour the dressing over the lettuce wedges and use your hands to coat them really well. Once the potatoes have had their 20 minutes, add the tray of lettuce to the oven and cook everything for another 15 minutes, or until the potatoes are brown and the lettuces charred at the edges, then take them out of the oven.

Meanwhile, in a large deep saucepan with a lid, heat a little olive oil on a medium heat, add the chopped spring onions and cook for a couple of minutes until brown at the edges. Add the stock and the olive oil and bring to the boil. Taste the stock, and if you think it needs it, add a little seasoning.

Add the broad beans and peas to the broth and cook for a minute or two, then stir through half the chopped herbs and take off the heat.

To serve, divide the potatoes and lettuce between four bowls, top with the broth, then break or spoon over the ricotta, the rest of the herbs and a drizzle of oil.

Roasted roots with wasted pesto

There is a movement in the food world to stop us wasting so much; a third of what we produce worldwide is thrown away, enough to feed 17 million people, and yet millions still go hungry. In the last few years I've been doing my best to tackle waste in my own kitchen.

Rigid sell-by dates and a squeamish attitude to imperfection encourage us to throw away perfectly good food: tops are cut off turnips, beetroot and carrots before we have even had a chance to think of using them; imperfect melon trimmings are abandoned to make our little pots of pre-chopped fruit more presentable. And that's without mentioning the fuel and water that has been used to produce and transport it all.

I have been cooking using the whole ingredient, trying not to throw any of the precious food I have bought in the bin (I hope you will excuse me a papery garlic skin). This is a pleasing tray of roasted roots with a pesto made from things you'd probably usually overlook. There is little more satisfying than making something out of nothing.

Preheat the oven to 220°C/200°C fan/gas 7.

Separate the green tops from the carrots and beetroots, then wash and put to one side for later.

Wash all the vegetables really well; the carrots and beetroots will need a particularly good scrub, as you're not going to peel them.

Cut the butternut squash in half lengthways and use a spoon to scoop out the seeds (keep these aside to use later), then slice the squash into 1cm moon-shaped wedges.

Slice the beetroot into quarters or halves if they are small, and the carrots in half lengthways, or quarters if they are really big.

Tip all the vegetables into a large baking tray and drizzle with a good glug of the oil from the olive jar. Sprinkle about 2 tablespoons of the caper brine over the vegetables – this will be your salt – then add the capers and give everything a good mix. →

SERVES 4

1 bunch of carrots with tops

1 bunch of beetroots with tops

1 small butternut squash

100g whole black olives in oil, pitted

2 tablespoons baby capers in brine

1 unwaxed lemon

1 bulb of garlic

a piece of hard, white cheese (Manchego, Parmesan, Cheddar; optional)

extra virgin olive oil

103

Grate over the zest of the lemon, then cut it in half and add to the tray along with the whole bulb of garlic. Bake for 30–40 minutes, until the vegetables are cooked through and golden around the edges.

Meanwhile, wash the squash seeds under cold running water to get rid of any fibrous bits. Coat with a little more oil from the olives, add with the olives to the tray and roast in the oven for 10 minutes, or until you can hear them pop and they look a shade darker.

Once the vegetables are cooked, remove the tray from the oven, carefully spoon out the lemon and garlic to make the pesto, and put the veg back in the oven to keep them warm.

To make the pesto, squeeze the roasted garlic out of its papery skin into the bowl of a food processor. Add the roasted squash seeds, whole roasted lemon halves (picking out any pips) and grated cheese if you're using it, and blitz to a coarse paste. Add the carrot and beetroot tops and about 4 tablespoons of olive oil (from the olive jar) then add a little more if you need to, (alternatively you could add a splash of water) and pulse until you have a chunky pesto. Season with a little caper brine.

Serve the roasted veg in the middle of the table, with the pesto for spooning. Freeze leftover pesto in ice cube trays for up to a few months or keep in a jar in the fridge, covered with a thin layer of olive oil, where it will keep for up to a week.

Ginger-spiked spring herb salad

The start of April brings the first home-grown soft herbs. It feels like a shift; the deep savouriness and rich oils of the woody herbs of winter are put away for a while to make way for the verdant grassy-green herbs of spring and summer.

Here I use a mixture of the ones I have at home. Picking the leaves into a bowl is a lovely thing to do – you'll be hit by a wave of fragrance and the bowl will get prettier and prettier as you pick.

The delicate herbs could just be dressed in lemon and oil and a good pinch of salt and would still be quite some salad, but here I toss them in a ginger-spiked dressing with some tiny shards of lightly pickled cucumber and some toasted coconut. It's a light salad, great next to curries and Asian food, but I most often eat it simply, with some flatbreads and thick yoghurt.

SERVES 4–6

¼ cucumber, chopped into tiny ½cm pieces

2 tablespoons white wine vinegar

the juice of 1 lemon

1 teaspoon flaky sea salt

1 teaspoon golden caster sugar

50g raw coconut chips or 25g unsweetened desiccated coconut

5 generous handfuls of mixed soft herbs

FOR THE GINGER DRESSING

the zest and juice of 2 limes

1 green chilli, finely chopped

1 shallot, finely chopped

½ teaspoon tamari or soy sauce

1 teaspoon brown rice vinegar

1 teaspoon runny honey or agave nectar

½ a small thumb-sized piece of peeled ginger

1 small clove of garlic

Mix the cucumber in a bowl with the vinegar, lemon juice, salt and sugar. Scrunch well to help begin the pickling, then cover with a plate and set to one side. Lightly toast the coconut chips in a dry frying pan on a medium heat, until they begin to brown and smell toasty, then tip on to a plate and allow to cool.

Roughly pick the leaves from the herbs, discarding any tough stalks, and wash well in a bowl of cold water. Lift into a salad spinner, and spin them to dry well – they'll retain more of the dressing and won't wilt immediately, which can sometimes happen when the leaves are wet.

Next, make the dressing. Mix the lime zest and juice, chilli, shallot, tamari, vinegar and honey in a bowl. Use a fine grater to grate in the ginger and garlic. Mix well with a fork and season to taste.

Drain the cucumber and pat dry with kitchen paper. Toss in a large bowl with the dried herbs and dress with the ginger-spiked dressing, turning the leaves a few times to coat them evenly. Sprinkle with the coconut and serve straight away.

Roasted radishes with sorrel, crispy lentils, and buttermilk dressing

This is a very cheerful dinner. Radishes and potatoes are roasted in a little honey and lemon to exaggerate their sweetness, offset by the crispy roast lentils. I use my favourite spring leaf here, sorrel. Its bright lemony flavour makes you sit up when you take a mouthful. This recipe is everything I want in the winter, brightness that somehow makes your mouth water.

If you can't get hold of sorrel, scrunch a couple of handfuls of spinach together with the juice of half a lemon and roughly shred. Scatter over the top in place of the sorrel. It won't be quite as pretty but it will taste great. Look out for the long breakfast radishes here or the unusual purple ones; they will add some extra good looks. The flavours in the salad are subtle, so be sure to season it carefully.

Preheat the oven to 220°C/200°C fan/gas 7. Tumble the radishes and potatoes into a roasting tray with a tablespoon of the olive oil, the juice from half the lemon, the honey and some salt.

In a separate roasting tray, mix the lentils with a generous pinch of salt, another tablespoon of olive oil and the zest of the lemon.

Place the tray with the radishes and potatoes in the oven for 30 minutes, giving it a shake once or twice during the roasting time. With 15 minutes to go, add the tray with the lentils to the oven. After 15 minutes they should be crispy and beginning to blister in places, and the radishes and potatoes should be soft and brown at the edges.

Meanwhile, make the dressing by whisking the buttermilk with a good squeeze of the other half of lemon and the remaining tablespoon of olive oil. Season well with salt and pepper, taste and add more lemon if you like and set aside.

Once the lentils and radishes have had their time, remove from the oven and mix everything in rough layers on a large platter with the sorrel, then drizzle the buttermilk dressing over the top.

SERVES 4

400g radishes, halved

400g new potatoes, halved

3 tablespoons olive oil

1 unwaxed lemon

1 tablespoon runny honey

2 x 400g tins of Puy lentils, drained and dried on kitchen paper

50ml buttermilk or thin plain yoghurt

2 handfuls of sorrel leaves

Crushed new potatoes, broccoli and blood orange cream

This is a gentle, soothing dish. The potatoes are warm, crisp and golden next to the bright broccoli stems, whose little tree-tops soak up the pale-pink blood orange cream. The garlic is sweet and subtle behind it all. I eat this for supper but also often serve it as part of a spread, as its subtle notes mean it goes well with an endless list of things.

If you are vegan you could make a cashew cream to use in place of the crème fraîche. (Soak 25g of cashews in cold water for at least 2 hours, then drain and blitz with 100ml of fresh cold water until you have a smooth cream – you'll need a powerful blender to get it totally smooth.)

Put the potatoes into a medium saucepan and cover with cold water. Add a generous pinch of salt and bring to the boil over a high heat. Once the potatoes are boiling, let them cook for a further 10–12 minutes, depending on the size, until a knife passes through them easily.

While the potatoes are cooking, trim the broccoli spears, nicking off any dry, tough ends and slicing any larger pieces in half lengthways.

Remove the potatoes with a slotted spoon, leaving the pan on the heat. Place them in a bowl and cover to keep warm. Lower the broccoli into the water that the potatoes were cooking in and boil for 3–4 minutes, until just tender. Leave to steam dry.

Find two frying pans whereby one fits inside the other easily and heat the olive oil in the larger one over a medium heat (if you don't have two frying pans you could just roast the potatoes in the oven, at 220°C/200°C fan/gas 7 at the beginning of the recipe and burst a few with a potato masher halfway through). Bash the garlic cloves with the side of a knife and put them into the hot oil, leave for a minute to flavour the oil, then take the garlic out and put to one side. Place the potatoes in the pan and cover with the smaller pan so that the potatoes are crushed by the weight of the pan. Cook the potatoes like this in the pan for 25 minutes, turning them 2–3 times during the cooking process and pressing down with the back of a wooden spoon on some to help them split and crisp. →

SERVES 4

600g new potatoes, large ones halved

300g purple sprouting broccoli

2 tablespoons olive oil

2 cloves of garlic, skin on

150g crème fraîche

the zest and juice of 2 unwaxed blood oranges

50g hazelnuts

Meanwhile, mix the crème fraîche with the blood orange zest and juice and season with salt and pepper. Toast your hazelnuts quickly in a dry pan over a medium heat until they turn from pale brown to rich golden brown, then remove and roughly chop.

Once the potatoes are crisp, split and golden, tip them out of the pan into a serving bowl and put the pan back on the heat. Peel and roughly chop the cooked garlic and add it to the pan with the broccoli. Cook until the edges of the broccoli begin to crisp – this should take only a few minutes.

Tumble the broccoli into the bowl, top with the blood orange crème fraîche and mix while everything is still warm. Scatter over the hazelnuts and serve in the middle of the table.

Pea and charred spring onion fritters

These flavourful little fritters have become a favourite on my table. Spring onions are something we are used to seeing year round but they are at their best in early spring, when they are British and mellow and sweet. You could use calçots (a delicious Catalonian spring onion) if you make this during their short season and you can get your hands on some.

I char the spring onions to give them depth and smokiness to offset the bright sweet little peas. And I serve them with a spring herb salad which is purposefully heavy on the herbs and brings an amazing fragrance to the table. The double mint yoghurt makes use of dried mint. As a rule I prefer fresh herbs to dried, but this is an exception, where both dried and fresh mint sing together and bring their own different notes.

─────────────────────

Heat a griddle until very hot. Add the spring onions and griddle until soft all the way through and charred all over. If you don't have a griddle you could roast them in a hot oven at 220°C/200°C fan/ gas 7 for 10 minutes.

Blanch the peas in salted boiling water until just cooked – about 30 seconds to 1 minute.

Toast the sesame seeds in a dry frying pan over a medium heat until golden, then tip into a bowl to cool.

Put the white beans into a food processor with half the cooked peas and blitz until they are mashed up but not pasty – you still want a few beans to be visible. You can do this with a bit of determination and a potato masher too, if getting the food processor out is a chore. Transfer to a mixing bowl.

Roughly chop the charred spring onions and place in the bowl with the rest of the peas and the flour, 2 tablespoons of the sesame seeds, the lemon zest and mint. Season well with salt and pepper.

Mix the yoghurt with the mint – dried and fresh – the zest of the lemon and the olive oil. Season well and put into a bowl, then top with the sumac and the remaining toasted sesame seeds. →

SERVES 4

3 bunches of spring onions

400g fresh or frozen peas, podded if fresh

3 tablespoons sesame seeds

1 x 400g tin of white beans, drained

2 tablespoons plain flour (I use spelt)

the zest of 1 unwaxed lemon

a few sprigs of mint, leaves picked and finely chopped

olive oil, for frying

warm flatbreads, to serve (optional)

FOR THE MINT YOGHURT

8 tablespoons plain yoghurt

2 teaspoons dried mint

a few sprigs of mint, leaves picked and finely chopped

1 unwaxed lemon

a glug of olive oil

1 teaspoon sumac

FOR THE HERB SALAD

a small bunch of dill

a small bunch of mint

a small bunch of chervil or tarragon

2 handfuls of pea shoots

113

For the salad, pick the leaves from all the herbs and mix with the pea shoots, then squeeze over the juice of half of the lemon you used in the yoghurt.

Heat a frying pan on a medium heat, add a covering of olive oil and spoon heaped tablespoonfuls of the fritter mixture into the pan – the mix will make 12 heaped tablespoon-sized fritters. Flatten each one a little with the back of the spoon and leave to cook for 3–4 minutes on each side until golden brown. You can keep the first batch warm in a low oven while you cook the rest if all 12 don't fit in your pan.

Serve with the double mint yoghurt, herb salad and some warm flatbreads if you like.

Staffordshire oatcakes

Oatcakes are a thing of beauty. These are the famed Staffordshire version, not the crisp biscuity ones; more of a chewy toothsome pancake. They are sold in shops in the north of England but it's hard to come by them where I live in London. We used to bring packs home in our suitcase from trips up north but they are actually surprisingly easy to make; you'll need a couple of hours to let the batter rise but the rest is very easy. The oatcakes can be made successfully with a gluten-free flour blend (if you use GF oats) and are naturally dairy free if you use oat milk, though normal milk works too.

In a small saucepan, heat the milk with 400ml of water until it's about body temperature, then take off the heat. Remove a couple of tablespoons of the warm liquid to a separate bowl and stir the yeast and sugar into it. Set aside for 10 minutes.

In a mixing bowl, combine the oats, flours and salt and whisk until no lumps are visible. Once the yeast mixture is frothy, make a well in the centre of the flours and pour in the yeast. Sprinkle some flour over the top. Set aside for another 10 minutes. Whisk the remaining milk and water through until you have a pourable batter that's a little thicker than a pancake batter. Cover with a damp tea towel and set aside for at least an hour, ideally two.

Heat a large frying pan with a splash of rapeseed oil on a medium heat. Give the batter a quick mix, then ladle it into the pan and tilt to ensure the base is evenly covered like a thick pancake. Cook for around 4 minutes on the first side, until it's bubbling and the colour has changed from dark to a couple of shades lighter; the batter will also look dry on the top. When the sides of the oatcakes start to come away from the pan, ease a spatula around them and gingerly flip them over. Cook for another 2 minutes on the other side. Top them as you wish (see overleaf for some of my suggestions) and serve warm.

Any leftovers can be left to cool and the oatcakes can be wrapped in greaseproof paper and stored in the fridge for up to 5 days or the freezer for a few months. Reheat them in a dry pan or under a hot grill for 30 seconds on each side. →

MAKES ABOUT 10

400ml oat milk

4g dried active yeast

½ teaspoon sugar

225g finely-ground oats
(or you could use oatmeal)

80g wholemeal spelt flour

80g white spelt flour

½ teaspoon sea salt

rapeseed oil, for frying

How to top your oatcakes

• Mustard, capers and rocket (enough for 4 oatcakes)

Mix a teaspoon of wholegrain mustard with 100g of grated Cheddar and 2 tablespoons of crème fraîche. Fry 4 tablespoons of capers in 2–3 tablespoons of olive oil until crisp, then add 2 handfuls of rocket and allow to wilt. Cover the oatcakes with the crème fraîche mixture, top with the capers and rocket and finish with a grating of lemon zest.

• Cheese and chutney

Top each oatcake with a thin spreading of chutney, then grate over some cheese and pop it under the grill to melt.

• Sunny egg florentine

Poach an egg per person; meanwhile wilt some spinach in a pan with a little cider vinegar and grated nutmeg. Top the warm oatcake with the wilted spinach and egg and finish with a good grind of salt and pepper.

• Cherries, yoghurt and poppy seed (enough for 4 oatcakes)

Put 100g of frozen cherries into a pan with a tiny splash of water and a teaspoon of vanilla paste and cook for 10 minutes until they are sticky and sweet. Mix 100g of plain yoghurt with a little honey and another teaspoon of vanilla paste. Top the oatcakes straight from the pan with the warm cherries and yoghurt, and sprinkle over some poppy seeds to finish.

Spring chickpea stew with salted lemons

This is a fresh spring stew, sustaining thanks to the chickpeas, fresh with a hit of lemon, with a pleasing savouriness from the caraway and chilli. Spring carrots and rocket along with the lemon lift this.

I use pumpkin seed butter here, which I keep on hand at home; it's great to use as you would a nut butter. If you can't get your hands on it you can make your own easily by blitzing pumpkin seeds with a little rapeseed oil and a pinch of salt.

The salted lemon recipe is my version of the quick preserved lemons from *The Modern Pantry Cookbook*; an easy way to make them without fuss. I have suggested you make more than you will need, as it's a very useful thing to have in the fridge. Use them as you would preserved lemons: chop into dressings, toss through pasta and to flavour stews.

Heat a large saucepan on a medium heat, add the carrots, onion and garlic with a drizzle of oil and a good pinch of salt and pepper, and cook for about 10 minutes until soft and sweet.

In the meantime make the salted lemons. Peel the zest of the lemons into long strips with a speed peeler, then put the strips in a pan with all their juice and the salt and bring to the boil. Simmer for 10 minutes, then remove from the heat and leave to cool.

Next add the caraway, chilli, thyme, tomatoes, chickpeas and their liquid, wine and stock to the carrots and onions and simmer for 15 minutes until you have a thick well-flavoured soup.

Bash the basil in a pestle and mortar, then add the pumpkin seed butter, a pinch of salt and a squeeze of lemon juice and mix well.

When the soup is nearly done, add three of the pickled lemon pieces and simmer for another 5 minutes. Taste and adjust, adding more salt, pepper or salted lemon as needed. Once cool, the rest of your lemons and their liquid can be kept in a jar in the fridge for months.

Once the soup is tasting great, stir though most of the rocket. Serve into bowls and top each one with a good spoonful of the pumpkin seed and basil butter. Finish with the last bit of rocket.

SERVES 4

- 2 carrots (about 300g), peeled and finely diced
- 1 red onion, finely chopped
- 3 cloves of garlic, finely chopped
- olive oil
- 1 heaped teaspoon caraway seeds
- a generous pinch of dried chilli flakes
- a few sprigs of thyme
- 1 x 400g tin of tomatoes
- 1 x 700g jar of chickpeas
- a 175ml glass of white wine
- 500ml good vegetable stock
- 2 big handfuls of rocket

FOR THE SALTED LEMONS

- 4 unwaxed lemons
- 1 teaspoon flaky sea salt

FOR THE HERB AND SEED BUTTER

- a bunch of basil
- 2 tablespoons pumpkin seed butter (see note above)
- the juice of 1 lemon

119

Easter egg and spring veg tart

This is what I have made on Easter Sunday for the past few years. The recipe makes a hero of the egg; it shows it off in all its sunny-yolked glory. As tarts go, this is quick to make – it unashamedly uses good shop-bought puff pastry, though a homemade flaky pastry would certainly elevate it to another level if you had the time. It is a wash of green and yellow, using the first baby vegetables and broad beans. I make this tart all through spring and summer, varying the vegetables as different things come into season – peas and leeks one time, asparagus and broad beans the next.

Most years I have in fact made two tarts, one as the recipe reads and a vegan version for my brother (most puff pastry is actually vegan, as it uses oil rather than butter), and I top it with a quick cashew cream (see page 110 for a quick recipe). For the non-vegans I use ready rolled all-butter puff pastry but if you buy a block or make your own, roll it out to just bigger than an A4 piece of paper, to about the thickness of a pound coin.

This tart is most delicious eaten straight out of the oven, and the eggs are best cracked over just before baking, so if you want to get ahead I'd suggest making the tart and topping it with everything but the eggs and adding them just before it goes in the oven. I like to double-pod my broad beans, but if you buy baby ones they will be sweet and you might not need to. I serve this with a simple lemon-dressed green salad and some buttered new potatoes.

SERVES 4

5 organic eggs, from the fridge

320g puff pastry (see note)

8 spring onions, trimmed

6 baby courgettes, halved lengthways

olive oil

100g small podded broad beans (400g unpodded)

200g crème fraîche

2 tablespoons Dijon mustard

1 unwaxed lemon

TO FINISH

soft herbs (I use chives, parsley, chervil, tarragon)

toasted hazelnuts, roughly chopped

Preheat your oven to 220°C/200°C fan/gas 7. Crack one of the eggs into a cup with a big pinch of salt, beat well and leave to one side. Fill and boil the kettle.

Spread your puff pastry out on a cold baking tray, roll the pastry out a little bigger than an A4-sized piece of paper, then trim a 1cm strip from each side and put to one side. Working quickly, prick the base all over with a fork and lightly brush with the beaten egg. Put the trimmed pastry pieces back on the base along each edge, forming a raised edge that will keep the filling in. Egg wash the top of those too. →

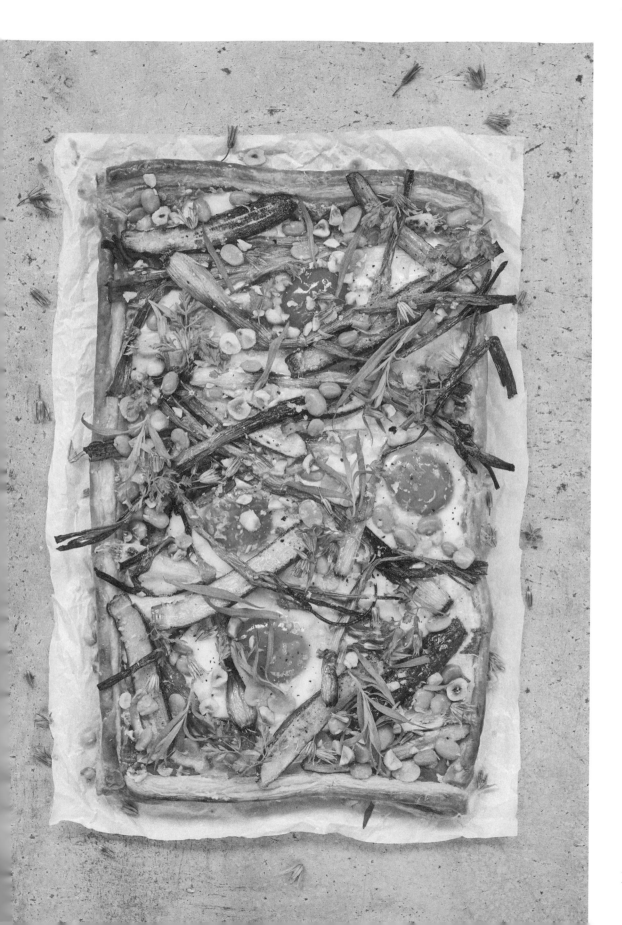

Put the spring onions and baby courgettes on a baking tray, drizzle with a little olive oil and season with salt and pepper. Bake, along with the puff pastry case, for 20–25 minutes until the vegetables are golden and the pastry is really crispy.

Meanwhile, pour a little boiling water over the broad beans, allow to cool, then pop each one out of its tough outer skin, leaving the bright green bean. If you have small young broad beans there's no need to do this – you can use them as they are.

As soon as the pastry comes out of the oven, press down the middle rectangle of the base (which will have puffed up a little), leaving yourself a nice border around the outside.

Mix the crème fraîche with the mustard and a little salt and pepper and spread it over the crispy pastry, keeping it within the border. Arrange the courgettes and spring onions over the top, then make four little spaces to crack the eggs into. Stop here if you are preparing the tart in advance, then cover and keep it in the fridge.

When you are nearly ready to eat, take the eggs out of the fridge and really carefully crack each one into a little cup. As an egg ages, some of the white turns watery and you want to lose this bit, leaving only the freshest part; it means the white will hold its shape during the cooking and won't run all over the tart. Pour the first egg into your cupped hand, with your fingers closed, and let the very watery part of the white drain off. Gently place the egg in one of the spaces, repeating with the other three, then sprinkle over the broad beans and bake for 15–20 minutes, until the egg whites are set and the yolks are still a little soft.

Remove the tart from the oven, grate over the zest of the lemon and scatter over the herbs and hazelnuts.

Caper and watercress cauliflower tart

This is a tart you could eat any day of the week. While I love a pastry tart and do eat them regularly, sometimes I want something that looks and feels as generous, without having to rely on pastry as the base. This tart uses cauliflower, almonds and oats to make a quick case, which is much, much easier and quicker than pastry and is a much lighter load. The base won't crisp up quite like pastry but it's baked twice, so it should be crisp on the outside and soft in the middle. I crown it with a quick ricotta, caper and watercress topping.

Preheat the oven to 220°C/200°C fan/gas 7 and line a baking tray with baking paper.

Blitz the cauliflower in a food processor until it has a fine, rice-like texture. Put it into a mixing bowl, add the ground almonds, oats, lemon zest, chopped parsley and a good pinch of salt and pepper, and mix with your hands. Make a well in the centre and add the eggs. Mix it all together, then use your hands to form it into a ball. It won't look like a traditional pastry dough, it will be a little wetter and less firm.

Rub the baking paper with some olive oil, then put the dough in the middle of the baking tray and use your hands to flatten it out until it is about 0.5cm thick, slightly thicker around the edges. Bake for 20 minutes, until golden all over and set into a crust.

Meanwhile, make the filling. Roughly chop the cornichons with the parsley and watercress and put them into a bowl with the capers and ricotta. Add the lemon zest, Parmesan and artichokes, then add the beaten egg and a good pinch of salt and pepper and mix well.

Remove the tart base from the oven and turn the oven up to 240°C/220°C fan/gas 9. Spread the topping over the base and finish with some more Parmesan, drizzle with a little more oil, then put back into the oven for another 15 minutes to cook the filling.

Once cooked, serve with some green leaves, a drizzle more oil and a little more Parmesan.

MAKES A LARGE TART TO SERVE 4–6

FOR THE BASE

1 medium cauliflower (about 800g), broken into florets

100g ground almonds

100g rolled oats

the zest of 1 unwaxed lemon

a small bunch of flat-leaf parsley

2 organic eggs, beaten

olive oil

FOR THE FILLING

150g cornichons

a small bunch of flat-leaf parsley

a small bunch of watercress or spinach

4 tablespoons baby capers

250g ricotta

the zest of 1 unwaxed lemon

a good grating of Parmesan (I use a vegetarian one)

200g jarred artichokes, quartered

1 organic egg, beaten

TO SERVE

a few handfuls of green leaves

Sweet potato and green chilli masala dosa

SERVES 4

75g chickpea flour

75g rice flour

2 green chillies, finely chopped

a small thumb-sized piece of ginger, peeled and grated

1 teaspoon mustard seeds

FOR THE FILLING

3 sweet potatoes (about 600g), peeled and cut into 2cm pieces

1 tablespoon cumin seeds

coconut oil

2 cloves of garlic, finely sliced

a large thumb-sized piece of ginger, peeled and grated

4 spring onions, trimmed and finely sliced

1 green chilli, finely chopped

a small bunch of coriander, leaves picked and stalks finely chopped

½ teaspoon ground turmeric

250g peas (defrosted if frozen)

TO SERVE

50g pea shoots

2 unwaxed limes

plain yoghurt

mango chutney, lime pickle or my green chutney (see page 36)

I first ate masala dosa on a trip to India years ago. We were at a faded old restaurant in the back streets of Cochin. It was breakfast time. We ordered masala dosa and when we saw it in the waiter's hands, on its way from the ramshackle kitchen, the thin roll of lentil pancake looked longer than my arm. It teetered on a plate, comically small for it, but the pancake was so crisp it held its shape. It looked like an impossibly huge meal, but the pancake was so light and lacy and perfect, and the mustard seed- and curry-leaf-seasoned potato inside so flavoursome that we ate one each. It was the start of my first Indian adventure and a lifelong love for the food of southern India. It's hard to pick out moments that shape you, but this one definitely had a hand in shaping how I cook. This one is for you Jon Abbey; thanks for a great adventure.

This is my version of masala dosa. I use sweet potato instead of the traditional potato, and make the most of the first peas and their shoots, though if you are making this outside of pea season then frozen ones will work well. The traditional way to make it is with rice and urud dhal, which are ground and then fermented. That makes a great dosa but isn't the most practical for a weeknight so I use chickpea and rice flour instead, which are easy to get hold of and work a treat. Sorry if it makes any traditionalists cross.

Put the flours into a food processor. Add the chilli, ginger and mustard seeds and 250ml of cold water and blitz until it's a little thinner than milk, then put into a jug or bowl to sit for 30 minutes or so.

Steam or boil your sweet potatoes for 8–10 minutes until cooked through, then allow to sit and steam dry.

Heat a frying pan, add the cumin seeds and toast for a couple of seconds, then add a tablespoon of coconut oil, the garlic, ginger, spring onions, chilli, coriander stalks and the turmeric. Cook for a minute, until the edges of the garlic begin to brown. Add the cooked sweet potatoes and fry for a few minutes until the sides begin to catch, then stir in the peas and most of the coriander leaves (keep a few back for serving) and keep warm on a very low heat.

Put a large non-stick pan on the heat, rub with a little oil, then use a piece of kitchen paper to wipe out any excess, keeping this paper for the next one. Pour one medium ladle of the batter into the pan, then lift the pan at an angle and rotate to allow the batter to flow over the surface of the pan. Cook for 30 seconds to 1 minute until the bottom of the dosa is golden, then flip and cook for a further 30 seconds. Pile on to a plate with greaseproof paper in between each one and keep warm while you cook the remaining batter – this should make about 6 small dosas or 4 medium ones.

Pile the warm dosas with the sweet potato mixture and top with pea shoots, coriander, lime for squeezing over, and yoghurt and chutney.

Fritters – a flavour map

Pick one thing from each column, using your tastes and instincts to guide you as to which flavours will work well. Remember to season with salt and pepper and fry gently in olive or coconut oil. Serve with a salad and rice, quinoa or wrapped in flatbreads as you see fit. These will make enough for a hearty dinner for two.

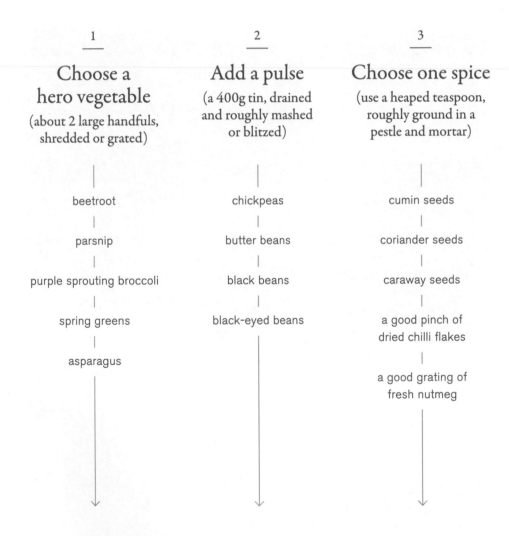

1	2	3
Choose a hero vegetable (about 2 large handfuls, shredded or grated)	**Add a pulse** (a 400g tin, drained and roughly mashed or blitzed)	**Choose one spice** (use a heaped teaspoon, roughly ground in a pestle and mortar)
beetroot	chickpeas	cumin seeds
parsnip	butter beans	coriander seeds
purple sprouting broccoli	black beans	caraway seeds
spring greens	black-eyed beans	a good pinch of dried chilli flakes
asparagus		a good grating of fresh nutmeg

4	5	6	7
Choose herbs	Add a top note	To bind	Serve with

Choose herbs
(a small bunch,
leaves picked and
roughly chopped)

|

thyme
|
coriander
|
mint
|
flat-leaf parsley
|
dill
↓

**Add a
top note**

|

the zest of
1 unwaxed lemon
|
the zest of
1 unwaxed lime
|
1 fresh chilli,
finely chopped
|
1 clove of garlic,
finely chopped
|
a grating of
fresh ginger
↓

To bind

|

1 tablespoon of flour
(I use spelt or
chickpea flour)
|
1 organic egg, beaten
↓

Serve with

|

mashed avocado
|
herb-spiked yoghurt
|
hummus mixed with
olive oil
|
good pesto
|
tomato salsa
|—

Roast leek, feta and lemon polenta cake

Polenta in a cake is something I love; it's toothsome and textured and adds a pleasing crunch to a slice. In fact I love polenta in all its forms: cooked with butter and Parmesan until soft and oozy like good mash, or bouncy slices of it griddled and charred. Though polenta can be a hard sell to some, I am convinced this savoury cake would persuade the most committed polenta-hater. It's easier and quicker than a tart but looks just as good. For a gluten-free version you can use Doves Farm gluten-free blend instead of the spelt.

SERVES 8

4 leeks (about 500g),
    cut into 1cm slices

2 tablespoons butter, plus
    extra for greasing

150g plain spelt flour

120g polenta

1½ teaspoons baking powder

½ teaspoon flaky sea salt

a good grinding of
    black pepper

2 tablespoons nigella seeds

the zest and juice of 1
    unwaxed lemon

1 red chilli, finely chopped

½ a bunch of thyme,
    leaves picked

150g feta, crumbled

4 organic eggs, lightly beaten

100ml milk

200g plain yoghurt

Preheat the oven to 220°C/200°C fan/gas 7. Butter a loose-bottomed 24cm cake tin and line with baking paper.

First, sauté your leeks in a tablespoon of the butter in a frying pan over a medium heat until soft and sweet – this should take about 10 minutes.

Melt the remaining tablespoon of butter and use it to brush the baking paper. Meanwhile, put the flour, polenta, baking powder, salt, pepper and a tablespoon of the nigella seeds into a bowl and whisk to get rid of any lumps of baking powder. Add the lemon zest, red chilli and thyme leaves and crumble in the feta.

Put the juice of the lemon into a small bowl and whisk together with the eggs, milk and yoghurt.

Mix the yoghurt mixture into the flour mixture until just combined (being careful not to over-mix). Once the leeks are cool, stir half of them through the batter. Pour the batter into the lined cake tin and scatter the rest of the leeks on top, then sprinkle over the reserved tablespoon of nigella seeds.

Bake for 35–45 minutes, until the top is golden and a skewer inserted into the cake comes out clean. Leave to cool in the tin for 5 minutes, then cool on a wire rack to room temperature before slicing.

128

Grilled kale with honeyed tofu and shallots

Kale is not just for deep winter, it's around until early spring. There seems to be no stopping the kale renaissance of recent years; despite it being annoyingly plastered on teenage T-shirts and liberally scattered on every restaurant menu for the last couple of years, people still seem to have an appetite for it – including me. I love the frilly, minerally deep green bunches and this is a fresh way to eat it, grilled so it's a little smoky, offset by the honeyed tofu but still fresh thanks to some mint and lemon in a bright tahini dressing. This is a salad that will make you friends.

Be sure to use a good firm tofu here, organic is best if you can find it – soy is one of our most processed crops, so organic is the best way to avoid GMO soy. If you are especially hungry you could serve this with some brown rice or quinoa.

SERVES 4

2 tablespoons runny honey

1 tablespoon tamari
or soy sauce

200g firm organic tofu, sliced
into 1cm-thick sticks

olive oil

3 banana shallots, peeled
and finely sliced

2 heads of kale (about 800g),
de-stalked and torn

a few sprigs of mint

75g almonds, toasted

FOR THE DRESSING

100g Greek yoghurt

1 tablespoon light tahini

2 tablespoons olive oil

the juice of ½ lemon

Mix the honey with the tamari and spoon it over the tofu, then toss everything well to coat each bit.

Heat 2 tablespoons of oil in a frying pan over a medium to low heat and slowly fry the shallots for 10–15 minutes or until they are golden. Remove with a slotted spoon and leave to drain and crisp up on some kitchen paper. Keep the pan for later.

Mix the dressing ingredients together, then season well with salt and pepper and taste, adjusting the seasoning and the amount of lemon or oil if needed – you can add a little cold water here if your dressing looks too thick.

Put a griddle on to heat up – you want it on a medium heat. Put the shallot pan back on a medium heat and add the tofu. Cook until it is golden on all its edges, then take the pan off the heat and keep warm. Toss the kale in a tablespoon of olive oil and season with salt and pepper. Drizzle with 3 tablespoons of water and mix well. Put a batch of kale onto the griddle and cook for about a minute on each side until it is wilted and charred, then put into a serving bowl while you char the rest – it should take 4–5 minutes in total.

To serve, tumble the tofu and crispy shallots into the kale, add the mint and the dressing. Toss well and top with the almonds.

Spring green rolls with almond satay

I love these rolls, they are fresh and lively, filled with spring greens and herbs, which is the perfect way to wake up our palates after the winter roots and woody herbs. They are much easier to make than you might expect and are brilliantly portable, making them a great snack for a picnic or a journey and, if you are organised, perhaps even a plane snack, though I've never quite managed it.

As the rolling takes a little while, I usually make these for a crowd; if you'd prefer to make fewer then halve the recipe. They will keep well in the fridge too for a few days if you have leftovers.

The key here is to soak your rice papers for just the right amount of time – you want to take them out of the water while they still feel a little stiff as they will continue to soften as they sit. I make these for parties too and cut them in half. If you can, rope a few early guests in to help with the rolling. The rolls are a great thing to make with kids too, just leave out the chilli from the dipping sauce if you are serving them to little ones.

MAKES 12–15 (TO SERVE ABOUT 6)

FOR THE TOFU

400g extra-firm tofu

2 cloves of garlic

2 teaspoons tamari or soy sauce

2 teaspoons runny honey or agave nectar

1 teaspoon of brown rice vinegar

2 tablespoons coconut oil

FOR THE ROLLS

200g spring greens

1 lime

100g wholegrain rice vermicelli noodles

a small bunch of mint

a small bunch of Thai basil, washed and dried

a small bunch of coriander, washed and dried

½ large cucumber, sliced into thin batons

a small bunch of chives, finely chopped

12–15 x 15cm rice paper wrappers →

First, make a marinade for the tofu by placing the garlic in a pestle and mortar and pounding it to a rough paste. Mix the tamari, honey and vinegar through and place in a bowl to one side.

Pat the tofu dry with kitchen paper and cut into 6 equal chunky slices. Gently toss the tofu in a bowl with the marinade and cover with cling film. Leave to one side while you make the rest of the filling for the rolls.

Peel the leaves of the spring greens away from the core and cut the core away from the middle of the leaves, leaving a thin V-shaped gap in each leaf. Layer four or five similar-sized leaves up together on the chopping board and roll them up tightly into a cigar shape. Slice into thin ribbons.

Place the spring green ribbons in a large mixing bowl and squeeze over the juice from half of the lime then sprinkle over a little salt. Scrunch the leaves with your hands firmly, pushing the juice and salt into the leaves as you go. The leaves will turn a deep green and should reduce in size by about half after a couple of minutes. Cover and set to one side. →

Cook the rice noodles according to the packet instructions and refresh under cold water. Drain well and set aside.

Pick the leaves from the herbs and discard the mint and basil stalks. Finely chop the coriander stalks to add to the dipping sauce later.

Next, make the dipping sauce by whisking all the ingredients together in a bowl with a fork, then stir through the chopped coriander stalks.

When you're ready to eat, heat the oil for the tofu in a wide frying pan over a medium heat and lay out the tofu in the pan so there's no overlap. Fry on each side for 4–5 minutes, or until golden. Allow to cool a little, then cut into pencil-sized pieces.

Mix the spring greens, noodles, cucumber and herbs in a large bowl with 3 tablespoons of the dipping sauce.

To assemble, get all your elements together. Fill a wide shallow bowl or plate with 1cm of warm water. Dip rice paper into the warm water for between 3 and 5 seconds – how long you need to soak it will depend a little on the brand of rice papers you use. Resist over-soaking them – even if the paper is a little bit stiff, it will continue to absorb water as you assemble the wrap.

Put the paper on a non-stick surface, like a plate or chopping board, and leave the paper to sit until just tacky. Pile all your ingredients in the centre of the wrapper, keeping a couple of centimetres clear at the top and bottom and 4–5cm on each side.

Now for the rolling. Fold the top and bottom of the paper over the filling, then quickly roll the whole thing over the filling to enclose everything, tucking in as you go and keeping the roll as firm as possible. Repeat with the remaining papers and filling, then serve on platters with the rest of the dipping sauce.

FOR THE DIPPING SAUCE

4 tablespoons almond butter

4 tablespoons white miso paste

the zest of 3 unwaxed limes and the juice of 4

3 teaspoons sesame oil

a large thumb-sized piece of ginger, peeled and grated

2 red chillies, finely chopped

3 tablespoons tamari or soy sauce

2 tablespoons runny honey or agave nectar

Double lime, cashew and ginger stir-fry

John, my husband, is the king of a healthy vegetable-packed dinner. The first few months after having my son I did very little cooking but John kept us going, cooking each night as I rocked Dylan to sleep. John makes a mean stir-fry. Somehow the word stir-fry feels a bit ungenerous; it conjures up old memories of raw chunks of red pepper and packet sauces. John's are nothing of the sort. They are fresh, filling and always have a rainbow of veg. This is the sort of thing he makes; mine are never as good.

I use pickled ginger here as I love the balance of sweet and tart it brings, but if you don't have it a little more ginger will stand in, no problem. I also use short-grain brown rice but white or brown basmati or jasmine would all work too.

Cook the rice in boiling salted water until cooked but with a little bite, then drain and leave to steam dry.

Meanwhile, grate the zest of 2 of the limes into a large bowl, add the juice of all 4 along with 2 tablespoons of the vinegar, the ginger and half the honey. Add half the spring onions, all the radishes and the sugar snaps.

Snap the ends off the asparagus and trim off the tips, then cut the remaining stalks into 1cm pieces and add these to the bowl too. Toss everything in the lime marinade to coat and leave it to sit while you get on with the rest.

Shred the spring greens finely. Pick the coriander leaves from their stalks, finely chop the stalks and add them to the bowl with the vegetables. Put the coriander leaves to one side for later.

Heat a large frying pan on a medium heat and add a little coconut oil. Once hot, add the cooked rice and fry for a couple of minutes so the edges begin to crisp, then add the pickled ginger and remaining tablespoon of rice wine vinegar and keep warm. →

SERVES 2

200g rice (I use short-grain brown rice)

4 unwaxed limes

3 tablespoons rice wine vinegar

a thumb-sized piece of ginger, peeled and grated

2 tablespoons runny honey

a bunch of spring onions, finely sliced

200g radishes, cut into quarters

200g sugar snap peas, cut in half

a bunch of asparagus

a head of spring greens

a small bunch of coriander

coconut oil

25g pickled ginger

2 tablespoons tamari or soy sauce

50g cashew nuts, toasted

135

Heat another large frying pan over a really high heat; it is important you have a large frying pan or a wok here so that there is enough room for the liquid to evaporate from the veg and for it to cook quickly. Put the vegetables into a sieve set over another large bowl to drain their marinade, keeping the marinade for later. Add the vegetables and fry for a few minutes until they have just lost their rawness but still have some crunch. Now stir through the spring greens.

While the veg is cooking, add the tamari and remaining tablespoon of honey to the bowl of marinade and mix well. Once the veg is cooked to your liking, add the marinade and cook for about 30 seconds until it has all evaporated. Serve in deep bowls with the ginger rice and top with the reserved spring onions, a sprinkling of coriander leaves and the toasted cashews.

Avocado and popped bean burritos

These are quick, fresh, spring-like burritos that I have found myself making over and over; they are loved by young and old. Making a dressing out of the avocado with loads of lime means that there will be no browning and makes these burritos quite portable, though if you plan to wrap them up for later I'd suggest letting the beans cool before you do.

If you want the burritos to be really sustaining you can add some cooked rice or quinoa tossed in a little lemon or lime juice and some salt and pepper.

First make your dressing. Place all the ingredients in a blender and blitz on a high speed until you have a smooth pale green dressing, adding a little water tablespoon by tablespoon until the dressing is the consistency of a thick smoothie (I usually end up adding about 3 tablespoons).

Toast the pumpkin seeds in a large non-stick frying pan with the lime zest and a good pinch of salt, then transfer to a bowl for later.

Put the spinach and kale into a bowl with the lime juice and a big pinch of salt and scrunch with your hands until the kale has broken down a little – this will take about 3–4 minutes. Add half the avocado dressing to the bowl and mix well.

Pat the drained beans dry with kitchen paper. Put the frying pan back on the heat and add the olive oil. Once it's nice and hot, add the beans and cook for a couple of minutes. Once they begin to pop and blister, add the coriander seeds and cook for another 2 minutes until all the beans have burst and are crispy.

Toast your tortillas by warming them through in a dry frying pan on a low–medium heat, or as I do, directly on the gas flame on the hob, turning them with tongs after a few seconds. Lay them out and divide the beans and greens between them. Top with a little more of the avocado dressing and the pumpkin seeds, then roll them up and enjoy.

SERVES 4

FOR THE DRESSING

1 ripe avocado, peeled and stoned

the zest and juice of 1 unwaxed lime

¼ teaspoon cayenne pepper

1 teaspoon runny honey

3 tablespoons olive oil

1 green chilli, finely chopped

a bunch of spring onions, roughly chopped

a bunch of coriander

50g pumpkin seeds

the zest and juice of 1 unwaxed lime

100g spinach or spring greens

150g curly kale

4 wholemeal seeded tortilla wraps

FOR THE POPPED BEANS

1 x 400g tin of cannellini beans, drained

2 tablespoons olive oil

1 teaspoon coriander seeds

137

Almond satay bowl with tempeh

SERVES 4

FOR THE ALMOND SATAY

1 small red chilli,
   roughly chopped

1 clove of garlic,
   roughly chopped

125g almond butter

2 tablespoons tamari
   or soy sauce

the juice of 1 lime

2 tablespoons runny honey
   or agave nectar

100ml full-fat coconut milk

400g new potatoes

2 tablespoons coconut
   oil, plus a little extra

4 carrots (about 250g),
   peeled into strips

a small head of spring
   greens, shredded

150g mung bean sprouts

a bunch of coriander,
   roughly chopped

2 shallots, sliced into rings

200g tempeh, sliced into
   long 1cm-thick slices

2 tablespoons maple syrup

2 tablespoons tamari
   or soy sauce

lime wedges, to serve

cooked brown rice, to
   serve (optional)

This dressing is so good I could spoon it straight from the jar. It perks up some humble vegetables and elevates this to a seriously flavourful bowl. I use tempeh here, a fermented soy bean cake, which is as good for you as it is delicious. It can be hard to get hold of, however, which is why I hold off from using it too much.

You can use other seasonal vegetables here: purple sprouting broccoli and asparagus when spring kicks in, tomatoes and corn in summer. Perhaps roasted roots in the winter. It's a pretty versatile bowlful. Other nut butters like peanut could be used instead of almond too.

_____

First make the dressing. Put all the ingredients into a food processor and blend on a high speed. If you are not a fan of chilli, add less or deseed yours. Add a little water until the sauce is thin enough to pour, but not watery. Taste and adjust the seasoning as needed.

Have all your vegetables ready. Put a steamer over boiling water and place the potatoes inside first; cover and set a timer for 12 minutes. Once tender, remove them from the steamer, toss with a teaspoon of the coconut oil, then cover to keep warm.

Fill the steamer with the carrots and greens and cook for 2–4 minutes until tender-crisp, then toss with the remaining coconut oil. In a large bowl combine all the steamed veggies with the sprouts and coriander. Sprinkle with salt and toss.

Heat a frying pan on a medium heat, add a little coconut oil and fry the shallots until crisp and golden but not burned, then drain on kitchen paper. Put the pan back on the heat and add the tempeh. Cook until crisp on each side, add the maple and tamari, then take off the heat.

To serve, layer everything in a bowl and top with the dressing. Serve with the lime wedges and brown rice if you are really hungry.

Bay and lemon-laced crème caramel

I can't tell you emphatically enough how much I love these. What I can tell you is that the first time I made them I ate two in succession. The lemon, vanilla and bay is a favourite combination: the gentle herbaceous bay, lifting lemon and warm sweetness of vanilla together is unexpected, comforting and refreshing. You need the best full-cream, blue-top milk here.

Making a caramel can put people off, but I have given easy instructions here so don't be nervous, it's really not hard at all. Be sure to check the wobble on the baked crème caramels — you want a very light wobble in the middle; they shouldn't be liquidy. You will need 6 individual ramekins or 170ml dariole moulds to make these.

Preheat the oven to 170°C/150°C fan/gas 3. Grease all the ramekins or dariole moulds with butter.

Start by infusing your milk. Pour the milk into a saucepan. Peel 4 strips of zest from the lemon with a speed peeler and add to the milk wtih the bay. Scrape the seeds from the vanilla pod and add to the milk along with the pod. Heat gently over a low heat and when it's just under a simmer, take off the heat and allow to cool a little and infuse for 15 minutes.

Next make the caramel by melting the caster and muscovado sugars together in a large, deep saucepan with the lemon juice and 2 tablespoons of water. Try not to it stir once it's heated (stirring will encourage the sugar to crystallise) — a gentle shake and tilt of the pan now and again will help the sugar to melt evenly.

Let the sugar mixture cook until it's bubbling, is a rich molasses colour all over and smells biscuity. It should take around 3 minutes from when it starts to bubble. If you're nervous and want to test that it's done, pour a small dot on to a cold plate and if it sets, it's done. Pour the caramel into your greased ramekins, distributing it evenly across all 6, and leave to one side to set.

Now on to the custard. Crack the whole eggs into a mixing bowl and whisk with the yolks and caster sugar until everything is combined. Gradually add the cooled milk to the eggs and sugar, gently combining with a whisk as you go. Fill and boil the kettle. →

SERVES 6

a knob of butter, for greasing

500ml organic whole milk

1 unwaxed lemon

2 bay leaves

1 vanilla pod

2 medium organic eggs, plus 4 egg yolks

75g golden caster sugar

FOR THE CARAMEL

60g golden caster sugar

60g light muscovado sugar

the juice of 1 lemon

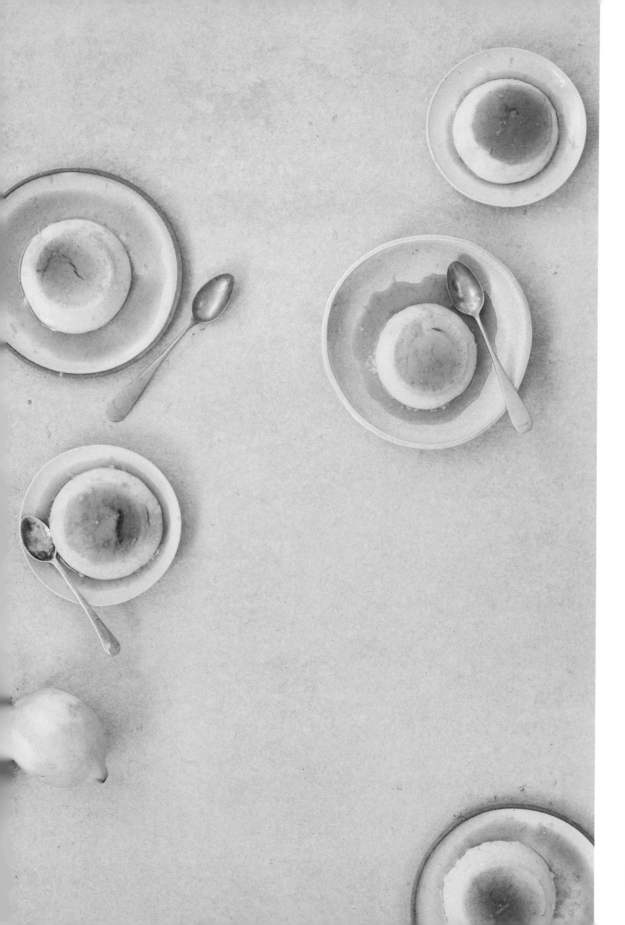

Pour the mixture through a sieve into a jug, then pour into the ramekins and place them in a deep roasting tray. Cover each ramekin tightly with foil. Carefully pour the hot water from the kettle around the ramekins to about halfway up the sides.

Bake in the centre of the hot oven for 15 minutes, then remove the foil and bake for a further 15–20 minutes, until they're set with a bit of wobble still in the centre. Cool on a roasting tray, then place covered in the fridge, ideally overnight, but definitely for at least 3–4 hours.

Remove from the fridge at least 30 minutes before you want to serve them. When you're ready, gingerly run a small palette knife around the edge and invert each one on to a plate.

Rhubarb and rose frozen yoghurt

This sweet-shop pink frozen yoghurt is as cheerful as it is delicious. Thanks to the bright bubblegum colour of the forced rhubarb and the gentle cloudy white of the Greek yoghurt it ends up the most beautiful tone of rosy pink. This year we ate it from good waffle cones in the garden on my birthday in early April, on one of the first warm days of the year; I couldn't have been happier. If you use outdoor rhubarb for this it will be less pink.

I infuse the rhubarb with some rose geranium leaves. I have a plant that sits on my windowsill but you may not, so you could use a couple of teaspoons of rosewater in their place. The rose geranium has a fresher, less perfumey rose note, though, so use it if you can.

Chop the rhubarb into roughly 2.5cm pieces and place in a medium saucepan with the sugar, rose geranium leaves, orange zest and a couple of tablespoons of water. Cover with a lid and place on a medium heat for 3 minutes, until everything is steamy and smelling fragrant, then turn the heat right down and let the pan blip away for a further 7 minutes, until the rhubarb is completely soft and bright pink. Transfer to a bowl to cool for at least 20 minutes.

Once the rhubarb has cooled, remove the rose geranium leaves and mash up any big pieces of rhubarb with a fork. Stir the yoghurt and salt through the rhubarb; you can leave a bit of a ripple here if you like, but I mix mine quite well.

Churn in your ice-cream maker until the frozen yoghurt has thickened to a scoopable consistency. Transfer to your freezer if you like a really set frozen yoghurt.

If you don't have an ice-cream maker, chill the yoghurt and rhubarb mix in the fridge for at least 1 hour, then transfer to a 1-litre Tupperware box with a lid. Freeze for 1 hour, until its wobble is no longer visible, and beat with a whisk or fork to incorporate all the frozen pieces and ensure the frozen yoghurt has an even consistency. Mix twice more over the next couple of hours, and remove from the freezer a few minutes before serving.

MAKES ABOUT 1 LITRE

500g rhubarb

200g golden caster sugar

6–8 rose geranium leaves, or 1–2 teaspoons rosewater depending on how strong it is

the zest of 1 unwaxed orange

800g Greek yoghurt

a pinch of flaky sea salt

Lemon and cardamom upside-down cake

As far as I am concerned there is no greater cake than a lemon cake and this one has the crown. It's an upside-down cake with an easy candied lemon bottom, which, once cool, is turned out to become a gilded lemon roof. The lemons burnish as the cake cooks, under a crumb of almonds, polenta and oats (so it's free of gluten, if that's something that's on your radar). The lemon comes with a back-up of cardamom and vanilla, a combination that's well used in my kitchen and for very good reason.

A vegan version can be made quite successfully with aquafaba in place of the eggs (use the method on page 459). It will need 135ml of aquafaba or 9 tablespoons. If you'd like to keep this totally gluten-free, be sure to use gluten-free oats.

SERVES 10

butter, for greasing

5 unwaxed lemons

175g golden caster sugar

75g rolled oats

seeds from 12 cardamom pods

150ml rapeseed oil

75g polenta

1 teaspoon baking powder

75g ground almonds

1 teaspoon vanilla paste

3 organic eggs

a generous pinch of flaky sea salt

plain yoghurt whipped with a little vanilla, to serve

Preheat your oven to 200°C/180°C fan/gas 6. Next, grease and line a 24cm springform cake tin with greaseproof paper.

Put the zest and juice of 2 of the lemons into a small bowl and set aside. Next, prepare the remaining lemons for the base of the tin. Using a really sharp knife, slice the lemons into wafer-thin slices (about 0.5cm is ideal). Remove any visible pips from the slices.

Put 50g of the sugar into a medium saucepan with 50ml of water and heat until the sugar has dissolved, then simmer for about 5 minutes until you have a syrup. Add the lemon slices and very gently simmer for another 10–15 minutes until they are starting to turn slightly translucent, then carefully scoop them out of the syrup and put them on to some baking paper to cool so that you can handle them. Reserve any syrup for later.

Meanwhile, blitz the oats in the food processor until you have a rough, flour-like consistency.

Bash the cardamom seeds to a rough powder. Beat the rapeseed oil and remaining sugar with a wooden spoon. Mix in the polenta, baking powder, almonds, cardamom, vanilla, eggs, ground oats and reserved lemon juice and zest. Sprinkle over the salt and mix well again. →

Arrange the sliced citrus on the bottom of the lined cake tin, leaving some little gaps for the batter to hit the bottom of the tin, which will allow some of the steam to escape. Pour the batter on top and level it out with the back of a spoon.

Bake in the middle of the oven for 35–40 minutes, checking at 30 minutes and perhaps covering with foil if it looks like it's getting very brown on top. Check that it's cooked through by piercing the cake with a skewer; if it comes out clean, the cake is ready.

After the cake has cooled for about 20 minutes, remove the tin, peel away the paper and carefully upturn it on to a plate. Pour any leftover syrup from the lemons over the top. Serve with yoghurt, whipped with a little vanilla.

Cheddar, swede and wild garlic scones

These might sound more wintry but this time of the year is filled with just as many cold days as warm ones and these warming, quick little scones are the kind of thing I make when we run out of bread, or if I want to make a bowl of soup look a bit more like a meal. These are hard to mess up, so if bread is a stretch for you these are a better bet. I use swede, as it's pretty much my favourite root vegetable through the winter: cheap, British and abundant and its season lasts a little longer than the other roots – into the early spring. Parsnip, celeriac or sweet potato would happily stand in.

Preheat the oven to 240°C/220°C fan/gas 9. Put the flour, baking powder and salt into a large mixing bowl and whisk together until smooth and well combined.

Grate in the butter, then rub it in with your fingertips until the mixture looks like fine breadcrumbs.

Finely grate in all but 25g of the cheese, then add the swede, wild garlic or chives and the mustard and stir to combine. Mix in the milk and water until the dough just comes away from the edge of the bowl; don't handle it any more than is necessary, as this will make your scones tough.

Tip the dough out on to a very lightly floured surface and flatten into a rectangle about 2.5cm high. Cut out with a fluted cutter (I use a 6cm one for 16 scones), reshaping as necessary while handling the dough as little as possible.

Carefully place the rounds on a lined baking tray and brush the tops with the egg and milk mixture. Grate the remaining cheese over the top and bake for about 12 minutes, until golden. Allow to cool slightly on a cooling rack before splitting open.

MAKES ABOUT 16

450g plain spelt flour, plus a little extra to dust

6 teaspoons baking powder

1 teaspoon salt

100g cold unsalted butter

100g Cheddar

200g swede, peeled and grated

25g wild garlic leaves or chives, finely chopped

1 heaped tablespoon wholegrain mustard

120ml cold milk

120ml cold water

1 organic egg, beaten with a splash of milk

First warm days

Best of the season
Asparagus
Garden herbs
Radishes
Sorrel
Baby spinach
Cauliflower
Broad beans
Peas
Beetroot
Globe artichokes
Samphire
Lettuces
Jersey Royals
Elderflowers
Gooseberries
Outdoor rhubarb
First strawberries
First raspberries

Flowers
Iris
Nigella
Daffodils
Cornflowers

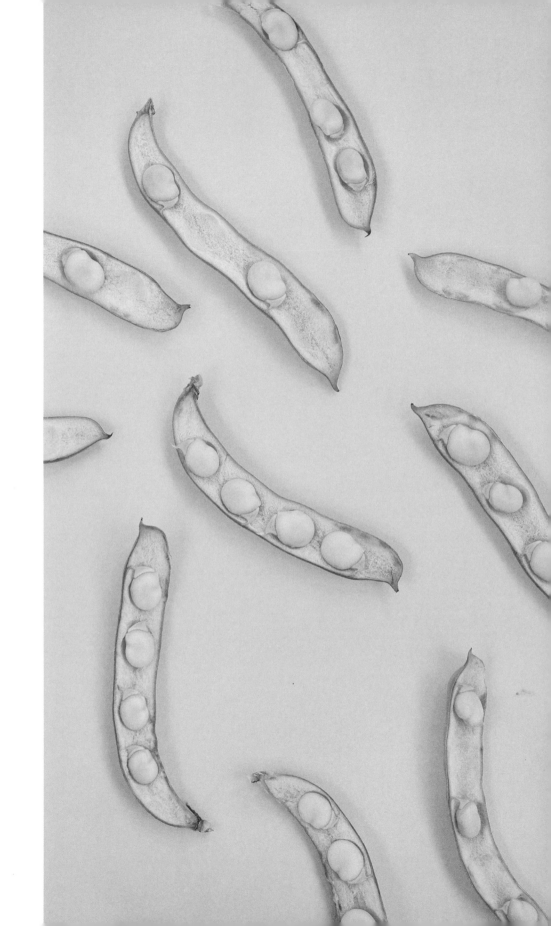

Roasted strawberry and chia breakfast bowls

I usually double this recipe and make enough for two days. The night before, stick a tray of strawberries in the oven for spooning on top the next day. The syrupy roasted red strawberries take this breakfast from holier-than-thou porridge to a proper food-lover's breakfast. If you have beautifully sweet strawberries there is no need to roast them.

Chia is a funny ingredient to cook with and, quite honestly, I'm not always a fan of it, but it works here. I find it a particularly good thing to eat in the morning – it gives me lots of energy without making me feel really full like porridge can. If you are new to chia seeds you could try starting with 2 tablespoons and 2 of rolled oats, which will make it a bit creamier.

MAKES 2 BOWLS

4 tablespoons chia seeds

300ml almond milk (or other milk of your choosing)

a handful of strawberries

a pinch of flaky sea salt

the zest of 1 unwaxed lemon

a splash of vanilla extract

2 teaspoons maple syrup or runny honey

FOR THE ROASTED STRAWBERRIES

500g strawberries

1 tablespoon olive oil

2 teaspoons maple syrup or runny honey

a pinch of flaky sea salt

TO SERVE

toasted coconut flakes

a drizzle of maple syrup or runny honey

The night before, combine the chia seeds with the milk and stir well. Mash a handful of fresh strawberries with the salt, lemon, vanilla and maple syrup then stir them into the chia. Refrigerate overnight so the seeds can bloom and soften.

For the strawberries, preheat the oven to 200°C/180°C fan/gas 6. It is important to use a baking tray with a lip or a large baking dish to prevent the juices running off the sheet on to the bottom of your oven. If you are using a baking tray, line it with baking paper.

Cut the strawberries in half. Put the berries on the tray and pour over the olive oil, maple syrup and the salt. Toss gently around the tray until coated.

Arrange the strawberries in a single layer and roast for about 40 minutes, just long enough for the berry juices to thicken and set slightly, but not long enough for the juices to burn. Watch the edges of the tray in particular. While still warm, scrape into a jar and put in the fridge for the morning.

Just before serving, sweeten the chia to taste with a little more maple syrup, if you like, then top with toasted coconut flakes and a spoonful of roasted strawberries.

Seeded spinach breakfast waffles

I love waffles. With their crisp chequered edges and their fluffy insides, I can't think of anything I'd rather eat for breakfast. In her book *I Remember Nothing* Nora Ephron lists waffles, as well as the idea of waffles, as things she will miss when she dies.

The idea of waffles is usually a sweet one. One morning I realised I'd never had a savoury waffle and about an hour later the waffle iron was heating up and then the batter was being ladled in. These are the result: rich with buttermilk (or plain yoghurt), buckwheat flour, cheese and spinach. The cheese melts when it hits the waffle iron, making the most delicious crisp cheesy exterior. I serve these with roast tomatoes and goat's cheese, but I've listed a few other options overleaf too.

I have made a vegan version with oat milk and 1 tablespoon of chia mixed with 3 tablespoons of water in place of the egg, and leaving out the cheese (or adding a pinch of nutritional yeast); they don't puff up quite as much but are still very good. If you want a gluten-free version you can use all buckwheat flour and skip the wholemeal. You can also fry the batter like a pancake.

MAKES 6

olive oil

4 spring onions, chopped

100g spinach

1 red or green chilli, finely chopped

400g cherry tomatoes on the vine

130g buckwheat flour

60g wholemeal spelt flour

1 heaped teaspoon baking powder

2 tablespoons little seeds (I use a mixture of linseed and poppy seed)

375ml buttermilk, kefir or thin yoghurt

1 organic egg, beaten

125g Lancashire cheese, plus extra to serve

125g soft goat's cheese

Preheat your waffle maker. I use an electric one but if you are using a hob iron leave it on a very low heat to warm up.

Heat a little olive oil in a frying pan over a medium heat, add the spring onions and cook for a few minutes until they have started to brown, then add the spinach and cook until most of the moisture has evaporated. Stir through the chilli, then tip the mixture on to a chopping board to cool and put the pan back on the heat.

Add the tomatoes to the pan (you can keep them on the vine) with a good pinch of salt and pepper, and cook on a high heat, letting the sides of the tomatoes brown and blister.

Meanwhile, put your flours, baking powder, seeds and a good pinch of salt and pepper into another mixing bowl and stir with a whisk to get rid of any lumps of baking powder.

In another bowl mix the buttermilk and egg and crumble in the cheese. →

Once the spinach mixture is cool, put it into a sieve and use the back of a spoon to squeeze out any excess liquid. Then, back on the chopping board, roughly chop it.

Add the spinach to the buttermilk and egg, then mix this into the dry ingredients. Season well with salt and pepper. This is your waffle mixture.

Brush your heated waffle iron with a little olive oil and pour a small ladle (about 125ml) of the mixture into each of the bottom waffle wells. (Depending on the size of your waffle maker you may need to add a little more or less.) Close the waffle maker and cook the waffles for 5–6 minutes, until golden brown on both sides.

Serve the crisp golden waffles with the roasted tomatoes, the goat's cheese and any of the other options below. These waffles freeze well and can be warmed in the oven from frozen.

Topping options

- Avocado mashed with lemon

- Crisp-edged mushrooms

- A spoonful of tomato chutney or the tomato kasundi on page 176

- Spiced refried beans

- Some leaves dressed with lemon and soft goat's cheese

Courgette *skordalia*

If ever there were a dip to give hummus a run for its money, it's *skordalia*. Traditionally it's a Greek dish of mashed then whipped potato, spiked with garlic and lemon and a generous amount of olive oil. I make mine with the addition of some buttery slow-cooked courgettes, which add to the comforting creaminess, and a little bit of veg.

My son eats hummus at almost every meal, so I was keen to find something he loved as much. This is it. I made it with a floury Cyprus potato, which is around at this time of year, its distinctive red soil still clinging to its skin. Cyprus are earthy in flavour, pale and fluffy when cooked – they make amazing mashed potato.

Skordalia should be absolutely smooth – use a potato ricer to mash the potatoes or push the cooked potato through a sieve with the back of a spoon.

Put the potatoes (skins on) into plenty of cold salted water and bring to the boil. Simmer for 25–35 minutes, depending on the size of your potatoes.

Put the courgettes into a frying pan with a good drizzle of olive oil and fry over a low heat for 20–25 minutes until they have broken down and are buttery and soft.

Meanwhile, chop the garlic finely, add a pinch of salt and use the side of a knife to crush the garlic into a fine paste.

Once the potatoes are cooked, drain and leave to steam dry. When cool enough to handle, peel them, then push them through a sieve, mouli or a potato ricer and add the garlic paste.

Once the courgettes are cooked, put them into a blender with half the oil and whizz until completely smooth – you don't want any lumps. You may need to add a little water if it needs loosening.

Bit by bit, beat the courgette mixture, remaining oil and lemon juice into the potato mix. Check the *skordalia* for salt and pepper and place in a bowl. Scatter the toasted almonds on top. Your *skordalia* should last for 3–4 days if kept covered in the fridge.

MAKES ENOUGH FOR A FEW DAYS' DIPPING

300g floury potatoes, such as Cyprus, unpeeled

300g courgettes, chopped into 2cm slices

140ml olive oil, plus a little extra to fry the courgettes

2 cloves of garlic

the juice of 1 small lemon

50g almonds, toasted and finely chopped

Green baked eggs

Through the winter I make breakfast eggs in a quick, gently spiced tomato sauce, but as the sky gets brighter and the vegetables greener, this is what I make. This is a light, bright, late-spring brunch of baked eggs, slow-cooked courgettes, jarred artichokes (use fresh if you like, though – see *Vignarola*, page 196), sweet roast shallots and bright greens, all doused in the sunshine-mellow yellow of saffron. It goes without saying that organic, free-range eggs should be used whenever possible – the sunnier the egg, the happier the eater.

In our house some people have two eggs and some one, so the filling and cooking method is generous enough that you can add the number of eggs that suits your eaters' appetites.

_____

SERVES 4

4–5 banana shallots

2 tablespoons olive oil

600g courgettes, cut into 1cm coins

2 cloves of garlic, crushed

2 heads of spring greens, finely sliced

4 artichoke hearts from a jar, drained and halved

a pinch of saffron, soaked in 50ml boiling water

1 tablespoon cider vinegar

4–6 organic eggs, depending on how hungry you are

TO SERVE

a small bunch of mint

a small bunch of parsley, chopped

plain yoghurt

dried chilli flakes

Preheat the oven to 220°C/200°C fan/gas 7.

Peel the shallots, then slice them into quarters from root to tip. Warm the olive oil in a heavy-based, shallow pan that can go in the oven. Add the shallots and a big pinch of salt and lightly brown them on both sides over a medium heat.

When the shallots are soft, push them to one side, add the courgettes and garlic to the other side of the pan, and cook for a few minutes until the courgettes begin to turn golden. Depending on the size of your pan, you may need to do this in two or three batches to make sure the courgettes don't overlap as they cook.

Next, add the greens, artichokes, saffron water, cider vinegar and another pinch of salt, cook for a minute or two until the greens have just wilted, then transfer the whole pan to the oven. Bake the vegetables for 15 minutes to allow the shallots and courgettes to roast and soften, then remove the pan from the oven.

Place the pan on a medium heat for 3 minutes to simmer away any excess liquid, then make four, five or six small, shallow hollows in the vegetables. Crack an egg into each, then return to the oven for 7–8 minutes, until the whites are set and the yolks are still runny.

Serve scattered with the mint leaves and parsley, a dollop of yoghurt and a sprinkle of chilli flakes, if you like.

English garden toasts

These little toasts are a riot of colour and represent all that is great about English gardens in the late spring. The first radishes, roasted until they sweeten, the sweet peas, and some allium or chive flowers, if you can get them, add some prettiness as well as a punch of flavour.

These go particularly well with a glass of ice-cold rosé outside on a warm day. I use the dip-dyed pink and white breakfast radishes here, but the regular round ones would work really well too. We eat this for a late evening dinner but I'd proudly serve this as a quick starter too. They are also great at a picnic or a party; just double or triple the recipe for a crowd.

Preheat your oven to 200°C/180°C fan/gas 6.

Put the radishes, keeping the tops intact (if you have them), on a baking tray, drizzle with olive oil, season with salt and pepper, then roast in the oven for 20 minutes, or until the tops are crisp and the radishes have turned a softer, more mellow pink.

Fill and put the kettle on. Put your sliced onion in a little bowl with a good pinch of salt and the lemon juice. Scrunch it all together with your hands. Leave to one side to continue to lightly pickle.

Pour the boiling water from the kettle into a small saucepan, add a pinch of salt and bring to the boil again. Cook the peas for a few minutes, then drain. Mash them a little with a potato masher or in a large pestle and mortar. Add the lemon zest, then a good pinch of salt and black pepper. Finely chop most of the mint (saving a few little leaves for later) and stir through the peas.

Once the radishes are roasted, toast or griddle your bread. Drizzle with a little olive oil or spread with a little salted butter. Pile the peas on the toasted bread, drain the now-bright-purple onions from their liquid and dot on top of the peas. Crumble the goat's cheese on top and scatter with radishes. Finish with the remaining mint, and some allium flowers or chopped chives, if you like.

MAKES 4

a bunch of radishes

2 tablespoons olive oil

1 red onion, finely sliced

the zest and juice of ½ unwaxed lemon

200g podded fresh peas

a small bunch of mint

4 slices of good bread, such as sourdough

salted butter (optional)

100g soft goat's cheese or ricotta

a few allium flowers, or chopped chives (optional)

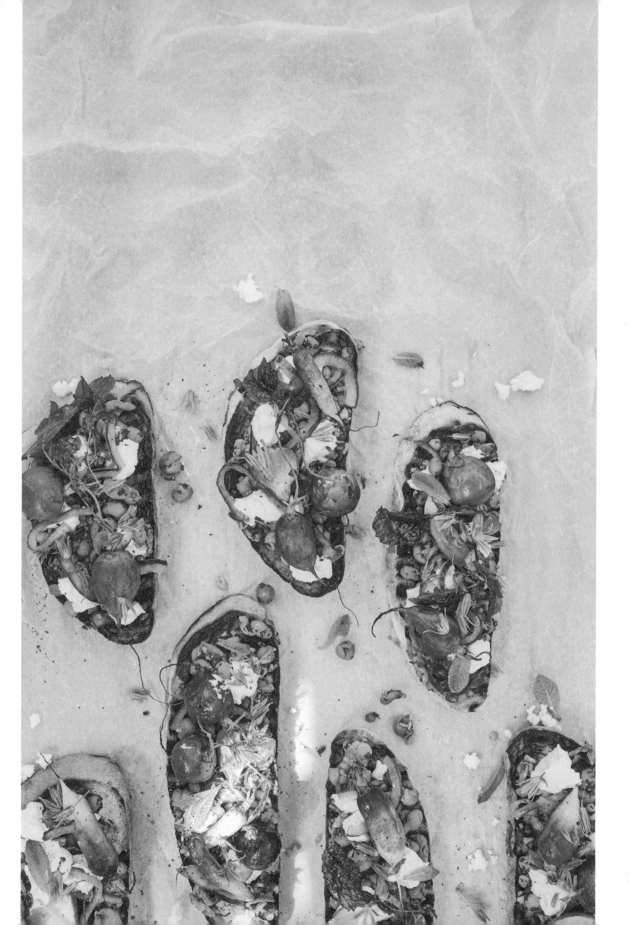

Quick tartines

'Tartine.' Such a nice word, isn't it? But whatever you choose to call them – bruschetta, open sandwiches, tartines – many a memorable meal can be made by piling simple ingredients on to good bread. Some of my favourite quick meals have come from moments where everything aligns: a few things pulled from the fridge and fruit bowl then added to bread have turned out unexpectedly triumphant. Here are a few I have remembered to make again.

Honey and pecorino

set honey

good pesto

toasted almonds

rocket

shaved pecorino
    (I use a vegetarian one)

lemon juice

Cheddar club

smoked tofu

mature Cheddar

gherkins

crispy romaine lettuce

cherry tomatoes

mustard

mayonnaise

Fridge raid

hummus

harissa

black olives

sun-dried tomatoes

peppery leaves

toasted seeds

Falafel and pickles

smashed falafels

chopped caper berries

tomatoes

hummus

pickled beets

spinach

lemon juice

Asparagus

shaved raw asparagus

avocado

toasted pumpkin seeds

rocket

lemon juice

shaved Parmesan
    (I use a vegetarian one)

All green

mashed avocado

feta

coriander

lime zest

green chilli

Beetroot

grated raw beetroot

soft goat's cheese

toasted almonds

black olives

orange zest

Full of veg

mung bean sprouts

grated carrot

spinach

mashed avocado

cherry tomatoes

pumpkin seed butter (see page 119)

Kale smash

sun-dried tomatoes

kale and lemon juice blitzed to paste

carrot dressed with lemon

mashed butter beans

crunchy lettuce

Asparagus and coconut soup

This is a quick and simple soup that puts asparagus at the centre. The greens add a little minerally depth and the coconut milk some gentle creaminess. I love using coconut milk in soups – it adds silkiness without having to use dairy or cream and the coconut flavour is subtle when mixed with vegetables. This soup comes together in a very short time, so it's a great spring staple at our house.

It works really well with other green veg too as the seasons change: peas, broccoli or courgettes. I have suggested my favourite ways to top and adapt it below.

Put a large deep pan over a medium–high heat, add the butter and leek and cook for 10 minutes, stirring, until the leeks are soft and sweet.

Next add the asparagus, the basil stalks and the greens and allow to cook for a minute or two, then add the coconut milk and stock and simmer until the asparagus is tender – this should take about 4–5 minutes.

Add the basil leaves and blitz in a blender or in the pan with a stick blender, until the soup is completely silky smooth. Squeeze in the juice of the lemon.

Next make any adjustments to the soup. Add more water if the soup is too thick, a pinch of salt if needed or more lemon. Once it is tasting great, ladle it into bowls and top with one of the suggestions below.

SERVES 4

2 tablespoons butter or coconut oil

1 leek, finely chopped

500g asparagus, trimmed and cut into 1.5cm pieces

a small bunch of basil, leaves picked, stalks finely chopped

400g spinach or greens

1 x 400ml tin of coconut milk

500ml vegetable stock

1 lemon

Topping ideas

- Toasted coconut flakes and a drizzle of olive oil

- Little basil leaves and a little tinned coconut milk

- Some pan-crisped white beans and lime zest

- Some chopped mint, lemon zest and yoghurt

- Grated hard-boiled egg and some spring herbs

- Lots of toasted sesame seeds and some pan-fried tofu

Four-herb and yoghurt soup

Four soft green herbs make an appearance in this soup – dill, tarragon, coriander and parsley – but really any combination of your favourite soft herbs would work. This soup is light and optimistic in flavour with lemon and herbs, but backed up with butter beans and yoghurt for some sustenance. The freshness of the herbs is answered by some anchoring spice: cumin, coriander and fennel. It's a pleasing yin and yang balance, and a great soup for filling that gap between the very cold and the warmer days. Vegans can use coconut yoghurt here.

_____

SERVES 4

olive oil

1 onion, finely chopped

2 sticks of celery, finely sliced

½ a small bunch of dill

½ a small bunch of tarragon

a bunch of coriander

a bunch of flat-leaf parsley

2 cloves of garlic, peeled and finely sliced

1 teaspoon ground cumin

1½ teaspoons coriander seeds

1 teaspoon fennel seeds

1 x 400g tin of butter beans, drained

1 litre weak vegetable stock

4 tablespoons Greek yoghurt

the juice of 1 lemon

sumac, to serve

Heat a good glug of oil in a large saucepan over a medium heat. Add the onion and celery, season with salt and pepper and fry for about 5 minutes, stirring from time to time, until the onion is really soft and translucent. Meanwhile, separate and roughly chop the herb stalks.

Once the onions are soft and sweet, add the garlic, spices and chopped stalks then cook for a further 2–3 minutes, until everything smells great.

Add the butter beans and the stock to the pan, then bring to a simmer and cook for 5 minutes.

Allow to cool a little, then blitz with a stick blender in the pan until you have a really smooth soup. Add the yoghurt, most of the herb leaves (reserving a few for garnishing the soup) and whizz again, until smooth.

Add the lemon juice and taste, adjusting the seasoning by adding more salt or pepper or lemon if you think it's needed. Ladle the soup into bowls and top with a sprinkling of sumac and a few of the reserved herbs.

Charred courgettes with mozzarella and lovage

British courgettes start showing up when the days get warmer and they stay around for most of the summer. I cooked this on a hot and heavy day early last year, at a supper club, and it's now a meal I regularly dream of. The sweetness of the charred courgettes paired with the cool, calm and creamy mozzarella and the verdant hit from the lovage is pure joy. It was the brainchild of the brilliant Robbin Holmgren, the head chef at Fifteen London. I am sure his version is much fancier, but this is how I do it at home.

The lovage oil is the crowning glory and simpler than you might think, though a good pesto would work too. Any leftover oil can be kept in a jar in the fridge for a few weeks. A mixture of parsley and celery leaves will also work.

First, make the lovage oil. Fill a bowl with boiling water and another with cold. Plunge the lovage into the boiling water, scoop it out immediately and immerse in the cold water to cool. Pat dry with kitchen paper; this keeps the lovage green.

Put the lovage into a food processor or blender, add the olive oil and a small pinch of salt, then blend until really smooth. Leave the food processor running for at least a couple of minutes to extract as much flavour from the lovage as possible. Pass the oil through a sieve, then transfer to a jar and set aside. Push any herb in the sieve down with a spoon to squeeze out the most flavour.

SERVES 4

a bunch of lovage

6 tablespoons good extra virgin olive oil

6 courgettes (I mix yellow and green)

2 balls of buffalo mozzarella or burrata

TO FINISH (OPTIONAL)

some courgette flowers

Next, heat your barbecue (or griddle) until it's smoking hot. While it heats up, cut your bigger courgettes into 1cm rounds and smaller ones into long slices or just in half. Once hot, char your courgettes on both sides until nicely charred and softened a little in the middle. This will take longer on a griddle, but try not to move them around too much otherwise the char marks won't form in even lines – about 2–3 minutes each side should do the trick, even less on a barbecue.

Serve the charred courgettes alongside the mozzarella, torn into pieces, and finish with a little sea salt, black pepper, a drizzle of the lovage oil and torn courgette flowers if using.

Elderflower broad bean toasts

I love elderflowers. When the floaty little blooms show up all over the parks near where I live, I know that the first days of summer are here. These toasts have a lot going on: the sweet but slightly sharp elderflower contrasts with delicate leaves (I use a mixture of rocket and pea shoots), milky burrata and the smokiness of the charred sourdough. You can make the salad and dressing ahead of time and keep them in the fridge, but make sure you griddle the toast at the last minute.

SERVES 6

a good loaf of
  sourdough bread

FOR THE SALAD

300g podded broad beans

400g delicate salad leaves

a drizzle of good extra
  virgin olive oil

1 unwaxed lemon

300g burrata or good
  buffalo mozzarella

FOR THE DRESSING

3 tablespoons elderflower
  and rose cordial
  (see page 221)

1 tablespoon white
  wine vinegar

4 tablespoons extra
  virgin olive oil

TO FINISH (OPTIONAL)

some fresh elderflowers

First, blanch your broad beans in boiling water for 2–4 minutes depending on their size, then drain and leave to cool. Once cool, peel the bitter skins from each one unless they are small and sweet, in which case you can leave them on.

Heat a griddle on your hob's highest heat.

Next, make your dressing by mixing all the ingredients in a jug, season well with salt and pepper and leave to one side.

Carefully pick through your salad leaves, wash and dry them well, then put them in a bowl with the broad beans.

Slice the sourdough loaf into 1.5cm-thick slices and griddle them until they have nice char marks on both sides. Drizzle all the toasts with olive oil, grate over the zest of the lemon and season well with salt. Put the toasts on a big platter or individual plates and tear over the burrata or mozzarella. Dress the leaves and broad beans with the elderflower dressing and pile on top of each toast. Finish with a scattering of confetti-like elderflowers if you like.

Butterhead lettuce and buttermilk dressing

This is my dream salad. I crave simple butterhead lettuce, and there is no better way to eat it than with a buttermilk dressing. Sometimes I just cut the lettuces into wedges and pour over the dressing, other times I pick the individual leaves as I have here. This salad sits well next to pretty much anything you might eat a salad with. I serve it as a simple start to a meal sometimes, and even as a light meal through spring and summer too.

This time of year sees some of the first British lettuces appear. I would encourage you to buy them whole. I use butterhead here, but oakleaf, lollo rosso, frisée, or a mix of more delicate leaves would all work well too. You can use yoghurt thinned with a splash of milk if you can't get your hands on buttermilk.

SERVES 4

FOR THE SALAD

2 slices of sourdough bread

2 heads of butterhead lettuce, washed and dried

50g almonds, skin on and chopped

FOR THE BUTTERMILK DRESSING

125ml buttermilk (or see note above)

1 teaspoon runny honey

2 tablespoons extra virgin olive oil

the zest and juice of 1 unwaxed lemon

a bunch of chives, finely chopped

Heat a griddle over a high heat for a few minutes to get the pan really hot. Grill the sourdough slices for a couple of minutes on each side until they are toasted and have dark char marks. Be bold here, as the charring imparts a smokiness that works as a great foil to the delicate lettuce and dressing.

Make the dressing. Whisk all the ingredients together in a jug or shake in a tightly sealed jam jar. Taste and add salt and pepper to season.

Quarter the lettuces, then lay them on a platter and drizzle over the dressing. Tear the charred toasts into rough chunks and scatter over the lettuce, then sprinkle over the almonds. Serve straight away.

New potato tortilla with halloumi and tomato kasundi

I ate something like this at a café near where I live, then went back twice in the following weeks for the same thing, until I realised I should probably just work out how to make it myself. It was spring, so I used new potatoes instead of the sweet potatoes the café had gone for. I have kept my tortilla pretty simple but you could also add any other spring or summer veg that you like.

The real star here is the tomato kasundi, which is an insanely good Indian tomato relish. It is a variation of kasundi, which is originally a sauce made from fermented mustard seeds. Mine is not much like the original. This recipe makes more kasundi than you will need, so your efforts will be rewarded beyond just one dinner. I have also suggested a few favourite ways to use the kasundi you are left with. If you don't have time to make it, a good tomato relish would work.

I cook some halloumi here to sit with the tortilla. I realise I am crossing a few continents but I don't really mind; it's a great combination.

SERVES 4

FOR THE TOMATO KASUNDI

2 tablespoons coconut
    or olive oil

1 tablespoon black
    mustard seeds

1 teaspoon ground turmeric

a small thumb-sized piece of
    ginger, peeled and grated

1 green chilli, finely chopped

2 cloves of garlic,
    finely chopped

1 teaspoon cumin seeds

1 x 400g tin of chopped
    tomatoes

1½ tablespoons light brown
    or coconut sugar

½ teaspoon flaky sea salt

2 tablespoons cider
    vinegar →

First make the kasundi. Melt the coconut oil in a large frying pan over a medium heat and add the mustard seeds. Cook until they start to pop, then add the turmeric, ginger, chilli, garlic and cumin seeds. Fry for a minute until everything smells fragrant.

Add the tomatoes, sugar, salt and vinegar and turn the heat right down. Simmer gently for 45 minutes to 1 hour, stirring occasionally. When the oil rises to the top of the pan the kasundi is ready.

While the kasundi is gently cooking, melt the tablespoon of coconut oil in a large ovenproof frying pan (I use one that's 28cm) over a medium heat and add the red onions. Cook for 6–8 minutes, stirring regularly, until the onions are completely soft and sweet, then add the potatoes along with the fennel seeds and a pinch of salt. →

Cook for 20 minutes, stirring from time to time, until the potato is soft and yielding but beginning to crisp at the edges. Meanwhile, finely chop the coriander stalks and add these to the pan too. After the potatoes have had their time, add the chilli flakes, lime zest and spinach and cook for a further 2–3 minutes, until the spinach has completely wilted.

Beat the eggs in a small bowl with a pinch of salt and pour into the frying pan. Turn the grill on. Cook the tortilla on a medium heat on the hob for 8 minutes, then place under the hot grill for a further 4 minutes to finish and brown the top.

1 tablespoon coconut
    or olive oil

2 red onions, finely sliced

800g new potatoes,
    sliced 0.5cm thick

1 teaspoon fennel seeds,
    roughly bashed

a few sprigs of coriander

a pinch of dried chilli flakes

the zest of 1 unwaxed
    lime, plus an extra lime
    cut into wedges

100g spinach

6 organic eggs

250g halloumi, sliced into
    1cm-thick pieces

salad leaves, to serve
    (optional)

While the tortilla is cooking, fry the halloumi in a non-stick frying pan for a couple of minutes on each side, until golden brown.

Serve the tortilla in wedges, with a couple of slices of halloumi and a spoonful of tomato kasundi. Finish with the coriander leaves and wedges of lime, and a few salad leaves if you like.

Ways to use your kasundi

- Stir it through fried rice and top with a fried egg

- In a toasted cheese sandwich

- In a wrap with falafel and salad

- Stir it through some mashed potato

- Use it to dress cooked green beans

Sorrel quinoa bowl with crispy greens

This is a take on a brunch dish I ate at one of my favourite LA spots. It makes the most of sorrel and is fine late-spring or early-summer eating. At Sqirl they serve it with rice and make it much fancier, but this is how I make it. If you can't get sorrel, any spring herb would work: basil, dill or lovage. The flavour will be different but all the other elements are quite neutral here, it's the sorrel oil that does the talking so you can confidently swap it for another herb. Vegans, try this with some pan-fried tofu (see page 28), adding a squeeze of honey to the pan just as you take it off the heat.

I toast quinoa before I cook it, as this gives it a deeper, nutty flavour that I really love. Be sure to use a mild-flavoured extra virgin olive oil for the sorrel oil – a peppery one will overpower the lemoniness of the sorrel.

First, make the pickled radishes. Mix the radishes in a large bowl with the lemon juice, vinegar, salt and honey and scrunch well with your hands to speed up the pickling. Place a plate over the top of the bowl and set aside.

Meanwhile, rinse the quinoa in a sieve. Fill and boil the kettle. Heat a pan over a medium heat, add the quinoa and cook until the residual water has evaporated and it has begun to smell toasty. Cover it with double the volume of boiling water from the kettle and add a good pinch of salt. Bring the pan to the boil over a high heat, then turn the heat down to low. Let the quinoa simmer for 15 minutes, until all the water has been absorbed and the germ comes away from the seed.

Meanwhile, make the sorrel oil by blitzing the sorrel in a blender with the olive oil and salt. Taste, and add lemon juice if you like a really punchy lemony flavour.

Bring a pan of water to the boil and lower the eggs in. Turn the heat down to a simmer and cook for 6 minutes with the lid on. →

SERVES 4

FOR THE PICKLED RADISHES

15 radishes, thinly sliced

the juice of ½ lemon

1 tablespoon white wine vinegar

1 teaspoon fine sea salt

a squeeze of honey or maple syrup

200g quinoa

4 organic eggs

olive oil

100g spring greens

50g pumpkin seeds

a pinch of flaky sea salt

the zest of ½ unwaxed lemon

FOR THE SORREL OIL

a large bunch of sorrel (about 50g)

6 tablespoons mild extra virgin olive oil

a small pinch of flaky sea salt

½ lemon (optional)

While the eggs are cooking, place a frying pan over a medium heat with a little olive oil. Tear any tough stems from the greens and roughly shred them. Add to the pan along with the pumpkin seeds and a little salt and cook until the pumpkin seeds start to pop and the greens have turned a deeper green and are starting to crisp at the edges. Take the pan off the heat and stir through the lemon zest.

When the quinoa is cooked and all the liquid has evaporated, take the pan off the heat, leave covered for 5 minutes, then fluff up with a fork.

Once the eggs have had their time, remove them with a slotted spoon, tap on a hard surface to break the shells then run them under cold water until they are cool enough to handle. Peel the shells away, then cut each one in half.

Drain the pickled radishes and roughly chop them into small pieces, about the size of the pumpkin seeds.

Divide the quinoa between 4 bowls and top with the greens, followed by the pickled radishes and the eggs. Spoon over the sorrel oil and serve warm.

Flash-roast green veg

It may seem a bit unusual to roast broad beans in their pods, but do give it a try. The pods sweeten, soften and char all at once, keeping the sweet little beans nestled safely inside, and you can eat the whole pod so nothing is wasted. I use the long, thin, pale, lime-green Turkish peppers here as they are readily available in the greengrocer's near where I live, but if you can't find them then a couple of normal green peppers, deseeded and cut into chunky strips, will do.

I like to use jarred chickpeas, as I find them to be more carefully cooked and hence more tender than tinned. The pulses tend to be bigger than those in the 400g tins, so use about 300g of drained jarred chickpeas, if you can get your hands on them.

Preheat your oven to 220°C/200°C fan/gas 7.

Put all the vegetables on a roasting tray – you may need two if you have smaller ones, then season liberally with salt and pepper and sprinkle over 2 good pinches of the pul biber. Drizzle generously with olive oil and put into the very hot oven to roast for 25 minutes. You want the oven to be quite fiercely hot, so that everything will catch and char. Turn your vegetables a couple of times while they cook.

On another tray, lay the whole block of feta on one side and the chickpeas on the other. Drizzle a splash of oil over the chickpeas and toss them to coat. Top the feta with a little more pul biber, half the lemon zest and the thyme tips. Put this into the oven on the rack underneath the veg.

Meanwhile, make the dressing. Chop all the herbs and put them into a bowl with the remaining lemon zest and almost all the juice plus 4 tablespoons of olive oil, the vinegar and the maple syrup.

When the vegetables are nearly done, squeeze the last of the lemon juice over the top, scatter with the garlic and return the tray to the oven for a couple of minutes.

Serve the roasted vegetables, topped with chickpeas, chunks of feta, the herb dressing and Turkish flatbreads.

SERVES 4

8 thin green Turkish peppers

4 red onions, cut into thin wedges

8 broad bean pods

4 Little Gem lettuces, halved

a bunch of radishes

a bunch of spring onions

Turkish chilli powder (pul biber)

extra virgin olive oil

200g feta

1 x 400g tin of chickpeas, drained

the zest and juice of 1 unwaxed lemon

a small bunch of thyme

2 cloves of garlic, finely chopped

Turkish flatbreads (see page 456)

FOR THE DRESSING

a small bunch of mint

a small bunch of dill

a small bunch of flat-leaf parsley

a splash of white wine vinegar

1 teaspoon maple syrup

How to make a hearty salad

1	2	3
Start with some leaves	**Add a hero vegetable**	**Add some texture**
(2 handfuls per person)	(½ a handful per person)	(a small handful per person)
spinach	roasted squash	olive-oil baked croutons
rocket	pickled beetroot	mixed toasted seeds
Little Gem	seasoned tomatoes	chopped toasted nuts (see page 459)
radicchio	roasted leeks	crumbled tortilla chips
mustard leaf	avocado	sprouted lentils and beans
shredded kale	sliced radishes	pomegranate seeds
shredded spring greens	ribboned courgettes	flash-fried breadcrumbs
	grated carrot	crushed poppadoms

4
Add a
top note
(a small handful
per person)

basil

mint

chervil

tarragon

parsley

coriander

fried crispy sage

fennel tops

celery leaves

5
Make it
hearty
(a few tablespoons
per person)

quinoa

drained beans

cooked seasoned lentils

cooked pearl barley

cooked bulgur wheat

a poached egg

crumbled cheese

6
Make a
great dressing
(follow the ratio, then
add your flavours and
seasoning, mix with a
fork in a jug, or put into
a jam jar and shake)

Oil (2 parts)

olive oil · hazelnut oil ·
rapeseed oil · blitzed
avocado · coconut milk ·
pumpkin seed oil

+

Acid (1 part)

citrus: lemon · lime ·
orange · grapefruit

vinegars: rice · white
wine · red wine · herb ·
balsamic

+

Flavours and seasonings

savoury juice (see page
86) · toasted spices ·
miso · red or green
chilli · mustard · capers ·
Parmesan · pecorino ·
salt and pepper

185

Golden six-spice paneer with lime pickle and smashed peas

I recently developed an obsession with paneer – its calm flavour and pleasing bouncy texture, the way it softens ever so slightly when it cooks but still holds its shape. What I do struggle with, though, is buying paneer made with good organic milk; I have only found one shop that sells it, so I often make my own. It's really very easy.

What I love most about paneer is its ability to take on flavour. Here I marinate it in six spices, then dry-fry it until it's crisp and golden. It sits next to a quick pea and coconut smash and an Indian slaw mixed with a clever little lime pickle that punctuates the slaw with little sherbet lime pops. I use fresh peas here but you could use frozen if you like. This recipe also works well on a barbecue if it's warm enough to eat outside.

SERVES 4

FOR THE PICKLE

2 unwaxed limes

1 tablespoon cumin seeds

1 teaspoon flaky sea salt

1 teaspoon golden
   caster sugar

FOR THE PANEER

400g paneer, sliced into
   2cm thick slices

2 tablespoons rapeseed
   or mild olive oil

1 teaspoon Kashmiri chilli
   powder

½ teaspoon ground turmeric

1 heaped teaspoon cumin
   seeds, ground

1 heaped teaspoon coriander
   seeds, ground

½ teaspoon fennel seeds,
   ground

a good grind of black pepper

½ teaspoon flaky sea salt →

To make the pickle, lightly peel the zest from the limes in long strips with a speed peeler. Put them into a saucepan and squeeze in their juice, then add the cumin seeds, salt and sugar. Bring to the boil over a high heat, then turn the heat down to low and simmer for 10 minutes, until the strips of zest have shrunk and started to curl at the edges. Once it's had its time, take it off the heat and leave to cool.

Toss the paneer in the rapeseed oil and all the remaining paneer ingredients and leave it to sit while you get on with a couple of other things.

While the pickle is cooking, fill and boil the kettle and place the peas in a bowl. Cover them with boiling water and set aside for a few minutes. Heat a frying pan over a medium heat and add a splash of oil, then the garlic, ginger, chilli and red onion, and sauté for a few minutes until everything is soft and sweet and smells fragrant. →

FOR THE PEA SMASH

200g podded fresh peas

rapeseed or mild olive oil

2 cloves of garlic, finely
  chopped

a small thumb-sized piece of
  ginger, peeled and grated

1 green chilli, finely chopped

1 small red onion, roughly
  chopped

the zest and juice of
  1 unwaxed lime

50g creamed coconut

FOR THE SLAW

½ spring cabbage

1 large beetroot (I use a
  pink candy cane one)

1 crisp red apple

2 spring onions

2 tablespoons mild olive oil

the juice of 1 lemon

TO SERVE

4 rotis or chapatis

Drain the peas well and return them to the bowl, then add the onion mixture (keeping the pan to use later), the lime zest and juice and a good pinch of salt and pepper. Crush the peas with a fork or a potato masher and grate the creamed coconut over the top. Stir the coconut through and check the seasoning. Set aside until you're ready to eat.

Next, make the slaw by removing the tough core from the cabbage (discard it). Shred the leaves finely and put them into a mixing bowl.

Peel the beetroot and grate it on the coarse side of a box grater, or cut it into small matchsticks and add it to the bowl. Grate the apple into the bowl, discarding the core and pips. Slice the spring onions finely and mix them through as well. Remove the pickled lime from the saucepan and chop it finely. Add this to the bowl with the oil and half the lemon juice and toss to mix well. Taste and add more salt, pepper and lemon juice as needed.

For the paneer, put the frying pan back over a medium heat and fry the slices for about 3 minutes on each side, until they are beginning to crisp and have turned a deep golden brown all over (you may need to do this in batches depending on the size of your pan).

Warm the rotis or chapatis in another dry frying pan or over an open flame, using tongs to hold them. Place a bread on each plate and spread a generous layer of pea smash down the centre. Put two or three pieces of crispy, spiced paneer on top and a heaped spoon of the slaw. Fold the sides over and eat while the paneer is warm.

Sri Lankan green bean and tomato curry

Where I live in London Sri Lankan food is having its moment in the sun. There have been a flurry of restaurants opening, serving traditional Sri Lankan hoppers and egg curries. This is a curry my friend Emily told me she'd eaten on a trip to Sri Lanka. It's a great thing to make with a glut of green beans, a curry that is even better the next day. If you want a really filling curry you could stir in some cooked lentils, sprouted mung beans or a tin of black-eyed beans just before serving.

This makes a jarful of Sri Lankan-style curry powder, which I keep on my spice shelf where it will last for a couple of months. It is deep and smoky and uses some roasted rice too, which adds an amazing crunch, and as the spices are already toasted you can use it to top hummus or mix it with a little olive oil for a spicy dip for bread. If it sounds like too much you can cut the quantity in half easily. I have suggested some other ways I like to use it overleaf.

First, make the curry powder. Place the rice in a dry non-stick pan. Heat over a medium heat until the rice starts to turn light brown. Add the spices and roast them for 3–5 minutes, until they start to brown, toast and become aromatic. Keep moving the pan to prevent the spices from burning. Remove from the heat and stir in the lemon zest, then leave to cool down.

Once the spices are cool, use a spice grinder (or a mortar and pestle) to grind them into a powder – you might need to do this in a few batches.

Next, on to the curry. Fry your onions in a little coconut oil until soft and sweet – it will take about 10 minutes. Once they are soft, add the garlic and turmeric and cook for another few minutes, until the garlic is starting to colour a little. →

SERVES 4

FOR THE CURRY POWDER

2 tablespoons basmati rice

4 tablespoons coriander seeds

3 tablespoons cumin seeds

2 tablespoons black peppercorns

1 tablespoon black mustard seeds

2 teaspoons whole cloves

1 heaped teaspoon cardamom seeds (from the pods)

1 heaped teaspoon fennel seeds

the zest of 2 unwaxed lemons

2 onions, roughly chopped

coconut oil

4 cloves of garlic, finely sliced

1 heaped teaspoon ground turmeric

2 tablespoons brown mustard seeds

20 fresh curry leaves

500g runner beans

1 x 400ml tin of coconut milk

4 tomatoes, roughly chopped

50g coconut flakes

the zest and juice of 1 unwaxed lime

TO SERVE

cooked basmati rice, rotis or flatbreads

189

Next add the mustard seeds and curry leaves and cook until the seeds start to pop, then take them off the heat. Add 2 tablespoons of the curry powder and stir for a minute until it has lost its rawness. The rest can be stored in an airtight container for up to 2 months.

Meanwhile, peel the rough strings from the edges of the runner beans and then chop the beans at an angle into 1cm pieces. Add to the pan with the coconut milk and tomatoes and cook for 15 minutes, until the beans are soft.

While the curry is cooking, toast the coconut flakes in a dry frying pan until golden, then add the lime zest and a pinch of salt.

Once the curry is ready, add the lime juice and take it off the heat. Serve the curry ladled into bowls, with the coconut flakes sprinkled on top and some rice or flatbreads on the side.

Ways to use your curry powder

- as a killer base for a curry (obviously)

- to top hummus

- mixed with olive oil and garlic as a quick dip for bread or veg

- scattered over a tray of veg before it goes into the oven to roast

- scattered over a cucumber and tomato salad

- tossed over some pan-fried paneer

- sprinkled on top of some lemon mashed avocado on toast

Lemon and fennel seed pizzette

I love the combination of fennel, chilli and lemon and it's well used in my kitchen – it gives these pizzette a freshness which so suits this time of year. We are lucky enough to have a pizza oven that lives in our small garden, so when the sun is out we make the little pizzas in there; you can mimic the effect by setting your oven to its highest heat and preheating a heavy baking tray or pizza stone.

These little pizzette are white, so they have no tomato, just the clean, simple slices of lemon which crisp and burnish in the oven, and some milky mozzarella with a hit of fennel from the quick salt. I make these for a crowd but you can scale the recipe back and make it for fewer without too much hassle. For the dough, I have given you two options: a slow sourdough, and a quick no-prove pizza dough which yields a result far better than the effort you have put in.

MAKES 12 SMALL PIZZAS

3 lemons, very finely sliced, ideally using a mandoline

1 tablespoon fennel seeds, bashed

a good pinch of dried chilli flakes

1 tablespoon flaky sea salt

flour, for dusting

1 batch sourdough or 2 x quick pizza dough (see page 457), rested and divided into 4 balls

olive oil

3 x 150g balls of mozzarella, roughly torn

a large bunch of basil

rocket and salad leaves, to finish

Preheat your oven to its highest temperature and put a pizza or baking stone inside if you have one. Put the lemon slices into a bowl and cover with boiling water, leave for 1 minute, then drain. Mix the fennel with the chilli and salt and put in a small bowl.

Sprinkle a little flour on the work surface. Take a ball of pizza dough and divide it into three pieces. Roll a small ball of dough into an oval or round, pulling and stretching the dough until it is as large as your hand. Repeat with a few more balls, then take a break while you start topping and baking the first batch of pizzas.

Once the first bases are ready, brush each with a little olive oil, then top with a little torn mozzarella, a few lemon slices, a sprinkling of the fennel salt and a scattering of basil leaves. Put on the hot baking stone and cook for 6–8 minutes, until blistering and golden. When the pizzas come out of the oven, top each one with rocket and salad leaves.

Return to the rolling when the first batch has gone into the oven and continue until all twelve pizzas have been baked.

One-pan pea, lemon and asparagus pasta

This pasta is a complete revelation. It's been one of the most popular recipes from my *Guardian* column, so I wanted to include it here. The sauce is magically made from the pasta water and asparagus as the pasta cooks – all in one pan. No fuss and a killer bowl of pasta.

The key to this recipe is to measure your water carefully and use the right pan: you need a large, shallow sauté pan or a casserole large enough to fit the pasta lying down. A large, deep frying pan or wok would work too. Keep tossing the pasta as it cooks to stop it sticking, as there is less water than you might be used to. Make sure your pasta is a type that cooks in 8 minutes; any longer will need water and more cooking.

I use sorrel here. It's a bright green, lemony, almost juicy leaf that I love. Be sure to add it if you can get your hands on it. If not, use watercress. The flavour will be more peppery than the sprightly lemon tang of sorrel but both work beautifully.

Fill and boil a kettle and get all your ingredients and equipment together. If you are using spinach or watercress, scrunch it between your hands with a little lemon juice and a pinch of salt.

Put the pasta into the pan. Snap the woody ends off the asparagus and chop the stalks into 0.5cm rounds, leaving the tips intact. Put the tips to one side and throw the rounds into the pan along with the garlic and peas. Grate in the zest of both lemons and add the oil and salt. Add 1 litre of boiling water, put a lid on the pan and bring to the boil. As soon as it comes to the boil, remove the lid and simmer on a high heat for 8 minutes, using a pair of tongs to turn the pasta every 30 seconds or so as it cooks.

Meanwhile, remove any big stalks from the watercress (if using). Once the pasta has had 8 minutes, take the lid off and stir through the asparagus tips, the sorrel and the basil or mint. Squeeze in the juice of 1 lemon and simmer for a final 2 minutes.

Once almost all the water has evaporated, take the pan off the heat and leave to sit for a minute or two, so the pasta can absorb most of the remaining water and form a lemony sauce. Tangle into four bowls and top with a little Parmesan.

SERVES 4

100g sorrel or watercress or spinach

2 large unwaxed lemons

400g spaghetti or linguine

400g asparagus

1 clove of garlic, thinly sliced

200g fresh podded or frozen peas

100ml olive oil

1 teaspoon flaky sea salt

a small bunch of basil or mint

40g freshly grated Parmesan (I use a vegetarian one)

Late spring stew of artichokes, peas and herbs

Vignarola is a Roman stew that is cooked in April in Rome and a little later here. It uses everything that is wonderful about this season. Mine is a little different from the classic Roman version as it is topped with some crisp seedy bread and a lot of herbs instead of the traditional crowning of prosciutto. I will probably be in trouble with purists and Italians, but this dish is so good I didn't want to stop making it when I stopped eating meat. It's a celebration of the vegetables of the hour, and the smoked salt and crisp cornered bits of bread add a depth that I think matches the classic version.

Artichokes are something I don't cook that much at home, mainly because they take quite a bit of preparing; but when I do I adore them. I use the small violet artichokes here, which are less time-consuming to prepare than their bigger cousins. If you are pushed for time you could use some good jarred ones.

SERVES 4

8 small violet artichokes

350g podded fresh baby broad beans

200g spinach or chard

a few slices of good seeded bread

extra virgin olive oil

2 small white onions, finely chopped

1 leek, shredded

350g podded fresh peas

the zest and juice of 1 unwaxed lemon

1 teaspoon smoked salt

a small bunch of fresh mint, leaves picked and chopped

a small bunch of fresh flat-leaf parsley, leaves picked and chopped

a few chive flowers, to serve (optional)

Preheat your oven to 220°C/200°C fan/gas 7.

First, deal with your artichokes. Put them into a large pot of cold salted water and bring to the boil. Once simmering, cook for about 10 minutes or until they are tender (check by inserting a knife into the heart to see if it is soft), then drain well and allow them to cool.

Fill the pot with 1.5 litres of water, add some salt and bring to the boil. Blanch the broad beans for a minute, then remove from the water with a slotted spoon and drain. Blanch the spinach or chard until just wilted. Keep this water. If you have the patience to double-pod your broad beans, now is the time to pop them out of their tougher outer casings.

Once the artichokes are cool, peel back the outer leaves of the flower part until you reach the pale tender edible ones; if you are unsure when that is, try one – if it's good to eat and not too tough you are there. Next, use a small sharp knife to cut 1.5cm off the top (this top bit can be tough), then cut the artichoke in half lengthways and use a teaspoon to scoop out the fibrous choke. Tear or cut the hearts into quarters. →

Tear the bread into 2-pence-sized pieces and lay it on a large baking tray. Drizzle with olive oil and scatter liberally with salt, then put the tray into the hot oven for 15 minutes for the bread to crisp up.

Heat a large saucepan (big enough to hold all the ingredients) and add a good splash of oil. Cook the onions and leek with a pinch of salt very gently for about 10 minutes, until soft, then add the reserved vegetable cooking water along with the peas and broad beans, and bring back to a gentle simmer.

Roughly chop the spinach or chard and add to the peas with the artichokes. Bring back to a simmer and let all the vegetables stew together for about 10 more minutes.

Taste, season with the lemon zest and juice, the smoked salt and some pepper, then stir together with almost all of the chopped herbs. Serve in bowls, with a generous drizzle of olive oil, the crisped bread on top and finally the flowers, if you are using them, as well as the remaining herbs.

Lemon, fennel seed and potato bake

I ate this in a restaurant many years ago and have never forgotten it. It's a simple dish that uses my two favourite ingredients as its stars. I eat this with a herby salad on the side but it would sit well next to most dinners.

It's a very flexible recipe; you can swap the fennel for other spices or woody herbs. And even add a little stock or cream before baking too, if you like.

Preheat the oven to 220°C/200°C fan/gas 7. Slice the potatoes as finely as you can – a mandoline can help here; you want the slices to be about 3mm thick.

Cut the top and bottom off the lemons, then slice them as finely as you can, keeping the rind on – you want the slices to be about the same thickness as the potatoes. The rind will soften and sweeten as it cooks.

Grease a medium ovenproof gratin dish with a little butter. Next lay some potato slices in a row across the end of the dish, propped up a little by leaning them at an angle against the side of the dish. Against this row, lay a line of lemon, not as many as the potatoes, but 2 or 3 slices.

Continue with potatoes and then lemon until you have filled the dish, shuffling the potatoes back a little as you go if you need to make enough space to fit them all in.

Pour over the stock then finish with a very good seasoning of salt and pepper and scatter over the fennel seeds. Dot the top with the butter. Cover the dish with foil and scrunch the edges to seal, then put into the hot oven for around 30 minutes, until the potatoes are cooked through.

Remove the foil and continue to cook for 30–40 more minutes, or until the potatoes are browned and the lemons are sticky and caramelised. Serve with a zippy lemon-and-olive oil dressed salad.

SERVES 4

1kg new potatoes, scrubbed but not peeled

2 small unwaxed lemons

50g butter, plus extra to grease the dish

200ml hot vegetable stock

1 tablespoon fennel seeds

Bright pink pasta

This is about as cheerful as dinner gets. It is super simple but will cheer up even the greyest day. Be sure to undercook your pasta in the water as it will cook for another couple of minutes with the beetroot, which will turn it bright fuchsia pink; nature's neon. I like to make this for kids and my son loves to jump up into my arms and watch as the pasta starts to turn pink.

If you like you can finish this with a crumbling of goat's cheese or feta, but I like it just as it is.

―――――――――――――

First, peel and coarsely grate your beetroot. Fill and boil a kettle. Heat a frying pan on a medium heat, add a drizzle of olive oil, then the beetroot and capers, and cook for about 7 minutes until the beetroot has lost its rawness and there is no liquid in the pan.

Meanwhile, fill a large pan with boiling water and add a good pinch of salt. Bring back to the boil, then add the pasta and cook for 3 minutes less than the packet instructions.

Once the pasta has had its time, drain it in a colander, reserving about 150ml of the cloudy pasta water to make your sauce. Put the pasta and the reserved water into the pan with the grated beetroot and simmer over a high heat for about another 3 minutes until all the water has evaporated and the pasta has turned deep pink and is perfectly cooked.

Take the pan off the heat and add the chopped dill, then squeeze over a little lemon juice and finish with a really generous drizzle of olive oil, more than you think you'll need, and salt and pepper.

SERVES 4

300g raw beetroot
extra virgin olive oil
2 tablespoons baby capers
400g wholewheat tagliatelle
a small bunch of dill
juice of 1 lemon

Vegetable shawarma

There is something so good about charred, soft flatbreads with some cooling yoghurt and warming spice. Some years ago on a trip to Granada in Spain I remember discovering their amazing shawarma stands. There is such a strong North African influence there, and the barbecue smoke and heady spices filled the streets. We sat outside and ate from our laps as we drank rosé mixed with lemonade, and ice-cold beers. For years since I have been trying to perfect a vegetable shawarma that didn't feel second best, and I think I've managed it.

I use spring carrots, little new potatoes and asparagus, which are spiced with cumin and coriander and charred and roasted in the oven, though on a hot day they could be blanched and then charred on a griddle or barbecue. They sit on top of warm flatbreads with a very good pistachio yoghurt spiked with coriander and sweetened with a drop of maple syrup. Vegans can use coconut yoghurt here to keep it free of dairy.

This dish is one I love in late spring and summer, but you can change the vegetables as they come into and out of season. Other favourite combinations are red peppers and aubergine; broccoli and runner beans; beetroot and cauliflower. Just be clever when you chop the veg – cut the veg that will cook slowly quite small and the quicker-cooking veg a bit bigger.

Preheat your oven to 220°C/200°C fan/gas 7.

Bash the cumin and coriander seeds in a pestle and mortar until roughly ground. Toss the carrots with a good drizzle of olive oil, a pinch of salt and pepper and half the cumin and coriander seeds. Transfer to a large roasting tray, cover with foil and roast in the centre of the oven for 10 minutes.

Meanwhile, make the yoghurt by mixing all the ingredients together with a pinch of salt.

After the carrots have had their time, push them to one side of the roasting tray, quarter or halve the potatoes and add to the other side. Drizzle over a bit more oil, and the other half of the cumin and coriander. Toss to mix the potatoes with the spices, put the foil back on and return the tray to the oven for 20 minutes. →

SERVES 4

1 tablespoon cumin seeds

1 tablespoon coriander seeds

400g bunch of baby carrots, scrubbed well

olive oil

250g new potatoes

½ a cucumber

1 lemon

200g asparagus, woody ends snapped off

4 flatbreads (see page 456) or round pittas

FOR THE HERBED PISTACHIO YOGHURT

100g Greek yoghurt

1 teaspoon maple syrup

a few sprigs of coriander, roughly chopped (stalks and all)

the zest of 1 unwaxed lemon

50g shelled pistachios, roughly chopped

While the potatoes are roasting, thinly slice the cucumber (I like to scoop the seeds out of the middle first), mix it with the juice from half the lemon, a good pinch of salt and pepper and a splash of olive oil, then put to one side.

Once the potatoes have had their 20 minutes, remove the tray from the oven, take off the foil and scatter over the asparagus. Squeeze over the remaining juice of the lemon, drizzle with a little oil and put back into the oven for 10 minutes until the asparagus are beginning to brown.

Toast or warm the flatbreads. When you're ready to eat, take the tray out of the oven and roughly crush the carrots with the back of a fork.

Spread some of the pistachio yoghurt over half of each flatbread and add the roasted carrots, then the potatoes and asparagus. Add a generous pinch of the cucumber and fold the warm flatbreads over to envelop everything. Eat straight away.

Farinata with slow-cooked courgettes

I have an obsession with pancakes; any opportunity to make or eat them for breakfast, lunch or dinner and I'll take it. So I've had to expand my pancake horizons beyond the Shrove Tuesday classics and the fluffy American ones. One of my favourite ways to make pancakes is with chickpea flour. All over the world chickpea (gram) flour is used to make *socca, farinata* and Indian *pudla. Farinata* are a distinctly Italian creation.

The pancakes come together easily and quickly and can be made in advance and warmed up if that's your kind of thing. I serve them with slow-cooked courgettes, 'trifolati' courgettes to give this kind their proper name, which means cooking them slowly in olive oil and garlic. It's also used for cooking mushrooms and truffles. I love cooking courgettes this way, as it brings out a sweet buttery character that you don't get when you cook them more quickly.

Start with the courgettes. Heat a large, deep saucepan over a low heat and melt the butter. Add the garlic, courgettes, fennel, lemon zest, a really generous pinch of salt and a few turns of the pepper mill. Cover and continue to cook over a low heat for 1 hour, stirring from time to time.

While the courgettes are cooking, make the batter by whisking the gram flour in a large mixing bowl with 800ml of cold water. Set aside for 20 minutes.

Preheat your oven to 220°C/200°C fan/gas 7.

When you are ready to cook, whisk in 60ml of the olive oil, the salt and half the reserved fennel fronds.

If you have two ovenproof frying pans of a similar size (25cm roughly), you can speed up proceedings here by cooking two pancakes at once, but if not, don't worry. Heat your frying pan(s) on the highest heat and add a tablespoon of oil. →

SERVES 4

FOR THE COURGETTES

1 tablespoon butter

1 clove of garlic, finely sliced

6 medium courgettes (about 1kg), thinly sliced

1 bulb of fennel, finely sliced (keep the fronds)

the zest and juice of 1 unwaxed lemon

3 tablespoons olive oil

a handful of mint

FOR THE FARINATA

350g gram (chickpea) flour

120ml olive oil

1 teaspoon flaky sea salt

half the reserved fennel fronds (see above)

TO SERVE

olive oil

2 tablespoons capers

100g soft goat's cheese or goat's curd

When the oil is so hot it's smoking, pour a quarter of the batter into the hot pan and let it cook for around 30 seconds so that it's bubbling on the sides. Place in the hot oven for 15 minutes, until the top is crisp and deep golden. Carefully remove the farinata from the pan; it should be crisp on both sides but still a little soft in the middle. Put it on a warm plate under foil to keep hot while you cook the others in the same way, adding a tablespoon of oil to the pan each time. You'll easily be able to do them all in the time it takes for the courgettes to cook.

After about 45 minutes, the courgettes should have completely collapsed and softened, almost to a rough purée. Turn the heat off, roughly chop the mint and add this to the pan with the lemon juice and remaining fennel fronds. Check the seasoning – you will probably need some more salt and perhaps a bit more lemon juice.

Heat 3 tablespoons of oil in the farinata frying pan and once it's hot, add the capers and cook for about 30 seconds so they are crispy. Scoop out with a slotted spoon and drain on kitchen paper.

Serve the courgettes over the farinata, with the goat's cheese and crispy capers dotted over the top.

Pistachio and ricotta dumplings with peas and herbs

These are light, bright dumplings that are quick and easy to put together. It is a plate which is all about late spring: white, green and fresh. I use freshly podded peas here and I don't cook them: I love their pop and sweetness when they've not been cooked and they work against the softness of the ricotta. If podding peas sounds a bit much or fresh peas are hard to get hold of for you, some briefly boiled frozen ones will work well too.

Chop your pistachios finely; you can do this in a food processor but be sure that you don't blitz them to a powder, as you still want them to have enough texture as if they had been finely chopped by hand.

Put the ricotta into a bowl with the pistachios, lemon zest, chopped chilli and the flour. Season well with salt and pepper and mix gently until it comes together as a dough.

SERVES 4

100g shelled pistachios, toasted

500g ricotta

the zest of 2 unwaxed lemons

1 red chilli, finely chopped

8 tablespoons light spelt flour, plus a little extra

a small bunch of spring herbs

150ml good olive oil

400g freshly podded peas

Half fill a large saucepan with water and place it over a high heat. Roll the ricotta mixture into about 20 little conker-sized balls. Very lightly dust in a little more flour and place on a chopping board while you wait for the water to boil.

Next, finely chop the herbs, put them into a bowl with the olive oil and the peas, and season with salt and pepper.

Once the water in the saucepan is at a boil, lower the dumplings in and cook them for 4–5 minutes, until they all rise and bob to the top. Drain on kitchen paper and serve about 5 per person, topped with the herby peas and olive oil.

Early summer gooseberry, elderflower and almond sponge

This is a favourite cake. The moment when elderflowers and gooseberries cross over is one of my favourite times of the year; everything is still verdant from spring but the bounty of the summer has started to arrive, it's a great time for food.

The sponge is quite a traditional one, spiked with almond, lemon and vanilla and then doused in elderflower and sandwiched with an easy gooseberry compote and a yoghurt icing. It is everything I love about summer cakes. It's not very fancy but this is on purpose, as unless it's a big occasion I like my cakes simple and natural, gently frosted, so that they tell the story of what's in them rather than hiding the ingredients behind a thick layer of butter and sugar.

If I make this for a special occasion I finish it with some elderflowers if I can get my hands on them, or some other fresh seasonal blooms (see page 296). If they aren't edible flowers, be sure to take them off before eating.

If you plan to eat this over a few days I suggest keeping the filling and sponge separate and icing each slice as you go, as the cake keeps better out of the fridge but the icing does need refrigerating. This cake can easily be made with frozen gooseberries if you want a hit of early summer at another time of year – who wouldn't.

MAKES A 20CM CAKE

200g unsalted butter, softened, plus extra for greasing

100g golden caster sugar

100g light muscovado sugar

250g light spelt flour

2 teaspoons baking powder

100g ground almonds

150ml milk (I use whole or oat milk)

3 organic eggs

the seeds from 1 vanilla pod

the zest of 1 unwaxed lemon

FOR THE GOOSEBERRY COMPOTE

300g gooseberries, topped and tailed

2 tablespoons elderflower and rose cordial (see page 221)

50g golden caster sugar

FOR THE WHIPPED YOGHURT ICING

200g Greek yoghurt

50g golden icing sugar

TO FINISH

fresh elderflowers (if you can get them)

Preheat the oven to 150°C/130°C fan/gas 2. Grease a deep 20cm springform cake tin and line it with baking paper.

In the bowl of an electric mixer, or with an electric hand whisk, cream the soft butter and sugars together until almost white and fluffy.

In a separate bowl whisk together the flour, baking powder and ground almonds to get rid of any lumps.

Add half the dry mixture to the butter and mix well, add the milk, eggs, vanilla and lemon zest, then mix in the remaining dry ingredients. Scrape around the bottom of the bowl and mix again.

Pour the batter into the tin, using the back of a spoon or a spatula to level out the top, then bake for 1 hour, until the top of the cake springs back and is soft to the touch. Cool for 15 minutes in the tin, then move to a rack to cool completely. →

While the cake is in the oven, get on with the compote and icing. To make the compote, place the gooseberries in a saucepan with the cordial and sugar. Place the saucepan over a medium heat, bring to a simmer and turn the heat down to low. Continue to cook gently for 20–30 minutes, until the gooseberries are completely soft, have burst to release their juices and have started to turn jammy. Leave to cool completely.

To make the icing, stir together the yoghurt and icing sugar until you have a spoonable icing and store in the fridge until needed.

Once the cake has cooled completely, use a long serrated knife to slice it horizontally through the middle. I find the best way to do this is to gently skirt around the edge of the cake with your knife, cutting just 1cm into the cake exactly halfway down so that you have a line to follow, then go all the way through following the line you have cut – this will give you a more even result.

Lift the whole cake on to a serving plate, then carefully lift off the top layer – you can slide it on to a plate to do this if you feel happier – and spread the bottom with the yoghurt mixture and then the gooseberry compote. Cover with the top of the cake and sprinkle over some elderflowers to finish.

Hedgerow food

I'm not a gardener. I wish I were but life seems to get in the way of growing. So for me my connection with the land comes when I head out to the marshes near my house and pick from the hedgerows. It might sound a bit whimsical and Enid Blyton but it's a lovely thing to do: to connect with the source of our food, to actually pick our own food when lots of us are so removed from that. I am not suggesting that you do this for a Tuesday-night dinner but a weekend afternoon spent picking and cooking is in my book one well spent.

Nettles

What and where: instantly recognisable for its ragged leaves; remember to wear gloves when picking and cooking, but once blanched they lose their sting.

Season: best picked from February to June; go for the younger-looking leaves.

How to use: often described as tasting like something between spinach and cabbage.

Wild garlic

What and where: long, flat deep green leaves, found in pretty much every British woodland or riverbank; you'll be able to smell it if you've picked the right stuff.

Season: late winter to mid-spring.

How to use: use anywhere you might spinach; my wild garlic and yoghurt baked eggs (see page 82) or the Cheddar, swede and wild garlic scones (page 149) are a favourite, and it's also great for simple pestos (see page 92) .

Elderflowers

What and where: the little cloud-like flowers are distinctive and you'll be able to smell them too. I pick mine on Hackney Marshes. Pick the ones higher up, and if you can, ones that face the sun.

Season: May to early July if you're lucky.

How to use: elderflower fritters, cakes (see page 220), cordial (see page 221), salad dressings (see page 172).

(Marsh) samphire

What and where: a thin, deep green, succulent, almost cacti-like grass that can be found in sea marshes and salt flats.

Season: best in July and August.

How to use: easy and delicious to pickle, or simply have steamed with a little butter. The most important piece of advice is to wash it very thoroughly to remove any sand or grit. The salty sweetness is like nothing else, with a very pleasing crunch. Think salty asparagus.

Chanterelles

What and where: distinctive golden, yolk-coloured mushrooms often found in conifer woods. A note of caution: mushroom foraging can be a dangerous business. Never eat a mushroom unless you are 100 per cent sure you know what it is. I am not a mushroom expert and there is plenty more information online or in numerous books so do check them if you're in any doubt about what you've picked.

Season: look from July onwards.

How to use: I love mine cooked in a little butter with wholewheat spaghetti, on toast (see page 315) or in a lasagne (see page 333).

Crab apples

What and where: look like tiny little apples – green with blushing red cheeks, which deepen in red as they ripen; they are the wild ancestors of the apples we eat today. Trees are found throughout the UK but are also an easy tree to plant in your garden.

Season: August to October.

How to use: nothing beats a classic jelly; the colour alone is spectacular and it's a favourite in our house with cheese on fresh sourdough. Adding crab apples to other jellies or jams can help them set.

Blackberries

Where: these are so easy to find across the UK; in towns and cities look for them on canal-side paths; I've even seen berries growing around some of London's tube stations. A good tip is to take an umbrella with a hooked handle with you to hook brambles and bring them closer to you. Avoid roadsides and berries that are low down.

Season: late summer to autumn.

How to use: ripe berries bursting with juice don't need much more than yoghurt and perhaps a bit of honey. But they're amazing in so many dishes; try them with fragrant bay leaves in a tart (see page 374), in a traditional cobbler or crumble, or in a savoury bake (see page 346).

Sloes

What and where: dusty, inky blue-black berries that are found on bushes on beaches and in woodland. Their bushes have spiky thorns and the berries have short stems and hug the branches.

Season: ready to be picked from the end of September to December; some people say to wait until after the first frost for the best flavour.

How to use: sloe gin, which is hard to beat; they're also lovely in a jam or a sorbet.

Strawberry and anise galette

Strawberries seem to be arriving on the shelves earlier and earlier. By my birthday in early April the shelves are full of British strawberries, but it's not until a bit later that I think they are at their best. The early French ones, though, are the ones to get excited about: the deeply perfumed Gariguette variety, then after that the good English ones start showing up.

This galette is quick and easy to make, and buttery and flaky to eat. The strawberries roast and melt to a pool of molten scarlet jam in the middle, some still holding their shape, but all of them releasing their juices to create a seriously good jammy centre.

What I love most about this, though, is that it uses very little sugar; the natural sweetness of the strawberries shines through. I have given an approximate weight for the sugar I use to sweeten the strawberries, as the amount you need will depend on the strawberries as well as your own tastes (I usually end up using about 60g).

The surprising element is anise seed, a sweet fennel-like seed which I love. The seeds can be harder to come by than other spices, but if you like you could replace them with fennel seeds or even just a grind of black pepper (you won't need as much as a tablespoon).

When you take the galette out of the oven it will look a little runny in the centre, but it will set within minutes as it cools.

_____

For the pastry, combine the flour, salt and sugar in a bowl. Add the butter and use the back of a fork or a food processor to cut the butter into the flour until you have a rough scruffy mixture, still with some bigger chunks of butter.

Add the ice-cold water bit by bit, until the pastry comes together – you will only need 4–5 tablespoons. Bring it together into a ball with your hands, or pulse a few times in the food processor. Handle it as little as possible, then wrap it in cling film and put it into the fridge to cool and rest for at least 45 minutes or so. →

SERVES 4–6

750g strawberries

1 tablespoon anise seed (see intro)

50–100g golden caster sugar

FOR THE FLAKY SPELT PASTRY

160g spelt flour, plus a little extra for dusting

a pinch of flaky sea salt

1 tablespoon golden caster sugar

100g cold unsalted butter, cut into cubes

a glass of iced water

1 organic egg, beaten

TO SERVE

coconut yoghurt, whipped with a little honey and vanilla, or thick Greek yoghurt, cream or ice cream

Meanwhile, hull the strawberries and cut them in half, or any larger ones into quarters. Put them into a bowl with the spice and half the sugar and leave to sit.

Once the pastry has rested, take it out of the fridge to soften a bit and preheat the oven to 180°C/160°C fan/gas 4.

Flour your work surface and, once the pastry has warmed slightly, roll it out quite thinly into roughly a 30cm round, then lift it on to a baking tray lined with baking paper.

Pile the strawberries in the middle of the pastry, leaving about a 4cm border of pastry to fold over. There's no need to be too precise with the strawberries, as they will shrink and change as they cook.

Next fold the edges of the pastry over the strawberries to hold them in. Brush the edge of the pastry with the beaten egg, then sprinkle the strawberries and pastry edges with the remaining sugar.

Bake in the hot oven for 55 minutes, until the strawberries are soft and bubbling and the pastry is golden and crisp. Serve with my choice of some coconut yoghurt stirred with a little honey and vanilla, or with ice cream, cream or thick Greek yoghurt.

Elderflower and rose cordial

Making cordial is actually much easier than you might think, and elderflower grows everywhere in May and June. Even in Hackney, in the middle of one of the world's biggest cities, I could probably show you 100 bushes near our house that bloom into floaty, starry blossoms.

Old wisdom suggests you should pick the flowers on a sunny day and only pick flowers that face the sun. I'm not sure I've been able to taste the difference but it does make the picking nicer.

It's best to use a rose from the garden; shop-bought ones tend to be sprayed, so aren't good to use in cooking. And don't worry that the infused liquid doesn't look very appealing: when the lemon juice is added, the rose's intense colour will return like magic. The cordial keeps in a sterilised bottle in the fridge for at least a month.

Fill and boil the kettle. Peel the zest from the lemons in long strips. Put the elderflowers into a large bowl with the lemon peel and rose petals. Pour over 500ml of boiling water and press down the florets, making sure they're submerged. Leave to cool, then cover the bowl and leave to infuse at room temperature for about 36 hours.

Strain the infusion into a medium saucepan, pressing the flowers with the back of a spoon, to release all the liquid, then discard the flowers, branches, peel and rose petals. Add the sugar and lemon juice to the infusion, then turn the heat to high and cook for 3–4 minutes, stirring until the sugar has dissolved and the liquid is starting to simmer. Take off the heat, leave to cool, then pour into a sterilised bottle. Seal and store in the fridge for up to a month.

MAKES 800ML

- 2 unwaxed lemons
- 100g elderflower heads (about 12 heads)
- 1 small red rose (see note above), petals picked
- 325g caster sugar
- 125ml lemon juice (3–4 lemons)

Herbal infusions

Herbs hold a special magic for me in the kitchen. As a young chef I remember listening to a talk by the amazing Jekka McVicar, the queen of herbs, a guardian of rare herb varieties and an expert on all thing herbal; she talked at length about the healing properties of herbs. She discussed how in days gone by basil would be infused into warm milk and given to infants to calm them before bed. I was totally charmed by this and went on to make a basil panna cotta, which I still make and love serving after a meal. It is soothing and gentle and a perfect end to a meal. I am sure I sleep better after eating it too.

I use herbs in almost everything I cook, picking bay and rosemary and lavender from the garden and softer herbs from my window sill or from the herbs I store in a little water in glasses in my fridge door.

I make infusions and tisanes with herbs. Their fresh verdant nature is amplified when they come into contact with hot water – the oils are released and gently flavour the water. It's a great way of making sure that you drink enough water too, as while I often forget to sip my water I'll always drink my tea before it's cold. It also a good way of making sure those bunches of herbs are used to their full potential and don't wither unused in the fridge.

It can be lovely to blend a spice with a fresh herb too: the grassy green top notes coming from the herbs and the warmer base notes from the spice e.g. rose petals with cinnamon, lemon verbena with fennel seed.

Brewing herbal infusions

— Pick herbs as you need them to keep them fresh.

— Two or three leaves or six to eight flowers per person is a good amount.

— Use heatproof glasses for maximum prettiness.

— Don't brew in the same teapot as caffeinated tea as the tannins can affect the taste.

— To preserve herbs dry them slowly out of direct sunlight. Either hang from the ceiling with string, or lay them flat in a paper bag, turning them every few days or whenever you remember.

— Infusions can be cooled and stored in the fridge and served over ice for amazing iced tea.

— For another way to make herbal teas see page 86 for how to juice their essence.

Favourite herbs

Wild fennel: great for digestion; pairs well with lemon zest.

Lemon balm and lemon verbena: good for digestion too; pairs well with fennel seeds.

Basil: green or purple; good for digestion; can be infused into milk for bedtime.

Lavender: calming and centring; strong so go lightly; good infused into milk.

Lemon thyme: the best of the thymes to infuse; pairs well with black pepper and honey.

Chamomile: good for sleep and to settle a stomach as well as for cramps; pairs well with vanilla and honey.

Mint: easy to grow, good for after meals; pairs well with orange blossom flowers or water and honey.

Elderflower: brew on its own or with another herb, needs some honey to sweeten.

Sage: only needs a short brew; good with honey and orange.

Nettle: grows everywhere; I like it paired with lemon.

Rosemary: good for digestion; also add to a bath to help with muscle or back pain; very good with honey and squashed blackberries.

Rosehip: vibrant red tea high in vitamin C; you can dry these yourself in a low oven or buy them dried.

Dandelion flowers: use the yellow flowers – one per person; can be bitter, which I love, but sweeten with honey if you need to.

Favourite herbal infusion blends

Rose and cinnamon: fresh or dried rose petals and a crumbled cinnamon stick.

Spiced mint: mint leaves, lemon, bashed fresh ginger, coriander seeds and black peppercorns.

Ruby vitamin C: dried hibiscus, dried rosehips, lemon zest and rose petals.

Hedgerow winter herbs: sage, rosemary, blackberries and lemon slices.

Moroccan mint: mint, orange blossom water, orange zest and honey.

Herbs can also be infused in water with fruit for extra depth and flavour and poured over ice in the summer. Add the herbs and fruit (see below) to a jug and leave to sit for at least half an hour before adding ice and drinking. You can infuse the water several times with one batch of herbs and fruit.

Favourite iced water infusions

— a couple of sprigs of sage and a handful of blackberries.

— a sprig of rosemary and a sliced apple.

— a few sprigs of mint, half a sliced cucumber and a sliced lime.

— a few sprigs of thyme and a sliced peach.

— a few sprigs of basil and a sliced lime.

— a couple of sprigs of marjoram and a sliced lemon or bergamot.

Summer

Best of the season
- Tomatoes
- Courgettes
- Corn
- Aubergine
- Peppers
- Chard
- Baby carrots and beetroots
- Radishes
- Runner beans
- Green beans
- Yellow beans
- Cauliflower
- Strawberries
- Cherries
- Blackcurrants
- Whitecurrants
- Raspberries
- Tayberries
- Loganberries
- Edible flowers
- Peaches
- Nectarines
- Greengage
- Blueberries

Flowers
- Hydrangea
- Yarrow
- Veronica
- Delphinium
- Dahlia
- Rose

Overnight summer birchers

On summer mornings I try to eat my breakfast outside. I sit in our garden and eat one of these bowls of bircher with my little boy running around me. I am not a morning person, and since Dylan's arrival there is even less time in the morning to focus on eating something good, so making this the night before has become a ritual for me and John so that all three of us start the day well.

These are my four favourite flavours for summer. They all work on roughly the same principle but you'll need varying amounts of liquid depending on the fruit you add. I encourage experimenting with your favourite flavours. And if by the morning the bircher is too thin, you could stir in a little yoghurt; too thick, a little more milk. I have also made a savoury version with almond milk and sesame seeds topped with flaked nori.

EACH SERVES 2

PEACH AND RYE

60g oats

40g rye flakes

1 apple, grated

1 tablespoon barley malt extract

350ml oat milk

TO TOP

1 peach, stoned and roughly chopped

4 tablespoons plain yoghurt

the zest of 1 unwaxed lemon

RASPBERRY AND HAZELNUT

100g oats

50g raspberries

50ml orange juice

250ml hazelnut milk

TO TOP

25g hazelnuts, toasted

50g raspberries

4 tablespoons oat or coconut yoghurt →

PEACH AND RYE

In a large screw-top jar, mix the oats, rye, apple and barley malt. Pour over the oat milk, cover with the lid and shake to combine evenly. Put in the fridge overnight.

The next morning, serve topped with the peach, yoghurt and lemon zest.

RASPBERRY AND HAZELNUT

Put the oats into a large screw-top jar. Roughly mash the raspberries and place them in the jar too, along with the orange juice and hazelnut milk. Cover with a lid and leave in the fridge overnight.

The next morning, roughly chop the hazelnuts and spoon the bircher into bowls. Top with the hazelnuts, raspberries and yoghurt. →

CHERRY AND POPPY SEED

80g oats

20g millet

2 tablespoons poppy seeds

200ml almond milk (I use
  unsweetened)

1 pear

1 tablespoon maple syrup

TO TOP

50g pitted cherries (frozen are
  fine)

the zest of 1 unwaxed lemon

poppy seeds

MANGO AND VANILLA

100g oats

the seeds from 1 vanilla
  pod, or 1 tablespoon
  vanilla paste

200ml ready-to-drink coconut
  milk

½ a mango, peeled and
  roughly chopped

¼ teaspoon ground cardamom

TO TOP

½ a mango, peeled and
  roughly chopped

4 tablespoons plain or
  coconut yoghurt

the zest of 1 unwaxed lime

2 tablespoons coconut chips

CHERRY AND POPPY SEED

Put the oats, millet and poppy seeds in a large jar and pour over
the almond milk. Grate the pear on the thickest setting on your box
grater and mix it through the other ingredients, along with the maple
syrup. Cover and leave in the fridge overnight.

Spoon into two bowls and divide the cherries and lemon zest
between them, then scatter over some extra poppy seeds.

MANGO AND VANILLA

Put the oats into a large jar with the vanilla paste and pour over
the coconut milk. Quickly blitz the mango in a food processor with
the cardamom, then mix it through the oats. Cover and leave in the
fridge overnight.

Spoon into two bowls and top with the mango, yoghurt, lime zest
and coconut.

Cherry and almond breakfast smoothie

For the few weeks cherries are at their best I eat them all day long. Straight from the paper bag on the way home from the shops, baked into cakes and brownies (see page 293), to top pancakes (see page 290) or laid over a bowl of ice for a quick dessert on a hot day. This is how I get cherries into my mornings and their cheering colour never fails to lift my spirits. Almond butter works here to give this smoothie an almost marzipan note; it works with frozen cherries, too once summer is gone.

_____

Place all the ingredients in a blender with a little ice if you'd like it really cold. Blitz until you have a thick, deep red smoothie.

SERVES 2

100g cherries, pitted

2 pears, cored and roughly chopped

1 orange, peeled

125ml coconut water or cool herbal tea

100ml almond milk (I use unsweetened)

1 tablespoon almond (or nut) butter

231

Summer morning bowl

MAKES A BOWL FOR ONE

200g berries

the cheek of 1 medium mango

2 tablespoons chia seeds

2 tablespoons thick Greek
   or coconut yoghurt

2 ice cubes

TOPPINGS

more berries

toasted coconut flakes

bee pollen

granola

toasted buckwheat

puffed rice or quinoa

chopped nuts

more yoghurt

This is a quick breezy summer breakfast for when porridge is a
distant memory. I first ate a breakfast like this in Brazil, where icy
açai bowls are the breakfast of choice in the juice bars that line
the streets off Rio's beaches. This is my British summer version. It's
essentially a thin frozen yoghurt, the right consistency for spooning,
with some chia seeds for texture and energy. I have left the toppings
up to you; use what you have on hand to add texture, flavour and
some prettiness. You can use frozen berries if you like, in which case
I'd recommend leaving out the ice cubes. I use a mixture of summer
berries (e.g. raspberries, strawberries and redcurrants).

Wash the berries and scoop the flesh out of the mango cheek
to remove the peel. Put all the ingredients into a blender and
blitz for 30 seconds, until everything is combined. I like mine to
have some texture from the chia seeds, but you may prefer yours
completely smooth.

Top with any of the additional toppings if you're using them.

Beetroot borani

There is something a bit 1980s about the word 'dip'. It makes me think of my parents' dinner parties, Mum in her turquoise and silver lapelled jumpsuit, passing around a bowl of tortilla chips and a layered Mexican creation we called 'The Dip'.

But a dip, spread or hummus is a very useful thing to have in your fridge. I make up a batch of some kind at least once a week. It means I have something on hand to dip a carrot in to fill the gap before dinner, or something flavourful to spoon into a bowl of greens and grains, or to spread into a sandwich with a sprinkling of feta and some peppery leaves.

This Iranian dip is a summer favourite. It's usually made with aubergine, but its flavours work with lots of different vegetables. I use different coloured beetroots here, sometimes the deep purple ones, sometimes the golden ones, or even the candy-cane ones, which give the borani a dusky pink hue; on the day we took the pictures I made all three. You can use vacuum-packed cooked beetroots here too if you want to make this in a hurry. If your dates are not soft, soak them in a little hot water first.

SERVES 4

500g raw or cooked beetroots

extra virgin olive oil

2 soft, pitted Medjool dates

1 small clove of garlic, finely chopped

4 tablespoons Greek yoghurt

a small bunch of dill, chopped

2 tablespoons red wine vinegar

100g feta cheese, crumbled

a small handful of walnuts, roughly crushed

½ teaspoon nigella seeds

TO SERVE

yoghurt flatbreads (see page 456)

crunchy vegetables

If you are cooking your beetroot, wash them, leaving the skins on, then cover with boiling water and simmer for about 40 minutes, or until they are tender to the tip of a knife. Top up the water when needed. Drain the beetroot, then leave them to cool.

Once cool, peel the beetroot and blend in a food processor with 4 tablespoons of olive oil, the dates and a pinch of salt until you have a totally smooth purée.

Transfer to a bowl and add the garlic, yoghurt, most of the dill, the vinegar and a pinch of salt if you think it needs it.

To serve, sprinkle over the feta, walnuts, nigella seeds and remaining dill, then drizzle with a little olive oil. Serve with the yoghurt flatbreads and crunchy vegetables, for dipping.

Flatbreads – a flavour map

Flatbreads or quesadillas are a weekly quick lunch or dinner in our house. They require little more than a few minutes' attention, one bowl and a pan, and with a few salad leaves or a bit of mashed avocado they make a perfect too-hot or too-lazy-to-cook lunch or dinner.

I make quesadillas a bit differently, leaving the seriously cheese-laden ones to fond childhood memory. Instead, I use vegetables, pulses, herbs and even eggs to make textured fillings with pops of flavour that move from Mexico to Italy, France, Morocco and back again. In fact, quesadillas are really just sandwiched flatbreads, which in some form or another you'll find in almost every culture. I use seeded tortillas, piadina flatbreads (see page 316 for my Quick squash piadina recipe) or large corn tortillas; all are easy to come across in good supermarkets these days, though for the really good, pure corn ones, you might need to order them online.

We make armies of them when we have a crowd to feed as they are the perfect vehicle for dipping, a great snack with a cold beer in hand, and are pretty fuss-free. A flatbread or quesadilla allows you to play around and use what you have to hand. It's important to fill them with something that will bind the two sides together – some cheese, egg or soft mashed vegetables or beans are ideal.

1

Choose your vehicle:
you'll need a pair of one of the following

seeded tortillas

wholewheat tortillas

corn tortillas
(see page 18)

piadina flatbreads

Turkish flatbreads

2

Create the base:
something soft or melty to help the tortillas stick together

mashed butter beans

mashed black beans

grated Cheddar

1 organic egg
(see Caper, herb and egg flatbreads on page 18)

torn mozzarella

mashed chickpeas

grated and sautéed courgette

3	**4**	**5**	**6**
Add back up:	Choose a top	Add a	Serve with
another soft texture	flavour note	soft herb:	something
to add interest	(one or two of these)	some freshness	to dip

3

Add back up:
another soft texture
to add interest

4

**Choose a top
flavour note**
(one or two of these)

5

**Add a
soft herb:**
some freshness

6

**Serve with
something
to dip**

sautéed grated sweet
potato

sautéed grated squash

chopped roasted
red peppers

chopped cherry
tomatoes

grated carrot

grated beetroot

sautéed shredded
greens or kale

a crumbling of feta

finely chopped
spring onions

chopped red chilli

baby capers

chopped pitted olives

smoky chipotle paste

finely chopped red onion

a spice mix (garam
masala, zatar etc.)

a grating of lemon or
lime zest

coriander

mint

basil

parsley

dill

guacamole

salsa

tahini and yoghurt dip

smashed peas with
mint and lemon

hummus

Corn on the cob with mustard-seed butter

There is something about corn and warm days that sits just right. Every single summer holiday I have been on has memories of corn; maybe I seek it out. Crunched straight off the cob, bathed in lime and butter, eaten with sandy feet on the beaches of Indonesia; little plastic cups piled with elote corn, trimmed from its kernels, topped with sour cream, mayonnaise, cayenne and a squeeze of lemon from stands that line Mexican beaches and roadsides; and tamales – little patties of fluffy cornmeal wrapped in their husks and steamed over fires on the Native American reservations of Arizona.

There is something about the sweet pop of a kernel of corn that makes it okay to eat when it's searingly hot, when almost nothing else (apart from an ice cream or an ice-cold coconut) will do. This is how I've been eating corn the last few summers: grilled and rolled in South Indian spiced butter, then topped with a punchy but fresh, green chutney (see page 36 for the recipe). If you don't have time to griddle the corn, this still works well on simply boiled corn; boil it for 8–10 minutes until the kernels are tender.

MAKES 4

4 ears of corn

100g butter or ghee

1 tablespoon mustard seeds

1 teaspoon cumin seeds

a sprinkling of dried chilli flakes

TO SERVE

green chutney (see page 36)

Heat a griddle or barbecue.

Pull the leaves from the corn cobs and when the griddle is hot, cook the corn, turning regularly, until the kernels are deep gold, brown here and there and tender – this will take about 10 minutes.

Warm the butter or ghee in a small pan and once it's hot, add the mustard and cumin seeds. Cook for a minute or so until the mustard seeds pop, then take the pan off the heat and add the chilli.

When the corn is ready, place it on a baking tray and pour over the warm spiced butter, then turn the cobs in the tray, anointing every last kernel. Take the lot to the table, spoon over the green chutney and eat hot.

Ajo blanco

I first tried this soup in a very hot kitchen during my first summer as a chef. It was made by one of my all-time favourite cooks, Steve Pooley. There are few people who have taught me more about cooking and the unbridled joy of eating. This soup is just that — a joy. Refreshing and richly satisfying all at once, with a perfect balance of mellow creaminess from the almonds, punch from the sherry vinegar-soaked bread and sweetness from the grapes.

If you don't have sherry vinegar, red wine vinegar will work in its place, though you might need a little less.

Put the almonds into a frying pan and place over a low heat. Shake them around for a minute or two, allowing the almonds to toast very slightly — just the very palest tinge, to accentuate the taste of the nut. Tip on to a plate and leave to cool.

Put the bread into a large bowl and cover with 100ml of cold water. Leave to soak for 10 minutes. Once the almonds have cooled and the bread has soaked, tear the bread into your food processor in little pieces, then pour away any water left in the bowl. Add all but a little handful of the almonds to the bread, then add the garlic, cucumber and 75g of the grapes. Add a little of the iced water and whizz until smooth.

Now with the motor running slowly add the rest of the water, the oil and vinegar and blitz until really smooth. If you have a powerful blender your soup may be smooth enough to eat without sieving. If not, use the back of a ladle to press the soup through a sieve into a bowl, forcing out every last drop of liquid.

Season your soup with a little salt and pepper, then taste and add more seasoning, vinegar or oil until it tastes good to you. Cover and chill in the fridge for at least 2 hours, along with four soup bowls.

Chop the remaining almonds into little shards, and slice the remaining grapes. Once cooled, divide the soup between the bowls, drizzle with a little good olive oil and top with the almonds, grapes and fennel fronds.

SERVES 4

220g blanched almonds

100g good stale bread
(I use sourdough)

2–4 cloves of garlic,
depending on taste

1 small cucumber, peeled
and roughly chopped

100g green grapes

600ml ice-cold water

200ml olive oil

3 tablespoons sherry vinegar

TO FINISH

good olive oil

dill or fennel fronds

Corn, courgette and coriander soup

While cold soups win the day when it's blistering, most of the soups I eat in summer are hot, but with a steer towards crunch and freshness. This one makes the most of the hero of the hour, papery husked corn on the cob, teaming it with chilli, green and yellow courgettes and crisp lettuce. The result: a soup layered with texture and freshness that cooks instantly. It's good cold too.

Coarsely grate 1½ courgettes; you will use the remaining half later. Heat 1 tablespoon of the butter or oil in a large, deep pan, then add the grated courgettes with a pinch of salt and cook for a few minutes, until they are soft and beginning to colour. Tip the lot into a blender and pulse a little, keeping a bit of texture. Put to one side.

Heat 2 more tablespoons of oil or butter over a medium heat and fry the onion for about 5 minutes until beginning to soften, then add the garlic and cook for a further couple of minutes without browning. Add the courgette mixture and cook for another couple of minutes.

Take a handful of the corn kernels and put to one side for later. Blitz the remaining raw kernels in the blender with up to 1 litre of water (depending on what consistency you like your soup to be), adding most of the coriander leaves (saving a few to finish) and all the stalks, the chilli and most of the shredded lettuce. Blitz until smooth.

SERVES 4

2 medium courgettes, or a few baby ones (about 500g)

4 tablespoons butter or olive oil

1 onion, finely chopped

2 cloves of garlic, finely chopped

4 ears of corn, kernels only

a small bunch of fresh coriander, plus more to serve

1 green chilli

2 Little Gem lettuces, washed and shredded

1 unwaxed lime

Add the corn mixture to the pan with the courgettes and onions, then cook on a medium heat for another few minutes, stirring and scraping the bottom of the pan to stop the mixture sticking. Meanwhile, cut the remaining half courgette into thin coins. Heat a frying pan with the remaining tablespoon of oil or butter and fry the courgettes, stirring frequently, for 5 minutes, until they start to brown on both sides. Push the courgettes to the side of the pan and add the handful of corn kernels. Continue to cook over a high heat until the corn starts to pop and blister. Remove from the heat and grate over the lime zest.

To serve, squeeze over the lime juice and season with more salt and pepper to taste. Ladle into bowls and finish with the remaining lettuce, coriander and the golden courgettes and corn.

Tarragon-blistered tomatoes with green oil

This recipe calls for quite a lot of tomatoes because they shrink as they cook, so make it when the season is in full swing and they are at their most affordable and tastiest. I serve these with the little herb cheese on page 246; they would be amazing in a tart too. I often make a double batch and keep half in a jar in the fridge under some olive oil; that way they will keep for a few weeks and are an incredible and speedy way to boost the flavour of a quick dinner.

Preheat your oven to 170°C/150°C fan/gas 3. First prepare your tomatoes. Cut larger ones into quarters, medium ones in half and leave the smaller ones whole, then place them all on a baking tray, keeping any cut sides up. Tuck the garlic cloves in around them.

Divide your tarragon into two. Put half to one side, then pick the leaves from the tough stems of the other half, and scatter these over the tomatoes. Drizzle with a good amount of olive oil (about 3 tablespoons) and season well with salt and pepper.

Place in the hot oven for 1½ hours, until the tomatoes have shrunk and are sticky and caramelised. Check them after an hour, as some of the smaller tomatoes may be done sooner; if they are, you can scoop these out and put the rest back in.

While the tomatoes are in the oven, make the green oil. Have ready a bowl of iced water. Put a small saucepan of water on to boil. Blanch the parsley for 15 seconds, then take the pan off the heat and immerse the herb in the ice-cold water to keep your parsley green. Strain the parsley using a sieve and use the back of a spoon to squeeze out as much moisture as you can; you can do this using a clean tea towel too — you don't want any moisture left. Use a good blender to whizz the herbs with the oil until they have broken down and the oil is bright green, then strain through a fine sieve. If you are particularly keen on a very smooth green oil, you could strain it through a sieve lined with muslin.

Toast your bread and spread it with the cooked garlic cloves. Pile the roasted tomatoes on top, with some herb oil drizzled over.

SERVES 4

FOR THE TOMATOES

1kg tomatoes on the vine (I use a mixture in all colours)

6 cloves of garlic, peeled

a bunch of tarragon

olive oil

FOR THE GREEN OIL

a small bunch of flat-leaf parsley

100ml rapeseed oil

TO SERVE

4 generous slices of bread

little summer herb cheeses (see page 246)

Little yoghurt and herb cheeses

I make these in summer when I have people coming for lunch. I like them with the tarragon-blistered tomatoes on page 244.

For the herbs I use tarragon, parsley, chervil or chives. You can add garlic – a grated clove is popular – but personally I find it too overpowering. I often add it to half the mixture to keep everyone happy.

Line a large sieve with a square of muslin and spoon in the yoghurt. Sit the sieve over a large mixing bowl and make space for it in the fridge, then let it sit overnight, squeezing out the bag to encourage it to drain before you go to bed and when you wake up. If you have space to suspend the sieve so that it doesn't sit on the bottom of the bowl, all the better.

Tip the strained yoghurt from the muslin into a bowl. Add the lemon zest and herbs and a big pinch of salt.

MAKES 6

1kg thick Greek yoghurt

the zest of 1 unwaxed lemon

a bunch of soft herbs, leaves picked and finely chopped

flaky sea salt

TO SERVE

more soft herbs and edible flowers

good olive oil

Line six little ramekins with some more muslin squares that are generous enough to overhang the edges. Spoon the yoghurt cheese into the ramekins and use a spoon to smooth out the surfaces. Fold the muslin back over the tops and use something heavy to weigh them down – a tin or a jar should work – then leave them in a cool place to firm up. You can leave them for anything from an hour to overnight depending on how firm you would like them.

To serve, unwrap them from their little wrappers, scatter with the herbs and flowers and drizzle with a little good oil.

Grilled Caesar salad with crispy chickpeas

A childhood spent in America meant a lot of Caesar salads: the clean crunch of Cos lettuce, the serious hit of flavour from the garlic-kissed dressing, the burnished golden brown of a crouton. This Caesar is a bit different to the ones I ate growing up. The dressing is spiked with tahini, and instead of bread I use crispy chickpeas for croutons (which incidentally are great on their own as a snack or to eat with a few drinks). The lettuce is charred too, adding a pleasing smoky edge to it all, though you could make this just as successfully without griddling the lettuce if you like. I've listed a few other ways of using the dressing opposite.

SERVES 4

4 Little Gem lettuces

1 x 400g tin or 300g jar of chickpeas, drained

1 tablespoon rapeseed oil

the zest of 1 unwaxed lemon

FOR THE CAESAR DRESSING

½ a clove of garlic

4 tablespoons light tahini

2 tablespoons Greek yoghurt

1 tablespoon olive oil

the juice of 1½ lemons

2 teaspoons Dijon mustard

a scant dash of soy sauce or tamari

TO FINISH

40g Parmesan (I use a vegetarian one)

a small bunch of parsley, leaves picked

Preheat the oven to 240°C/220°C fan/gas 9. Heat a griddle pan over a high heat.

While you're waiting for the oven and griddle to come up to temperature, slice the Little Gems in half lengthways. Toss the chickpeas in a roasting tray with the rapeseed oil and a pinch of salt and pepper, then place in the centre of the hot oven for 25 minutes, shaking now and again, until you hear the chickpeas popping and they are blistering and crisp.

Meanwhile, griddle the Little Gem halves for a couple of minutes on each side until deep char marks form and they collapse a little. Lay the charred lettuces on a platter and leave to one side.

Next, make the dressing: finely grate the ½ clove of garlic into your food processor, then add all the other ingredients with 6 tablespoons of water, and blitz until smooth. Taste and adjust the seasoning, adding more lemon/salt/pepper/soy to taste.

When the chickpeas have had their time, scatter over the lemon zest then put them on to kitchen paper to drain and crisp.

To serve, toss the charred lettuce in a few tablespoons of the dressing, then put it on to a platter, scatter the chickpeas over the lettuce and grate over the Parmesan. Serve with some more dressing, a good grind of black pepper and a few parsley leaves.

Other ways to use your Caesar dressing

- In a sandwich with smoked tofu and lettuce

- To spoon on top of a soup or stew

- To dress leftover quinoa or grains

- Thickened with a little more yoghurt for dipping crudités

- To spoon on to baked potatoes

249

Herb, lentil and lime brown rice salad

Until recently I was never a fan of rice salads – they conjured up memories of 1980s barbecues. But my mother-in-law, Sian, is the queen of them; hers are always packed with flavour and perfectly dressed, so I've been converted. A rice salad is one of those things which gets better after a day in the fridge, making this a good dish to prepare ahead if you have lots of people to feed.

This recipe is now a firm favourite all summer. It's half rice, half lentils, with a spiced dressing that works well with pretty much any pulse or grain.

SERVES 4

100g raisins or currants (I use golden raisins)

4 tablespoons red wine vinegar

250g basmati rice (I use brown basmati)

olive oil

2 red onions, finely sliced

1 x 400g tin of cooked lentils, drained (or 250g home-cooked, see page 461)

4 sticks of celery, finely chopped, any leaves reserved

a large bunch of herbs (e.g. basil, parsley and coriander), leaves picked

FOR THE DRESSING

1 tablespoon cumin seeds

1 teaspoon coriander seeds

the seeds from 4 cardamom pods

¼ teaspoon ground cloves

a few gratings of fresh nutmeg

4 tablespoons olive oil

2 tablespoons cider vinegar

the zest and juice of 2 unwaxed limes

1 tablespoon maple syrup

1 tablespoon Dijon mustard

Soak the raisins in the vinegar and leave to one side.

Fill and boil your kettle. Rinse your rice under cold running water until the water runs clear. Heat a drizzle of oil in a heavy-based pan, then add the rinsed rice and stir to coat in the oil for a couple of minutes. Pour in twice the amount of boiling water. Bring to the boil, then cover with a clean tea towel then the lid (making sure the towel is tightly secured, away from the heat source), and cook for 8 minutes for white basmati and 25 for brown. Take the pan off the heat and, with the lid on, leave it to sit and steam without peeking.

Heat a pan on a medium–high heat. Once hot, add a drizzle of oil and the red onion and cook for 5–8 minutes, until crisp but not burnt. Remove to a plate lined with kitchen paper to keep them crispy.

Make the dressing. Toast all the seeds in a dry pan for a couple of minutes until they smell fragrant. Add the ground spices, stir quickly, then take the pan off the heat and tip the lot into a mortar. Bash with the pestle until they are broken down a bit. Tip into a jug, add all the rest of the dressing ingredients and mix well.

Take the lid off the rice – it should be light and fluffy and have absorbed all the liquid but if there is any excess water, drain it off. Use a fork to fluff up the rice, then tumble it into a bowl. Drain and add the lentils, chopped celery and the dressing. Roughly chop the herbs and add these too along with the raisins. Season with salt and pepper, mix well and taste, adding more salt, pepper, lime, oil as needed. Remember it will mellow a little as it sits. When you are ready to eat, scatter over the crispy onions and pile into bowls.

Summer taco salad

I love tacos more than I love salad, and putting taco flavours into a salad makes me love salad a bit more. This is an all-in-one salad; it's a meal on its own, with slow-roast tomatoes, crumbled tofu, black beans and a crumbling of crispy tortilla chips. The sweet notes of the tomatoes and the tomato-rich dressing seem to make this a hit with people of all ages, even small ones.

If you want to make this more quickly you can skip cooking the tomatoes and use 200g of sun-dried or sun-blushed ones in their place.

Preheat your oven to 170°C/150°C fan/gas 3.

First put the tomatoes on a baking tray, cut-side up, and roast in the oven for 30 minutes. Use your hands to crumble the tofu into small bite-sized pieces. Heat a medium frying pan on a medium heat and pour in a little olive oil. Add the tofu and a good pinch of salt and pepper and cook until it is crisp on all sides. While this is happening mix together the chilli, paprika, cumin, garlic and lime zest. Add to the pan for the last minute of cooking and stir a couple of times to take the rawness out of the spices and garlic, then take off the heat and cover to keep warm.

Combine all the dressing ingredients in a bowl and mix well.

Thinly shred the heads of lettuce and put them into a large salad bowl. Toss with half the salad dressing, then quarter and stone the avocados, scoop them from their skins and slice into little pieces. Add them to the bowl with the black beans, spring onions and coriander leaves. Crumble in the tortilla chips and feta then toss through along with the tofu. Serve in the middle of the table with the rest of the dressing on the side for spooning over.

SERVES 4

400g cherry tomatoes, halved

200g firm tofu

olive oil

a pinch of chilli powder

¼ teaspoon sweet smoked paprika

¼ teaspoon ground cumin

1 clove of garlic, finely chopped

the zest of 1 unwaxed lime

2 heads of romaine lettuce

2 avocados

1x 400g tin of black beans, drained (or 300g home-cooked, see page 461)

4 spring onions, thinly sliced

a small bunch of coriander, leaves picked

2 handfuls of tortilla chips

crumbled feta or manchego (optional)

FOR THE DRESSING

4 tablespoons passata

4 tablespoons cider vinegar

3 tablespoons rapeseed or mild olive oil

2 tablespoons maple syrup

½ teaspoon chipotle paste or smoked paprika

Smacked cucumbers with orange and Sichuan pepper

SERVES 4–6

2 cucumbers (about 600g in total)

2 tablespoons flaky sea salt

FOR THE DRESSING

3 cloves of garlic, finely chopped

3 tablespoons tamari or soy sauce

2 tablespoons brown rice vinegar

1 tablespoon toasted sesame oil

1 tablespoon runny honey

a pinch of dried chilli flakes

½ teaspoon ground, toasted Sichuan pepper

the zest and juice of 1 unwaxed orange

TO SERVE

50g peanuts, toasted and roughly chopped

Cucumber has been a staple in our house this last year. It's been chopped into batons and devoured by my son, the cooling crispness soothing his little teething gums. Dylan's on to something, as when the weather heats up cucumber is what I crave: crunchy, refreshing and altogether summer food. Seek out the knobbly home-grown cucumbers if you can, as their flavour is much more intense.

This salad is my take on a Fuchsia Dunlop classic: orange and Sichuan pepper provide top notes and interest. It goes well with a bowl of simple honey and soy dressed noodles and a bit of crisped tofu, if you are after something more filling.

———————————————

Lay the whole cucumbers flat on a chopping board and bash them with a rolling pin all over (about 10 firm whacks should do the trick).

Cut each cucumber into quarters lengthways, then cut each quarter into roughly 1cm diagonal slices. Place the slices in a bowl with the salt and toss to coat. Set aside for 15–20 minutes.

Mix all the dressing ingredients in a bowl with a fork.

Drain the cucumber in a sieve to remove the excess liquid that may have been released, then toss in the dressing and scatter with the peanuts.

Corn, tomatoes and crispy bread

This is everything I love about late summer. I keep the corn and tomatoes raw here, countering their natural sweetness with a good hit of red wine vinegar. The golden on the outside, chewy on the inside croutons make this summer salad more of a meal. It's finished with some pistachios and pecorino, but feta or Parmesan would work too.

I eat this as a lunch or light supper, and to make it even more substantial I often pair it with some avocado smashed with a little lime juice and some chopped green chilli. You could also roughly chop a couple of avocados through the salad if you like.

SERVES 4

2 slices of good bread (I use sourdough)

olive oil

2 ears of corn

500g tomatoes (all shapes, sizes and colours)

4 spring onions

2 tablespoons red wine vinegar

100g shelled pistachios

50g pecorino (I use a vegetarian one)

a small bunch of mint, leaves picked

a small bunch of basil, leaves picked

extra virgin olive oil

Preheat your oven to 220°C/200°C fan/gas 7.

Tear your bread into small rough chunks and lay on a baking tray. Drizzle generously with olive oil (about 4 tablespoons) and sprinkle with salt and pepper. Roast in the hot oven for 10–15 minutes: how long you cook them for will be dependent on the density of your bread. You want the croutons to be crisp on the outside but chewy on the inside, so try to take them out before they are hard all the way through.

Next, on to the salad. Cut the corn kernels from the ears; I do this by resting the end of the corn in a large mixing bowl, which stops the corn flying everywhere. Cut the tomatoes into bite-sized chunks – it's nice to keep the shapes and cuts different here – and add them to the bowl. Finely slice the spring onions and add these too. Add a good pinch of salt and pepper and the vinegar and leave the lot to sit for a while.

When the croutons are ready, take them out of the oven. Roughly chop the pistachios and finely crumble or coarsely grate the pecorino – I like mine crumbled into pieces about the size of a grain of rice. Tear the herbs into the bowl, then add the pistachios and cheese and about 50ml of extra virgin olive oil and toss everything together. Finish by tossing the croutons through just before you serve.

Melon, tomato and mozzarella with two chillies

This is perfect for a hot day; it's cooling and invigorating all at once. This offbeat salad uses one of my new discoveries in the kitchen: pickled red peppers. You can buy them jarred, ranging from mild to hot. I go for the hot, slightly sweet ones, which add a perky, enlivening hit of sunny spice for very little effort. The second chilli is the Scotch bonnet, and their flavour always makes me think of the rich fragrance of cantaloupe melon; I'm not sure why it took me so long to pair them up. This salad is a meal in itself; all you need is a couple of slices of good toasted bread to pile everything on to.

SERVES 4

600g ripe mixed tomatoes

600g sweet, ripe cantaloupe melon

2 unwaxed limes

50g pickled peppers

1 Scotch bonnet

a small bunch of basil

extra virgin olive oil

2 x 120g balls of buffalo mozzarella

First cut all your tomatoes into different-sized chunks and pieces, the more irregular the better. Deseed the melon and use a spoon to scoop it out into little petals, then put it all into a bowl and add a generous pinch of salt and a good grind of pepper, the juice of both the limes and the zest of one.

Roughly chop the pickled peppers and finely chop the Scotch bonnet. Add these to the bowl with the basil leaves and a good drizzle of the olive oil (roughly 3 tablespoons).

Tear the mozzarella on to a plate and scatter the salad around it. Eat with a glass of ice-cold pale rosé.

How to make the perfect green salad

Each week, a small unassuming bag arrives in my vegetable box, labelled 'Hackney salad'. The leaves are piercing greens, acid yellows, deep emeralds and rich purples. Each leaf has a unique flavour and so full of personality. Small salad growers are cropping up all over the country growing interesting leaves, micro salad, salad herbs and flowers – seek them out when you can.

But even leaves from a supermarket bring the possibility of a really good bowl of salad. I like to buy whole lettuces, cutting and washing them in one go, filling the fridge with a few days' worth of leaves. There is a lot to choose from on the supermarket shelves: the bitter crunch of chicory, the soft frill of lamb's lettuce, spiky rocket as hot as peppercorns, sweet and crisp Little Gems and red-fringed Cos.

A good salad is all about the balance of the leaves, the perfect dressing and each mouthful being unique: a pop of lemon, a crunchy leaf, the frond of a delicate herb. I favour cooling, calm leaves to make up most of the plate, with a scattering of hot, peppery, earthy or citrus notes. For me this is what makes a simple green salad one of the most pleasing things to eat.

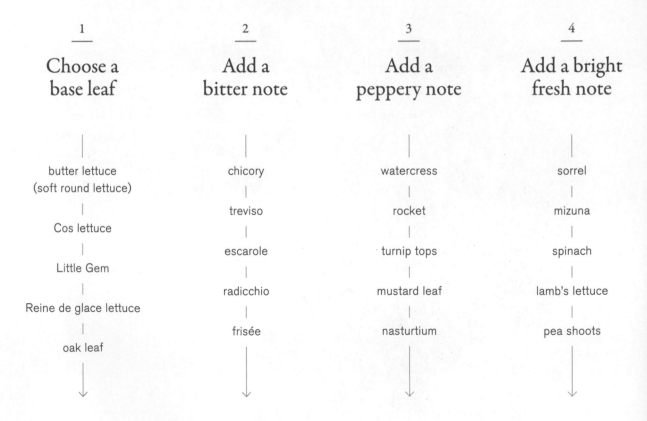

1	2	3	4
Choose a base leaf	**Add a bitter note**	**Add a peppery note**	**Add a bright fresh note**
butter lettuce (soft round lettuce)	chicory	watercress	sorrel
Cos lettuce	treviso	rocket	mizuna
Little Gem	escarole	turnip tops	spinach
Reine de glace lettuce	radicchio	mustard leaf	lamb's lettuce
oak leaf	frisée	nasturtium	pea shoots

How to wash salad well

This may be totally obvious to some but washing and storing salad well will extend its life and crispness. I like to wash my lettuce as soon as I can after buying, in a big sink full of very cold water, running my hands gently through the leaves. Drain then spin it dry. If you are using it immediately, spin it totally dry, if you are keeping it in the fridge then leave a little water on the leaves and store it in a bag or the salad drawer lined with a clean tea towel until needed. This way it will last for over a week.

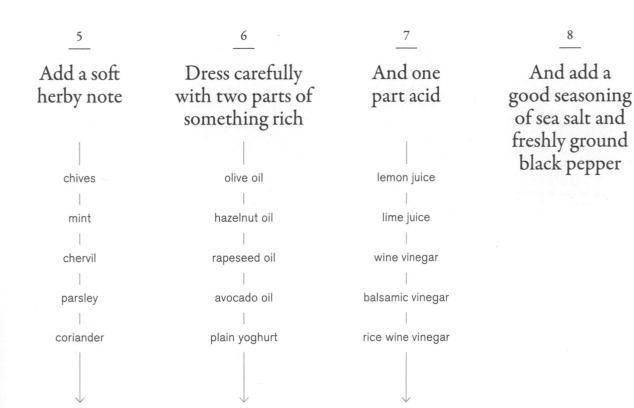

5
Add a soft herby note

|
chives
|
mint
|
chervil
|
parsley
|
coriander
|
↓

6
Dress carefully with two parts of something rich

|
olive oil
|
hazelnut oil
|
rapeseed oil
|
avocado oil
|
plain yoghurt
|
↓

7
And one part acid

|
lemon juice
|
lime juice
|
wine vinegar
|
balsamic vinegar
|
rice wine vinegar
|
↓

8
And add a good seasoning of sea salt and freshly ground black pepper

Summer beet salad with orange blossom water and curd cheese

In this salad I use every colour of beetroot I can get my hands on: the deep pinky-purple beetroots of my childhood, next to the candy-cane striped Chioggia beets and the paint-pot yellow ones. It makes for the most beautiful plate of food.

I use orange blossom water here, which I think works particularly well with the earthy flavour of beetroot; however, its delicate fragrant flavour can split opinion, so if you are not a fan just stick to the orange zest.

SERVES 4 AS A STARTER OR A SIDE

800g raw beetroot (see note above)

a small bunch of coriander, leaves picked and roughly chopped

125g goat's curd

50g walnuts, toasted and lightly chopped

FOR THE DRESSING

juice of 1 orange

2 teaspoons orange blossom water or rose water

2 tablespoons extra virgin olive oil

1 teaspoon runny honey

Scrub or peel the beetroot; if the skin is thin and tender, as it should be at this time of year, a good scrub should do. Use a mandoline or your very good knife skills to slice the beetroot into 1cm-thick rounds and place them in a bowl.

Make the dressing by combining all the ingredients and seasoning with salt and pepper to taste. Pour half the dressing over the raw beetroot and leave to rest for 15 minutes so the flavours can meld and mingle.

Toss the beetroots with the coriander, then arrange in a bowl or on a platter and top with the rest of the dressing. Dot the goat's curd over the top and scatter over the walnuts.

Black sesame noodle bowl

SERVES 4

200g rice noodles (I use brown rice noodles)

100g unsalted cashews

4 tablespoons black sesame seeds

4 tablespoons unsweetened desiccated coconut

a small bunch of coriander, leaves picked, stalks finely chopped

a small bunch of mint, leaves picked

a few large handfuls of mixed greens

2 spring onions, very finely sliced

½ a red chilli, finely sliced

150g sugar snaps, sliced in half lengthways

FOR THE DRESSING

3 tablespoons tamari or soy sauce

2 tablespoons toasted sesame oil

2 tablespoons runny honey

2 tablespoons brown rice vinegar

the zest and juice of 1 unwaxed lime

1 small clove of garlic, grated

a thumb-sized piece of ginger, peeled and grated

I first made this noodle bowl for a picnic and it's been made many times since. The dressing is a favourite for summer noodles; I finish it with lots of shredded greens and some final crunch from cashews and black sesame seeds (regular sesame seeds, well toasted, would work just as well), which elevates this from a one-textured noodle salad to something much more interesting. I use brown rice noodles here, as I prefer their depth of flavour and find them more filling and satisfying, but use what you can get your hands on. Swiss chard, kale or spinach will all work here. The salad is great served just warm or cold.

———————————————

Preheat the oven to 220°C/200°C fan/gas 7. Cook the noodles in a medium saucepan according to the packet instructions, breaking them up with chopsticks or a fork from time to time to ensure they don't stick together. Drain and refresh under cold water, then transfer to a large bowl.

Put the cashews on a baking tray in the oven for 4 minutes, then, once they have toasted for 4 minutes, add the sesame seeds and the coconut. Cook for another 4–5 minutes, or until golden.

Meanwhile, whisk the dressing ingredients together. Pour half the dressing over the noodles and toss well to coat, then stir through the chopped coriander stalks.

Finely chop the coriander leaves and mint leaves and set aside. Wash the greens, then spin them dry. Remove any tough stalks, stack the leaves, roll up and slice into thin ribbons, then add to the noodles with the spring onions and the chilli.

Once the nuts, seeds and coconut are golden, allow them to cool and roughly chop the cashew nuts.

Toss the herbs, sugar snaps and the toasted mixture through your noodles and serve with the rest of the dressing for spooning over.

Ricotta gnocchi with brown butter tomato sauce

This is another favourite recipe from my *Guardian* column. We made it at the photoshoot and that night I made it again for dinner – that's when you know something is really tasty. These are a forgiving ricotta dumpling; they use a little flour and sit in a cherry tomato sauce spiked with the toastiness of brown butter. I use cherry tomatoes as I find they make the sauce perfectly sweet but you can use larger ones; you may just need to cook the sauce for a little longer.

The ricotta you use here is important: the watery ricotta that you can buy in most supermarkets is a lot wetter than the strained ricotta which I prefer to use for these dumplings, as well as for dishes such as baked ricotta and desserts. You can buy it in good Italian delis, or you can strain supermarket ricotta yourself. Simply wrap it in muslin and hang it over a mixing bowl for 4 hours or overnight (500g fresh ricotta yields about 400g strained).

SERVES 6

150g pasta flour (tipo '00')

500g strained ricotta
(see note above)

1 teaspoon flaky sea salt

¼ of a whole nutmeg

1 organic egg, beaten

FOR THE TOMATO SAUCE

3 tablespoons extra
virgin olive oil

2 cloves of garlic, thinly sliced

750g cherry tomatoes

a generous pinch of
flaky sea salt

a small bunch of basil,
leaves picked

TO FINISH

50g butter

Parmesan (I use a
vegetarian one)

a few basil leaves

To make the gnocchi, spread half the flour out on a work surface in a rough circle and crumble the ricotta on top. Sprinkle over the salt and grate the nutmeg on top. Use your fingers to delicately gather the ricotta into a mound, picking up the flour as you do. Make a well in the middle of the mound big enough to house the beaten egg. Pour the egg in and use a fork to work it carefully into the flour and ricotta until it has become a rough dough. Gently knead the dough, adding a little more flour if needed, until you have a smooth dough (you may not need to use all the flour). Try to be delicate here, as being rough will develop the gluten in the flour and make your gnocchi tough. Once smooth, wrap the dough in cling film and put it into the fridge for 1 hour.

While the dough is resting, you can get on with the sauce. Put the oil into a large frying pan with the garlic and place on a medium heat for a couple of minutes. Add the cherry tomatoes and salt and cook for 30 minutes, pushing down on the tomatoes occasionally with the back of a wooden spoon until they have all burst and you have a bright red sauce. Add the basil leaves and put to one side. →

When you are ready to roll your gnocchi, lightly flour your work surface and have a lightly floured large tray nearby. Unwrap the dough and shape it into a 2.5cm-thick circle, then divide this into quarters. Take one quarter, and roll it into a log about 1.5cm thick, rolling it back and forth with both hands until it is even. Be delicate, touching the dough lightly; the lighter the hand the lighter the dumplings. Cut this log into 2.5cm pieces and transfer them to the flour-dusted tray. Repeat with the remaining three quarters of dough. You can keep the gnocchi in the fridge until you are ready to cook them.

When you are ready to serve, put a large pan of salted water on to boil, and warm the tomato sauce gently. In a small frying pan, cook the butter over a medium heat until it turns a couple of shades darker and smells nutty, then take off the heat and stir it into the tomato sauce.

Drop the gnocchi into the boiling water and cook until they rise to the surface – this should take about 2 minutes. You may need to cook the gnocchi in batches or have two pans going if they are small. Toss the drained gnocchi in the tomato sauce. Add a grating of Parmesan and more basil leaves before serving.

Quick orzo with fennel, almonds, capers and olives

This is a fresh and clean pasta dish with a super quick sauce made from sautéed caramelised slices of fennel, almonds, buttery green olives and fragrant dill with some coriander seeds, which may seem a little off track but trust me, they work amazingly. I serve this just warm, as I think the flavours come out better that way.

This recipe should come together in 15–20 minutes, so it's perfect for weeknight dinners and quick lunches. It also keeps really well; I often make a batch of it to take on long journeys as it's good cold.

You can make the olive sauce in advance and it will sit well in the fridge – just cover the top with a layer of olive oil. It's also great spread on toast, next to some roasted vegetables or spooned on top of mozzarella.

First, bring a large pot of salted water to the boil and cook the orzo according to the packet instructions. Heat a large pan on a medium heat and add a good glug of olive oil and the fennel. Season with a little salt and cook for 10 minutes, until starting to brown and caramelise.

Put the bread into a bowl and pour over the vinegar and a couple of tablespoons of cold water to soften it. Pound the garlic to a paste with a tiny pinch of salt in the pestle and mortar, then add the coriander seeds and bash to a coarse powder.

You can continue to make the sauce in a pestle and mortar or switch to a food processor. Either way, add the capers, almonds, most of the dill and olives one by one, bashing or blitzing or as you go. Rip up and add the soaked bread and finally the olive oil little by little, until the sauce comes together to a nice dropping consistency.

By now the pasta should be cooked; drain it well and add it to the fennel. Take off the heat and stir through the olive sauce. Taste for salt, vinegar and balance and add a little more of whatever is needed. Serve with a little lemon zest for a final sherbety punch, grated pecorino and the rest of the dill.

SERVES 4

250g orzo pasta (I use wholemeal)

olive oil

2 bulbs of fennel, trimmed and finely sliced (save any fronds)

a thick slice of good bread (I use sourdough)

1 tablespoon white wine vinegar

1 clove of garlic, peeled

1 tablespoon coriander seeds

4 tablespoons baby capers

50g almonds, skin on, toasted

a bunch of dill or fennel tops

200g green olives, pitted

4 tablespoons extra virgin olive oil

TO SERVE

1 unwaxed lemon

pecorino (I use a vegetarian one), for grating

Creamy spiced chickpeas, burnt lemon and runner beans

A light but filling summer dinner, these chickpeas get an outing at least once a week in my house; they take under 15 minutes to cook but the layers of flavour that are imparted would suggest they took much longer.

Often I eat these with a fried egg or some steamed greens and yoghurt, but this is my favourite way to serve them in the summer, with some lemon that's been charred on the grill, which adds some mellow acid and sweetness, and green beans cooked in the same way, which lends a pleasing smokiness to things. You could do the lemons and beans on the barbecue if you like.

Warm the olive oil in a large pan over a medium heat, add the cumin seeds, nigella and chilli and cook for a couple of minutes until they smell fragrant. Add the turmeric, sliced garlic and onion and a good pinch of salt and pepper. Cook slowly for 10 minutes until the onion is soft and sweet. Put a griddle on to heat.

Add the chickpeas to the pan of spices, along with all their liquid (about 300ml if using home-cooked), and cook for 30 minutes or until most of the liquid has evaporated.

Peel the strings from the sides of the beans using a speed peeler. When the griddle is smoking hot, add the runner beans and char for about 4 minutes on each side, until they are blistered and blackened in places. Squeeze a little of the juice from half a lemon into a bowl, then griddle all the lemon halves cut side down until well charred.

Put the yoghurt, crushed garlic, a couple of tablespoons of extra virgin olive oil and some salt and pepper into a bowl with the lemon juice and mix well. Spoon out a tablespoon of the yoghurt mixture into another mixing bowl and whisk with a tablespoon of olive oil.

Once the runners and lemons are all cooked and the chickpeas are creamy, you are ready to eat. Cut the runners into long widths at an angle, then mix them with the smaller amount of yoghurt and oil. Pile on to plates next to the chickpeas, yoghurt and half a burnt lemon.

SERVES 4

50ml olive oil

1 tablespoon cumin seeds

½ tablespoon nigella seeds

a good pinch of dried chilli flakes

1 tablespoon ground turmeric

2 cloves of garlic, finely sliced, plus an extra clove, crushed

1 white onion, finely chopped

700g jarred or home-cooked chickpeas (see page 461) or 2 x 400g tins

600g runner beans, tops trimmed

2 lemons, cut in half

150g Greek yoghurt

extra virgin olive oil

All-summer salad

This is a salad I make from May to September, while the days are warm. I start making it as the asparagus and new potatoes arrive, and stop when the nights begin to draw in, varying the vegetables with the seasons. This midsummer version, which makes the most of the best tomatoes and runner beans, is my favourite.

First put your new potatoes into a medium saucepan with a good pinch of sea salt and cover with cold water – you want a good amount of water here, as you will be adding other things to the pan later. Bring the potatoes to the boil, then allow to simmer for 12–20 minutes depending on their size.

In another small pan bring some salted water to a rolling boil, add the eggs and boil for 6 minutes, so that the middles are only just set. If you'd like them hard-boiled, go for a minute more. Crack the shells on a hard surface then run them under cold water for 30 seconds to stop them cooking, then leave to cool.

While the eggs are cooking, whisk together all the dressing ingredients, then taste and season. You want it to be quite punchy, as it will mellow when it hits everything else.

Pit your olives and rip them in half. Peel the cucumber and halve it down the middle, use a teaspoon to scoop out the watery seeds in the middle, then cut it into chunky slices. Roughly chop the tomatoes into different-sized pieces. Put them all into a large bowl.

When your potatoes are nearly cooked, add the beans to the pan and cook for the final 3–4 minutes. Drain everything and leave to steam dry. Once the potatoes have steamed away all of their moisture, add them to the bowl while they are still warm, along with the beans, and pour over the dressing. Use the back of a spoon to lightly crush the potatoes and allow them to split and soak up some of the dressing.

Peel the eggs, half or quarter them, then dot over the bowl and finish with some chopped herbs or lemon zest if you have some to hand.

SERVES 4

500g new potatoes

4 organic eggs

100g Kalamata olives

1 small cucumber

300g ripe tomatoes

200g green or runner beans, topped and tailed

FOR THE DRESSING

3 teaspoons Dijon mustard

2 teaspoons wholegrain mustard

4 tablespoons olive oil

3 tablespoons white wine vinegar

1 teaspoon runny honey

TO FINISH

chopped soft herbs

lemon zest

Lemon poha

I first ate poha on a yoga course in London. It was cooked by an incredible cook from the Ashram of Isha Yoga in Tamil Nadu, which I long to visit. Poha, or pawa, is flattened rice that really needs no cooking, just a quick soak to soften it. Poha can be bought easily from any Asian shop and there are different types, according to thickness; for this recipe you are looking for the thick poha – if you can't get hold of it you could use cooked basmati rice instead. Poha is often eaten for breakfast in India but I like it any time of day and often make it to sit next to curries instead of normal rice, or eat it on its own as a summer supper.

Soak your peanuts in cold water for at least 30 minutes but ideally overnight. Put the poha into a sieve and wash under running water for a few minutes, moving it around in the sieve – you want the running water to touch it all.

Put a large frying pan with a lid on a medium heat and add the oil, cumin and mustard seeds, chilli and curry leaves. Once the mustard seeds pop, add the spring onions and cook for 5 minutes, until soft and sweet.

Next, add the potatoes and cook for a minute until the edges begin to catch, then add 100ml of water, cover with the lid, bring to the boil and cook for 6 minutes or until the potatoes are cooked through.

Add the turmeric to the pan and stir with a wooden spoon to distribute it evenly. Add the soaked poha, lemon juice and a good pinch of salt and mix well, then cook for 3 minutes to warm through.

Take the pan off the heat and add the soaked, drained peanuts and the coriander, tasting and adding more lemon juice and salt if needed.

SERVES 4

5 tablespoons unsalted red-skinned peanuts

240g thick poha

3 tablespoons rapeseed oil

1 teaspoon cumin seeds

1 tablespoon black mustard seeds

1 green chilli, finely chopped

2 small handfuls of fresh curry leaves (about 25)

a bunch of spring onions, finely sliced at an angle

250g potatoes, peeled and cut into small cubes

½ teaspoon ground turmeric

the juice of 2 lemons

a small bunch of coriander, roughly chopped

Harissa, lime and halloumi with flatbreads

Halloumi is a real crowd-pleaser. I have never understood the blanket fascination with it, but I do like its texture when it's cooked just right, charred and crisped a little on the outside and perfectly melting inside.

Here, the halloumi has a quick dip in a rose harissa and lime marinade, which is backed up by a grilled relish that combines smoke from charred red onions, some piquancy from a good drizzle of pomegranate molasses, sweetness from red peppers and a salty olive kick. A cooling yoghurt tempers the chilli a little as well as providing a pleasing temperature contrast for the grill-hot halloumi.

This is a perfect recipe for the barbecue. The relish is also great in flatbreads, burgers and toasted sandwiches.

Combine the halloumi, lime zest and juice and harissa in a bowl and use your hands to mix everything and coat the halloumi. Set aside.

Light your barbecue (or heat a griddle over a medium–high heat). Let the flames die down a little, then grill the onions, turning them occasionally, for 10 minutes or until soft and sweet (they will catch and blacken on the outside). Char the peppers alongside until black all over, then put both into a bowl and cover with a tea towel while they cool.

Meanwhile, ripple the yoghurt with the harissa, tahini and lime juice, season, then sprinkle with the sumac and refrigerate.

To finish the relish, peel the skins from the peppers and deseed them, then peel the papery outsides from the onions. Chop the peppers with the onions and green olives, then add 1 tablespoon of the pomegranate molasses and mix well. Taste and add more pomegranate molasses, if needed, and a good pinch of salt and pepper.

Stoke the barbecue or put the griddle back on a medium–high heat. Cook the halloumi for 2–3 minutes on each side, or until just charred and a little blistered, and softly melting inside. Meanwhile, warm the flatbreads on the other side of the barbecue or griddle for a minute or so on each side.

Pile the halloumi on to the flatbreads, top with the relish and yoghurt, and scatter with sesame seeds, mint and a few salad leaves.

SERVES 6

2 x 250g packs of halloumi, cut into 2cm-thick slices

the zest and juice of 1 unwaxed lime

1 tablespoon rose harissa

a handful of dried rose petals, crushed (optional)

FOR THE RELISH

2 red onions, cut into 6 wedges, root intact

2 red peppers

a handful of pitted green olives

2 tablespoons pomegranate molasses

FOR THE HARISSA YOGHURT

6 tablespoons Greek yoghurt

1 tablespoon rose harissa

2 tablespoons light tahini

the juice of 1 lime

1 tablespoon sumac

TO SERVE

6 yoghurt flatbreads (see page 456) or wraps

2 tablespoons sesame seeds, toasted

a few sprigs of mint, leaves picked

a few handfuls of salad leaves

Vegetable-centred barbecues

We've moved quite happily towards eating less meat in our kitchens, but the barbecue hasn't quite kept up and traditionally vegetarians are ill considered where charred food is concerned – a limp vegetable kebab or an incinerated pepper being the standard token offerings. In restaurants, though, this caveman-esque style of cooking is not all about meat; in fact vegetables sit centre stage in many fire-led chefs' kitchens, from Norway to London.

A bit of char and smoke can complement a beloved vegetable or boost a neutral cheese, such as halloumi or feta. An aubergine is an obvious pairing with a bit of smoke – baba ganoush is a friendly blend of vegetables and smoulder, as is a halved aubergine grilled and basted in white miso. Onions, too, work well grilled slowly then tossed through plump pearl barley grains. Even halved Little Gems are transformed when quickly charred and simply dressed in oil, vinegar and chopped herbs.

This charring is, of course, possible on a griddle pan or even a good heavy-based frying pan, but its natural habitat is the barbecue. The resolution to cook outside to me seems most welcome on a weeknight, when taking the kitchen into the fresh air brings a holiday feeling to an otherwise normal Tuesday or Wednesday.

Tips for barbecuing vegetables

—Cook on charcoal or wood if you can as it will impart that smoky flavour that gas barbecues won't.

—Use lumpwood charcoal. It's more expensive but will hold heat longer so you will use less. Avoid firelighters if you can.

—Wait for the right moment to cook. This may sound basic but wait for the flames to properly die down. You want the coals white hot, grey and glowing as they give the most even heat.

—Control the heat just as you would if you were using a gas hob. If things are too hot then take your food off and let the coals cool down.

—If you are cooking more than one thing it might be useful to have two temperatures on your barbecue. To do this, once the coals are hot pile most of them to one side which will be hot for grilling, and a few on the other side for warming bread and gentler cooking.

—Don't oil your vegetables before they hit the grill. Instead, dress them carefully in good olive oil, citrus or vinegar after grilling, while they are still warm.

Vegetables and other things that work on the barbecue

All of these can be eaten on their own or mixed into a warm salad with crumbled cheese and chickpeas or beans to make a meal.

Aubergine: grill them whole until soft and blackened all over (see page 286), then cut open and season or mash into baba ganoush; or halve and grill them cut-side down, turning every so often and basting them with white miso throughout the grilling.

Avocado: peel and stone halved avocados, season and grill until well charred on the outside. Dress with soft herbs, lime and chilli.

Beetroot: wrap in foil with some woody herbs and whole garlic cloves and bake in the embers as you would a potato for 30–40 minutes. Or cut into thin slices and grill until soft and charred, turning every couple of minutes. Dress with orange juice and chopped thyme or marjoram

Cabbage: grill summer cabbages in wedges with the root still attached so they stay together and char until soft and crisp on the outside. Dress with a mustard, honey and lemon dressing (see page 40).

Carrot: cut into thick strips and cook until soft and charred. Dress with toasted cumin seeds, lemon, oil, coriander and pomegranate seeds.

Chicory and radicchio: cut in half down the middle and grill until softened and well charred. Dress with orange zest, wholegrain mustard, vinegar and good oil. Great with grilled pear too.

Courgette: cut into thin slices or peel into thin strips and grill until soft and charred (see page 170), then dress in lemon, mint and herbs. Good with milky soft cheese.

Potato: wrap in foil with some whole garlic cloves and lemon and bake in the embers for 40 minutes to 1 hour or slice and grill until soft and charred, turning all the time. Serve with chopped soft herbs, capers, oil and lemon zest.

Sweet potato: cut into long 1cm slices, cook until soft throughout and well charred, turning all the time. Serve with chopped coriander, yoghurt, chilli and lots of lime zest and juice.

Tofu: press to get rid of any excess liquid, then slice thickly and marinate in citrus zest and harissa, or miso and soy. Grill, turning and basting as you go, until crisp. Or marinate in lemon, thyme and honey and grill until crisp, then eat crumbled into flatbreads (see page 236) or over a salad or barbecued veg.

Peach: cut in half and remove the stone, then grill until charred on both sides. Serve with tomatoes, mozzarella and torn basil or mint.

Pineapple: peel, cut into wedges, then toss with honey or brown sugar and barbecue until charred on the outside and soft inside. Serve with ice cream or yoghurt.

Lime leaf and cashew tofu cakes

SERVES 4

100g cashew nuts

a large thumb-sized piece of
    ginger, peeled and grated

1 clove of garlic, peeled
    and grated

2 stalks of lemongrass,
    outer layer removed,
    finely chopped

1 red chilli, roughly chopped

2 lime leaves, roughly sliced

400g firm tofu

3 tablespoons nut butter
    (cashew or peanut)

200g green beans, topped,
    tailed and finely chopped

rapeseed or olive oil

steamed rice, to serve
    (optional)

FOR THE SALAD

200g sugar snaps, cut
    in half lengthways

8 radishes, finely sliced

3 medium carrots, peeled

a small bunch of coriander
    and/or mint, leaves
    picked and chopped

FOR THE DRESSING

the zest and juice of
    1 unwaxed lime

2 tablespoons tamari
    or soy sauce

a squeeze of runny honey

1 tablespoon white miso paste

These little cakes are packed with freshness and flavour. They also go with a lot of things: brown rice; soy and lime dressed noodles; or next to a salad. They are great both hot and cold, so are a good thing to take to a barbecue or on a journey. I make a batch on a Sunday for quick lunches and dinners.

Use firm tofu here; if yours feels spongy and full of liquid you can put a plate on top of it, then place a tin on top of that and leave it for 30 minutes for some of the moisture to drain off.

I buy a load of lemongrass stalks and lime leaves when I am in an Asian supermarket and store them in my freezer so I always have them on hand; they really elevate the flavour.

———————————————

Soak your cashew nuts in cold water to soften them – a minimum of 10 minutes but as long as you have.

Put the ginger, garlic, lemongrass, chilli and lime leaves in a food processor and blitz until you have a fine paste; you could do this in a pestle and mortar too. Add the tofu and blitz again until you have a rough paste. Transfer the mixture to a bowl, then add the nut butter and the green beans. Drain and roughly chop the cashews and add these too. Mix well, working the mixture together with the back of a spoon. Shape into about twelve 5cm cakes and put them in the fridge to firm up a little.

For the salad, put the sugar snaps into a bowl with the radishes. Use a speed peeler to shave the carrot into ribbons, add them to the bowl along with the herbs, and keep in the fridge until needed. Mix the dressing ingredients in a small jar and put to one side.

Heat your oven on its lowest setting. When you are ready to eat, put a large frying pan on a medium heat, add a little oil and fry as many cakes as will fit into the pan, cooking them for 2–3 minutes on each side until burnished and golden brown. Keep them warm on a plate in the low oven while you cook the rest.

Dress the salad and serve it next to the cakes, with a little steamed rice if you are really hungry.

Beetroot tops tart

SERVES 6–8

coconut oil or butter

1 red onion, finely sliced

2 cloves of garlic,
    finely chopped

a few sprigs of fresh
    thyme or oregano

2–3 raw beetroots
    (about 250g)

200g beetroot tops or leafy
    spinach, shredded

1–2 tablespoons cider
    vinegar (or lemon juice)

3 medium organic eggs

a small bunch of mint,
    leaves picked and
    roughly chopped

125g soft goat's cheese

50g walnuts

about 2 tablespoons
    runny honey

FOR THE PASTRY

50g rolled oats

100g white spelt flour

50g ground almonds

150g cold unsalted butter
    or coconut oil, plus
    extra for greasing

4–6 tablespoons ice-
    cold water

TO SERVE

peppery green leaves (rocket,
    lamb's lettuce, mizuna)

Beetroots are beginning to show up this time of year in all their sweet-shop colours. First come the smaller, sweeter ones with deep green and magenta veined stems. I adore them and the fuchsia kiss they give everything they touch. This tart is a riot of pink and makes the most of the often forgotten minerally tops too.

There is such a beauty to a really good tart or quiche: crisp pastry and a just set, quivering filling; for me they have to be handled with a lightness of touch and put vegetables at the centre. Here beetroots are the heroes, grated and paired with some slow-cooked onion, thyme, a little soft goat's cheese, fresh mint, some walnuts, which toast as the tart cooks, and a final drizzle of honey.

I use oats and almonds here to make my pastry, and a slimmer amount of butter than you might expect; the result is a deeply flavoured buttery crust with back notes of toasted oats and linseeds. It means that I'll just as happily eat this on a Monday as I would as part of a Sunday lunch.

Don't worry if you can't find beetroots with their tops; you could use some spring greens or spinach on its stem instead. At a pinch you can use shop-bought shortcrust pastry here if time is tight.

———————————————

Preheat your oven to 200°C/180°C fan/gas 6. Grease a 25cm loose-bottomed tart tin.

First, make the pastry. Put the oats into a food processor and blitz until you have a scruffy flour, then add the spelt flour and ground almonds and a good pinch of salt and blitz again until everything is mixed together. Cube and add the butter and pulse until the mixture looks like breadcrumbs. Add the water a tablespoon at a time, pulsing after each addition until the pastry comes together in a rough ball. You may not need all the water.

Form the pastry into a ball with your hands, wrap in cling film and chill in the fridge for about 30 minutes. →

Next, place the pastry between two sheets of baking paper and use a rolling pin to roll it out until you have a rough circle about 0.5cm thick. Remove 1 layer of paper and lay the pastry over the tart tin then push it down, making sure it is snug and there are no air bubbles. Take off the other piece of paper and trim off any excess. Alternatively, if the pastry is really cold, you could grate it into the tart tin using the coarse setting on your grater, then push down to fix up any gaps with your fingers.

Now blind-bake your pastry. Use a fork to prick the base a few times, scrunch up a bit of baking paper, smooth it out and place over the pastry. Fill with baking beans (or uncooked rice) and bake for 10 minutes. Lift out the paper and beans then put the pastry back into the oven for another 5 minutes. Leave to cool.

While the case is in the oven, place a large frying pan on a medium heat. Add a knob of coconut oil or butter and fry the onion for 10 minutes until soft and sweet, then add the garlic and thyme and cook for another couple of minutes.

Meanwhile, peel the beetroots and grate them coarsely on a box grater or in a food processor, which is less messy (and won't stain your fingers). Add the grated beetroot to the pan of onions and fry for about 30 seconds before adding the beetroot tops or spinach – you may need to add half first and allow it to wilt down before adding the other half.

Cook for 5 minutes until everything has dried out a little and there is no liquid left in the pan. Next add the vinegar and season well with salt and pepper. Transfer the lot to a bowl to cool.

Beat the eggs with the mint, then add to the beetroot mixture and crumble in half of the goat's cheese. Spoon the mixture into the tart case, crumble over the remaining cheese, break over the walnuts and drizzle a little honey on top, adding as much as is to your taste. Bake for 30–35 minutes or until the filling is golden on top and firm. Serve in generous slices with a shock of peppery green salad.

Roast avocado tacos with charred tomato salsa

Tacos are summer food. I spend every trip to see my sister in LA seeking out the best that California has to offer; that means a lot of tacos. These avocado tacos are, if you like, a greatest hits of all the things I have loved about tacos in LA: charred corn tortillas, a smoky chilli-spiked salsa, pickled jalapeños and some polenta-crusted avocado. It might seem a little out of the ordinary to cook avocados but it brings out a totally different character in them, still grassy and buttery but crisp on the outside – do give it a try. These tacos take me back to the palo-santo-scented boutiques and the brightly painted stairs that lead up to my sister's house on the hill.

If you can get your hands on tomatillos all the better, they make a great salsa; if not, vine tomatoes will do just fine. I encourage you to seek out corn tortillas made from 100 per cent corn masa (dough). They have a totally different texture and flavour from the softer corn and wheat tortillas we are used to in the UK.

Preheat your oven to 200°C/180°C fan/gas 6.

Cut the avocados in half and take out the stones. Cut them in half again lengthways and remove the skins. Put into a bowl and sprinkle with the lime zest, juice and chilli. Toss well to coat. In a separate bowl, mix the polenta with the smoked paprika, cheese, chipotle and a generous pinch of salt and pepper.

Put the polenta mix on to a plate and roll the avocados in it, then transfer to a baking tray, drizzle with olive oil and bake for 25 minutes. Alternatively, shallow-fry them in a good bit of olive oil.

While the avocados are baking, make the pickled chillies. Place the cider vinegar in a saucepan with 150ml water. Bash the garlic cloves and place them in the pan with the coriander seeds, agave and salt. Bring to the boil. Slice the chillies into rounds 0.5cm thick, leaving the seeds in. When the liquid has boiled, stir in the chillies and remove the pan from the heat. Leave to sit for at least 15 minutes. Any leftovers can be stored in the fridge covered in the liquid for up to 3 weeks. →

SERVES 4

FOR THE ROAST AVOCADO

4 just-ripe avocados

the zest and juice of 1 unwaxed lime

1 green chilli, chopped

50g fine polenta

½ teaspoon hot smoked paprika

25g hard cheese (Manchego or pecorino work well), grated

a pinch of dried chipotle or chilli flakes

olive oil

FOR THE PICKLED CHILLIES

150ml cider vinegar

2 cloves of garlic

1 tablespoon coriander seeds, bashed in a pestle and mortar

2 tablespoons agave nectar

1 tablespoon flaky sea salt

6 jalapeños or other green chillies →

FOR THE CHARRED SALSA

4 ripe, vine tomatoes
 or tomatillos (unripe
 green tomatoes)

4 spring onions

2 red chillies

2 cloves of garlic

1 tablespoon red wine vinegar

lime juice (optional)

agave syrup or runny
 honey (optional)

TO ASSEMBLE

12 small corn tortillas
 (see note above)

1 spring cabbage, shredded

a handful of coriander,
 roughly chopped

100g Manchego or feta
 cheese, crumbled

limes, to serve

Meanwhile, make the salsa. Put a griddle on a high heat. Once hot, char the tomatoes, spring onions and chillies until soft and blackened all over, turning with tongs every 30 seconds or so. You may need to remove the chillies and spring onions before the tomatoes. Once the whole lot looks good, cut off the chilli stalks and spring onion roots and transfer the charred veg to a blender with the garlic, the red wine vinegar and a generous pinch of salt and blitz until you have a punchy salsa. Taste and check it is nicely balanced: add more vinegar, lime or a little agave nectar or honey if it needs sweetness (depending on the sweetness and ripeness of your tomatoes). Put the salsa into a big bowl.

Drain the chillies. Warm the tortillas in a dry frying pan on a medium heat or over an open flame, turning them with tongs. Once they are warm and a little charred around the edges, pile them on to a plate. Put them in the middle of the table with the avocado, salsa, cabbage, pickled chillies, coriander, cheese, and limes for squeezing over, and let everyone make up their own tacos.

A wedding-worthy tomato tarte Tatin

Last year on a balmy July day, John and I got married in a tiny church on an island off the Anglesey coast; a little tidal island 30 metres across, separated from the beach by a rocky path that you can only tread at low tide. That morning I walked across the island in my wedding dress, in sea mist that made me feel like I was in a gothic novel. The tiny church held just 40 people and was lit only by candles. When we came out the sun was shining and we drove to the reception in my dad's old soft-top, and surrounded by our friends we ate this tart. I don't think I could be more fond of a recipe.

This is the simplified version – a perfect summer offering. Roasting the tomatoes takes a few hours but requires very little effort, so don't be put off. The tart can also be assembled ahead of time and kept in the fridge. Tomatoes are the star of the show here, so buy beautiful, different colours and shapes if you can. A special mention to Sarah and Stuart who cooked our wedding feast with such grace and care; nothing I make will ever taste as sweet.

Preheat your oven to 120°C/100°C fan/gas ½. Cut the tomatoes in half and put them cut-side up on a baking tray with a little salt, pepper and a couple of tablespoons of olive oil. Put them in the oven for 3–4 hours to slowly roast and sweeten. You may need to take some of the smaller tomatoes out a bit earlier, so keep an eye on them. Once cooked, remove and allow to cool a little. (Sometimes I find it easier to cook the tomatoes overnight: I roast them at 120°C/100°C fan/gas ½ for 1 hour, then turn off the oven and leave them until the morning.)

Next make the caramelised onions. Heat a tablespoon of olive oil on a medium heat and add the sliced onions. Cook for 10 minutes to sweeten and soften before adding the vinegar, sugar, the leaves from a few sprigs of the thyme or oregano (saving the rest for later) and a good pinch of salt and pepper. Cook on a low heat for 30–40 minutes until really soft and sticky.

Butter a cast-iron or heavy ovenproof frying pan (about 24cm in diameter) – a well-buttered pan will mean the tart comes out easily. Lay the tomatoes cut-side down in a kind of mosaic, fitting them all together; don't worry if there is a little bit of overlap. Once they are all squeezed in, scatter the onions over the top. →

SERVES 4–6

1kg good, ripe tomatoes

olive oil

3 red onions, freshly sliced

1 tablespoon red wine vinegar

1 teaspoon brown sugar or runny honey

a small bunch of thyme or oregano

25g butter, for greasing

flour, for dusting

1 x 375g pack of all-butter puff pastry

1 organic egg, beaten

50g baby capers, drained and dried on kitchen paper

283

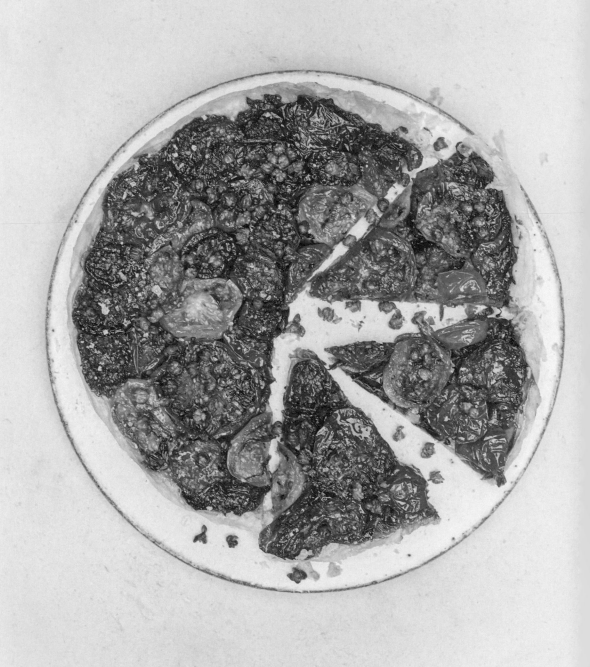

Lightly dust a work surface with flour and roll out the pastry until it's about 1cm thick, then cut out a circle just bigger than your pan. Lay it over the onion mixture and tuck the sides around the onion inside the pan. You can stop here and put the tart into the fridge if you like.

Once you are ready to cook, preheat the oven to 220°C/200°C fan/ gas 7. Brush the pastry with a little of the beaten egg and put it into the oven for 25–30 minutes, until golden all over and bubbling around the edges.

While the tart is cooking, heat a few tablespoons of olive oil in a frying pan. Have a plate lined with some kitchen paper and a slotted spoon to hand. Once the oil is good and hot, add the capers. They will bloom into little flowers and crisp in just 30 seconds or so. Lift them out and quickly drain them on kitchen paper.

Once the tart is ready, take it out of the oven and allow it to sit for 5 minutes before running a knife around the edge and carefully turning it out on to a plate. Scatter the capers over the tart before serving.

Buttery aubergines with toasted couscous

This is a perfect recipe for a crowd and works brilliantly on the barbecue rather than the grill if you like. One thing to ensure here is that your aubergines are buttery and soft; raw aubergine has to be one of the worst things to eat. Aubergines are pretty resilient vegetables, so be brave when you cook them, and give them long enough to make sure they are cooked right through. Try to get your hands on the longer thin aubergines here, as the short fat ones will take much longer to cook through.

SERVES 4

FOR THE PEPPERS

4 red peppers, deseeded and cut into thin strips

2 tablespoons olive oil

4 cloves of garlic, finely sliced

1 red onion, finely sliced

2 tablespoons sherry vinegar

½ teaspoon smoked sweet paprika

FOR THE AUBERGINES

1 teaspoon ground cumin

1 teaspoon ground coriander

1 tablespoon olive oil

4 long, thin aubergines

plain yoghurt, to serve (optional)

FOR THE COUSCOUS

300g wholewheat giant couscous (mograbieh)

1 heaped teaspoon vegetable stock powder

small bunches of mint, parsley, basil, leaves picked and roughly chopped, stalks reserved

the zest and juice of 1 unwaxed lemon

6 tablespoons extra virgin olive oil, plus extra to serve

1 teaspoon sumac

First, the peppers. Put the peppers into a frying pan with the olive oil, garlic and red onion and cook for 20 minutes over a low to medium heat, until softened and sweeter and the edges are beginning to pick up some golden colour. Add the vinegar and paprika and cook for another 20 minutes, then season well and take off the heat.

While the peppers are cooking, heat your overhead grill or barbecue to medium. Mix the cumin and coriander with the oil and a good pinch of salt. Prick the aubergines all over and rub them with the oil. Put them under the hot grill or on the barbecue for about 25 minutes, turning them a couple of times. You are aiming for the aubergines to almost completely collapse, so be brave.

Fill and boil the kettle. Toast the couscous in a dry frying pan over a medium–high heat for a couple of minutes until it smells toasty but before it colours. Cover with 1 litre of boiling water and add the stock powder and herb stalks. Turn the heat down to medium and let the couscous simmer for 8–10 minutes.

Put the lemon zest and juice into a small bowl with the olive oil. Add the chopped herb leaves and sumac and mix well. Once the couscous is cooked, drain well, remove the herb stalks and dress with half the dressing while still warm.

Place an aubergine on each plate, cut lengthways with a sharp knife and season the insides well with olive oil, salt and pepper. Serve with a heaped spoonful of the couscous and peppers on the side. Finish with the remaining dressing and some yoghurt if you like.

Smoky roast carrot burgers

Summer barbecues are often when I feel a bit short-changed as a vegetarian; these burgers are an attempt to remedy that. They are flavour-packed, with umami from the smoked tofu and smoky paprika, and some buttery sweetness from the mashed roast carrots. These burgers hold up well on the barbecue – just be sure to make them in advance and give them some time in the fridge to firm up.

I roast the carrots in the oven, as I usually like to make these in advance, but if you were so inclined you could roast them wrapped in foil in the embers of the barbecue. Vegans can replace the Parmesan with a teaspoon of nutritional yeast and the mayo with a vegan mayo.

First, roast your carrots. Tumble the carrots on to a tray with the smoked paprika, cumin, some salt and pepper and a good drizzle of olive oil. Cover with foil and roast for 20 minutes, then remove the foil and roast for a further 10 minutes, until completely soft and starting to brown.

While these are roasting, finely crumble half the tofu into a bowl and add the breadcrumbs, parsley, lemon zest, Parmesan and sesame seeds.

Once the carrots are ready, take them out of the oven (leave the oven on if you want to bake your burgers) and allow them to cool a little before blitzing in a food processor with the remaining tofu, until everything is evenly distributed and the mixture is pretty smooth. Allow to cool a little, then add this to the breadcrumb mixture and mix well, using a spoon to mash and persuade everything to come together. If your mixture looks a little dry, add a couple of tablespoons of olive oil or water until it comes together nicely.

Shape the mixture into 6 patties, lay them on a plate and put them into the fridge for 20 minutes. →

SERVES 6

600g carrots, peeled and cut into 1–2cm rounds

1 teaspoon smoked sweet paprika

1 teaspoon cumin seeds, roughly bashed in a pestle and mortar

olive oil

200g smoked tofu

100g rye breadcrumbs

a small bunch of flat-leaf parsley, chopped

the zest of 1 unwaxed lemon

50g grated Parmesan (I use a vegetarian one)

50g sesame seeds, toasted (see page 459)

TO SERVE

6 good burger buns or slices of rye bread

2 avocados

a punnet of salad cress

6 tablespoons good mayonnaise

smoked paprika

12 small lettuce leaves

Once you are ready to cook, put a large frying pan on a medium heat and add a little olive oil, swirling it to coat the pan. Add the burgers and cook for 3–4 minutes on each side, flipping them once they are well coloured. Alternatively you could cook them in the hot oven for 25–30 minutes. If you are barbecuing the burgers, brush them with oil before cooking on one side, flipping only when they are coloured and crisp enough to come away from the bars easily.

While the burgers are cooking, split and toast your buns, slice your avocados and snip your cress.

Spread the bottom of each bun with a spoonful of mayonnaise, add a pinch of paprika, then top with the lettuce leaves, avocado, the burger and a crown of cress. Cover with the lid of the bun and eat straight away.

Supper pancakes with pickled cherries

Cherries are hands down my favourite fruit, and for me British ones are the best. Sweeter than their foreign cousins because they are allowed to ripen on the trees for longer, and fresher when they arrive in your kitchen for not having travelled across the oceans, they are as much a part of my summers as barbecues and flip-flops. When they start filling my shopping basket they are all I eat for breakfast, and often pudding, until they are gone again. Accept nothing but the best: glossy deep cerise exteriors and bright green stems. For me they are the taste of pure summer.

This is a savoury take on cherries: they are quickly pickled and wrapped in warm buff-coloured buckwheat galettes, topped with a good spoonful of goat's cheese and a shock of greens.

The buckwheat grain comes from a leafy plant, not like the grass from which wheat is made, and has a deep distinctive flavour; it is also naturally free of gluten. If you have time, leave the batter overnight as it makes a softer, silkier and more tender pancake; if not, as long as you have will do.

SERVES 4

265g buckwheat flour

2 medium organic eggs

600ml milk (unsweetened almond or cow's milk works best)

300g cherries, pitted

150ml red wine vinegar

a good squeeze of runny honey

3 sprigs of tarragon, leaves picked and roughly chopped

2 tablespoons melted butter or ghee

200g soft, rindless goat's cheese or goat's curd

4 handfuls of peppery green leaves (watercress, lamb's lettuce, rocket)

You can make the batter as far as 24 hours in advance – the longer it sits the better your pancakes will be – but 30 minutes' sitting time will do if you are in a rush.

Whisk together the flour, eggs, milk and a good pinch of salt, then put the batter into the fridge for as long as you have.

Next, get your cherries going. Put them into a deep bowl and pour over the vinegar and honey, then throw in the tarragon. Season with a little salt and leave to one side.

Turn your oven on to 110°C/90°C fan/gas ¼. Once you are ready to cook, heat a large frying pan (about 25cm in diameter) over a medium heat. Using a paper towel, rub a little of the melted butter around the pan, then add a small ladleful of batter. Let the galette brown on one side, then flip it over. Once cooked, remove the galette from the pan to a plate and place in the low oven to keep warm while you cook the remainder.

Fill each galette with a little goat's cheese, a few cherries, a sprinkle of pickling juice and some peppery greens. Wrap up and devour.

Rigatoni with aubergines and tomatoes

I grew up eating this simple Sicilian pasta dish. There was a little Italian restaurant down the road from our house that made this classic; they called it 'penne Siciliana' but it's also often called 'penne alla Norma'. They added mozzarella to theirs, which gave it all a pleasing creaminess; I prefer to use *ricotta salata*, which is aged salted ricotta, but if you can't get this you could use some feta; just crumble it over at the end.

Slice your aubergines into 1cm-thick rounds. If you have a big seedy one you might want to salt the slices first; I find that most firm small aubergines don't need salting but the bigger ones with more seeds do. To salt them, lay them in a colander, sprinkle both sides with salt and leave for an hour. Pat dry with kitchen paper.

Next, heat a drizzle of olive oil in a large frying pan, add the garlic and cook for a few minutes until golden at the edges but not burnt. Scoop it out and put the pan back on the heat. Add a little more oil to the pan and cook the aubergines over a high heat in a single layer until they are browned on each side and soft in the middle – you can do this in a few batches. Once they are all cooked, put the lot back into the pan.

Add the tomatoes with the oregano and chilli, a good pinch of salt and a grind of pepper. Cook the lot for about 10 minutes, scraping the goodness off the bottom, until you have a nice soft juicy sauce – the veg will still hold its shape a little.

While this is happening, bring a large pot of salted water to the boil and cook the pasta until it is al dente. Follow the guidance on the back of the packet, though I usually cook it for a minute or so less. Scoop out a mugful of the cooking water.

Drain the pasta and add it to the pan of aubergines and tomatoes. Stir everything together and add a little of the pasta water to loosen the mixture to a generous sauce, remembering that the pasta will keep absorbing liquid as it sits. Taste and add more salt, pepper and chilli as you like, then top with a grating of ricotta, some pistachios and more olive oil.

SERVES 4–6

500g aubergines (2 small ones)

extra virgin olive oil

2 cloves of garlic, finely sliced

500g small or cherry tomatoes

a few sprigs of fresh oregano or marjoram

a pinch of dried chilli flakes

400g wholewheat penne or rigatoni

50g *ricotta salata* or feta (see note above)

50g shelled pistachios, toasted and roughly chopped

Strawberry and rose thumbprint cookies

Childishly simple to make but very good to eat, these little cookies are made of the good stuff: oats, dates, coconut oil and a quick jam sweetened with coconut sugar. While they are still a treat, this line-up of whole ingredients means I eat these with even more of a smile on my face. They are also great for little ones.

I love rose geranium and use it to infuse berries and rhubarb. I have a little pot of it on my windowsill and tear off a few leaves to add to a pan every few weeks. If rose geranium is a bridge too far for you, you could mimic the fragrant rose notes with a tiny splash of rose water or orange blossom water or leave it out altogether.

I make these cookies year round, with apricots or peaches in summer, pears in autumn and frozen berries in the winter.

MAKES ABOUT 24

FOR THE JAM

500g strawberries

5 rose geranium leaves or rose water (optional)

1 vanilla pod, split in half lengthways

3 tablespoons coconut sugar

the juice of 1 lemon

FOR THE COOKIES

100g coconut oil

150g rolled oats

100g pitted Medjool dates (about 8)

150g ground almonds

a pinch of flaky sea salt

the zest and juice of 1 unwaxed orange

Wash and hull the strawberries. If they are really large, cut them in half. Place in a pan with the rose geranium leaves, vanilla pod, sugar and lemon juice. If you're using rose water instead of rose geranium leaves, add it in small quantities after the jam is cooked and cooled, tasting after each addition to get the right balance. Cook the strawberries over a low heat for 30 minutes, until they have completely softened and gone jammy.

Meanwhile, make the cookie dough. Preheat the oven to 170°C/150°C fan/gas 3. Melt the coconut oil in a small saucepan and take off the heat. Blitz the oats in a food processor until you have a scruffy flour. Add the dates and blitz again until the dough is pinchable between your fingers. Add the almonds and pour the coconut oil in slowly, until the dough is starting to come together, then add the salt, orange juice and zest.

Line a baking tray with greaseproof paper – you may need two trays if yours are small. Take a tablespoon of cookie dough and shape it into discs about 1½cm deep with your hands. Place the discs on the baking tray, then stamp an indent into each one with your thumb. Remove the rose geranium leaves from the jam and spoon a teaspoon of jam into each little indent.

Bake for 30 minutes until golden around the edges and jammy and dark in the middle, then transfer to a wire rack to cool.

Cherry and black pepper streusel muffins

Not too sweet and filled with good things, these are a muffin I can happily eat for breakfast. I love them studded with cherries, so I make them most in summer, but in truth they could be made with other berries – frozen or fresh – or slices of summer stone fruits. The tops are crumbly and crunchy with their little hats of streusel topping flecked with black pepper and orange zest. These flavours are more subtle than you might expect and add a pleasing warmth and fragrance. The muffins will last for a couple of days in an airtight tin.

I use raw cane sugar in these muffins, also called rapadura sugar. It is less processed than lots of commercial sugars, and while a little more expensive I think it tastes much better too. I use it where recipes call for brown sugar, so you can use light brown sugar here instead. Vegans can use coconut oil and aquafaba (see page 459).

Preheat the oven to 200°C/180°C fan/gas 6. Grease a 12-hole muffin tray or line with muffin cases.

First make the streusel topping by placing all the ingredients in a bowl and rubbing through your fingers until it resembles rough crumbs. Set aside for later.

Melt the butter in a saucepan. Pour it into a bowl and set aside to cool slightly. In a large mixing bowl, combine the flour, baking powder, ground almonds and salt and use a balloon whisk to break up any lumps.

In another bowl, whisk together the eggs and sugar until it turns a smooth, light caramel colour. Slowly pour in the milk, whisking gently as you pour, then add the melted butter, the vanilla and the orange juice. Gently whisk the wet ingredients into the flour mixture. Toss the cherries in the teaspoon of flour (this stops the juice from 'bleeding' into the batter as it bakes) and fold them into the batter.

Fill the muffin cases or holes with the batter to just below the top. Sprinkle the topping over the muffins and bake for 30 minutes, until the tops of the muffins are golden and a skewer inserted in the centre comes out clean. Leave the muffins to cool for about 15 minutes before removing them from the tray.

MAKES 12

FOR THE STREUSEL TOPPING

50g unsalted butter, cut into 1 cm cubes

70g white spelt flour

40g raw cane sugar

the zest from 1 unwaxed orange

a pinch of flaky sea salt

1 teaspoon freshly ground black pepper

150g unsalted butter, or coconut oil plus extra to grease

300g white spelt flour, plus 1 teaspoon

2 teaspoons baking powder

100g ground almonds

a generous pinch of flaky sea salt

3 medium organic eggs

200g raw cane sugar (see note above)

200ml milk (I use oat or unsweetened almond)

1½ teaspoons vanilla paste

the juice from 1 orange

350g pitted cherries, cut into quarters

Coconut raspberry cakes for Mum

Since becoming a mother the love and respect I have for my own mum has grown and grown. Not only was my mum the most incredible mother to me, my brother and sister, but now she and my dad are helping me raise my son. Sometimes things in life are so huge and far-reaching that it's hard even to know where to start to say thank you. I started with these cakes: two of Mum's favourite flavours – raspberry and coconut, perfectly light and not too sweet.

    These are topped with a whipped coconut frosting that I use a lot. You can use four tablespoons of golden icing sugar in place of the honey if you want a more traditional-style vegan buttercream finish. Vegans can coconut oil and aquafaba here (see page 459).

MAKES 12 LITTLE CAKES

1 x 400g tin of coconut milk

200g softened unsalted butter, plus extra for greasing

150g coconut sugar or light brown sugar

4 medium organic eggs

1 teaspoon vanilla extract

a pinch of flaky sea salt

the zest of 1 unwaxed lemon

150g white spelt flour

175g ground almonds

2 teaspoons baking powder

150g raspberries

2 tablespoons set honey

a handful of coconut flakes, toasted

First put your tin of coconut milk into the freezer for 20 minutes to cool. Once cool, open it carefully, without disturbing the contents. Scoop out the set cream on the top and put it back in the fridge. Keep the more watery coconut milk for later in the recipe.

Preheat the oven to 200°C/180°C fan/gas 6. Butter a 12-hole muffin tin.

Beat the butter and sugar until light and fluffy, then add the eggs one by one, beating as you add each one. Add the vanilla, salt, lemon zest, flour, almonds, baking powder and 4 tablespoons of the watery coconut milk from the bottom of the tin and mix until you have a thick batter.

Fold in the raspberries, then divide the mixture between the holes of the buttered muffin tin. Bake for 25 minutes, until risen and golden brown.

To make the icing, use an electric whisk to beat the set coconut cream with the honey in a metal bowl at full pelt. Put it straight back into the fridge to cool.

Allow your cakes to cool completely before generously icing them with the coconut cream and scattering them with the coconut flakes.

Flowers in the kitchen

Flowers are part of how I cook in the summer months. Even in the middle of the city where I live there are flowers we can eat everywhere. Outside my house, a little 1-metre bit of earth is full of nasturtiums and marigolds. Greengrocers and even supermarkets have started selling edible flowers and mixing them into their salad blends.

I am a sucker for the colour and prettiness flowers add, but most add flavour too, from the punch of chive flowers to the subtle perfumed notes of a viola. I know I verge on sounding a little niche here, but I pick and buy flowers to put on my table so why not put them on my plate too, particularly as they are often free and easy to find.

A note of caution: some flowers are poisonous and cause real problems if you eat them so please stick to the flowers suggested below. If you are unsure whether something is edible do not go near it. Even decorating a cake with a flower and then taking it off before eating can be harmful if the flower isn't edible.

Borage: vivid, blue star-shaped flowers that are delicious in gin and tonics and Pimm's as well as to top cakes; they freeze into pretty ice cubes.

Broad bean flowers: look like little irises; white and velvety black, sometimes with lilac hues. Delicately flavoured, lovely in salads.

Chives and allium flowers: vibrant purple and shaped like little stars these have a strong chive flavour so use sparingly; they're delicious with scrambled eggs, spring stews (see page 196) and in salads.

Coriander flowers: these delicate white frond-like flowers are amazing, their flavour mimics the leaves and can be used wherever you might use coriander.

Cornflowers: beautiful blue in colour with a sweet almost spicy taste, they're great for adding to teas (see page 222) and decorating cakes.

Courgette flowers: sunshine yellow and bigger than most edible flowers, they have a sweet nutty flavour and can be stuffed and pan-fried or even battered and deep-fried; you can also tear them over salads.

Elderflower: delicate blooms of tiny off-white star-shaped flowers famously used to make elderflower cordial (see page 221), they are also delicious in gin and tonics, on salads (see page 298) and to top cakes (see page 210).

Lavender: particularly good in baking and brewed into herbal infusions and hot drinks (see page 222). Go lightly.

Nasturtiums: both the flowers and the flat-topped leaves have a lovely spicy flavour and the flowers come in a range of fabulous neon colours with soft velvety petals. I like to add them to salads and their peppery flavour works well in pesto.

Pansies: extremely versatile thanks to their gentle flavour; they have a long flowering period and crystallise beautifully. I use them in salads, to top summer toasts and to decorate cakes.

Rose: generally the more scented the better the flavour will be. Always use garden roses as most shop-bought ones will be sprayed with chemicals, unless you buy organic ones; good in cordial (see page 221), jam and baking (see page 292).

Sage flowers: these come in blue, purple and white hues and their shape can vary from one sage to the next. They are wonderfully savoury but have a very strong flavour so are best if cooked quickly; good with tomato dishes and sprinkled on pizzas.

Sunflowers: the petals have a bittersweet nutty flavour and a good crunch; they add an amazing burst of colour to salads.

Wild primroses: a delicate fragrant flavour; they look beautiful as a spring garnish.

Wild garlic: pretty white flowers with a gorgeous texture; a sign of spring (see page 214).

Ways to use flowers in the kitchen

- Freeze them into ice cubes

- To top a pavlova or meringues (see page 302)

- Stirred into cocktails

- Added to a green salad

- To top cakes

- Infused in cream, frozen yoghurt, ice cream and sorbet

- To make cordial (see page 221)

- Stirred into honey and left to infuse

- Added to pesto (nasturtiums work well here)

Summer fruit and elderflower salad

Hot days call for cooling puddings, refreshing fruits and everything ice cold. Most summer nights our pudding will be a few cherries and a snap of dark chocolate. If we have guests I'll put the cherries in a bowl of ice to keep them cool while we pick at them. Other nights it's a ripe peach, cold from the fridge and cut into slices. But sometimes I want something that feels a bit more put together and this is it. I largely make this in summer, when the peaches and cherries are at their best; that means that in London the elderflowers have all bloomed and gone, but if you live further north you might be lucky enough to have a few blooms left that you can scatter over the top. If not, other edible flowers would be pretty but by no means necessary.

SERVES 4

4 ripe flat peaches

250g cherries

a 500g piece of watermelon

2 tablespoons elderflower cordial (see page 221)

1 unwaxed lime

TO SERVE

1 head of elderflower, flowers picked (optional)

Start by washing all the fruit. Cut the peaches in half and remove their stones. Slice each half into three or four wedges depending on the size of your peaches.

Next, halve the cherries and if they're ripe you should be able to wiggle their stones out. Cut the rind away from the watermelon and any white edges too. Cut into 2cm bite-sized bits.

Combine all the fruit in a bowl and stir through the elderflower cordial. Grate the lime zest into the bowl, then add the juice.

Arrange the fruit on a platter and scatter the elderflowers over the top if you're using them.

Peach and cardamom tart

Summer desserts are tricky territory. They need to be sweet and satisfying but light and bright at the same time. This tart centres around ripe summer peaches, the ones which run down your chin as you eat them; sweet and custardy inside. You could use nectarines too, or even plums or apricots if you were making this outside the window of time when peaches are at their best.

This is an easy and unusual tart. It's light thanks to a crust made from oats, nuts and coconut oil, spiked with some heady cardamom, and is topped with a quick peach filling which is set not with eggs, but using the binding power of chia seeds.

Preheat the oven to 200°C/180°C fan/gas 6. Grease a 24cm loose-bottomed tart tin with a little coconut oil and line the base with baking paper.

Put all the crust ingredients into a food processor and pulse to mix. Press the crust mix evenly into the bottom of the tin – there's no need to push it up the sides.

Prick the base all over with a fork, then scrunch up a bit of baking paper, smooth it out and place it over the pastry and fill the paper with baking beans (or uncooked rice). Bake the base for 20 minutes or until lightly golden, then remove from the oven, take out the baking paper and baking beans then set aside to cool.

Combine the chia seeds with the apple juice or water and set aside until they come together to form a gel.

When the base has cooled a little, mix the peaches with the sugar, vanilla, cinnamon and zest, stir until well combined, then add the chia gel. Pour the peach filling into the tart case and spread evenly. Bake for 35–45 minutes, until the peaches are jammy and set.

Allow the tart to cool completely before removing it from the tin. Serve with coconut yoghurt or whipped cream.

SERVES 8–10

60g coconut oil, melted, plus extra for greasing

2 tablespoons chia seeds

100ml apple juice or water

6 peaches, cut into 1cm slices

60g light brown sugar or coconut sugar

the seeds from 1 vanilla pod

½ teaspoon ground cinnamon

the zest of 1 unwaxed lemon

coconut yoghurt or whipped cream, to serve

FOR THE CRUST

140g rolled oats

75g wholemeal flour

60g pecans, chopped

90g runny honey

100g coconut oil or melted butter

the seeds from 1 vanilla pod

8 cardamom pods, seeds removed and finely ground

½ teaspoon ground cinnamon

a good pinch of flaky sea salt

Summer pudding

Summer pudding is without doubt my favourite summer dessert and I wait all year for the blackcurrants to be able to make and eat it. Blackcurrants apparently aren't a traditional addition but I love their tartness. I make my pudding with sourdough, not the sliced white that even respected chefs favour. This does mean you will need to patch up any holes in the slices, as the crumb is looser, but the flavour is worth it.

Grease a 1-litre pudding basin or mixing bowl with butter and lay a sheet of cling film inside, leaving quite a bit of overhang.

Warm the berries in a small saucepan over a low heat with the sugar, vanilla, rose water and orange juice for about 10–12 minutes, until the fruits start to break down and it all smells fragrant.

Slice the sourdough into ½cm slices with a very sharp bread knife and trim away the crusts. Cut a round the size of the bottom of the pudding basin and place it inside. Arrange the slices around the sides of the basin, leaving some overlap of bread above the rim of the basin – you will cut this off later. Push the slices into the sides of the bowl, making sure there are no gaps; patch up any holes with smaller pieces of bread to make sure it's completely lined.

When the fruit is done, allow it to cool a little, then taste and add a bit more sugar if it needs it. Strain the fruit through a sieve over a bowl, and return the strained liquid to the pan. Spoon the fruit into the basin on top of the bread. Arrange some more slices of bread over the top of the fruit to make a lid, again making sure there are no gaps, then trim off the excess bread.

Pull the cling film over the top and place a snug-fitting saucer on top of the pudding with a little weight on top (a full jar of jam would do). Put the bowl, weight and all, into the fridge for at least 3 hours, but ideally overnight, for the bread to absorb all of the deep purple juices.

When you're ready to eat, bubble the remaining liquid in a saucepan to reduce it by half and use to pour over the top of the pudding. Serve with crème fraîche or good pouring cream.

SERVES 6

butter or oil, for greasing

300g blackcurrants

300g redcurrants

300g raspberries

4 tablespoons golden caster sugar

1 teaspoon vanilla paste

1 teaspoon rose water

the juice of ½ an orange

½ a loaf of stale sourdough bread

TO SERVE

crème fraîche or good pouring cream

Wedding meringues

This was the dessert I ate on my wedding day. I found it hard to choose what we might eat that day, especially as the end of the meal, the pudding, has always been my favourite part. It happened that we got married in mid-July – prime cherry season – so we decided on this: caramelly brown sugar meringues topped with a lemon-curd spiked Chantilly, crème anglaise and cherries three different ways, as well as a syrup made from fresh myrtle, a symbol of everlasting love, a very sweet touch from the wonderful people who cooked for us. This is a simplified version, no myrtle syrup and only a few simple processes, but well, well worth the bother. A very precious pudding.

Vegans can make the aquafaba meringues on page 459, use coconut yoghurt and leave out the curd.

Preheat the oven to 150°C/130°C fan/gas 2 and line a baking tray.

Put the brown sugar into a bowl, break up any lumps, then add the golden caster sugar and mix them together.

Whisk the egg whites until stiff peaks form. Gradually add the sugar while mixing on a high speed until the mixture is thick and glossy. It's ready when you can pinch it and not feel any granules of sugar.

Spoon the meringue mix into 8 mounds on the baking tray and bake for 1½–2 hours (depending on how chewy you like your meringues – less time means chewier middles). The meringues are ready when they are set and light to pick up. Put to one side to cool.

While the meringues are cooking put a handful of the pitted cherries into a pan with the honey, the lemon juice and half the vanilla seeds or paste, bring to a boil, then lower the heat and simmer for a few minutes before turning off the heat and letting the cherries macerate.

Mix the rest of the cherries with a little lemon zest – you only want a touch. Mix the yoghurt with the remaining vanilla and ripple through the curd.

To serve, I like to make a huge tower for sharing on a big plate but individual plates work just as well. Layer the meringues with the yoghurt and fresh cherries and finish with a whole cherry.

SERVES 8

FOR THE BROWN SUGAR MERINGUES

100g soft light brown sugar

100g golden caster sugar

4 medium organic egg whites

FOR THE TOPPING

400g cherries, pitted, 8 left whole for serving

2 tablespoons runny honey

1 unwaxed lemon

the seeds from 1 vanilla pod or 2 tablespoons vanilla paste

150ml Greek yoghurt

4 tablespoons lemon curd (shop-bought is fine) or my grapefruit and honey curd (see page 66)

Five summer ice lollies

**EACH RECIPE MAKES
8 × 75ML OR
6 × 100ML LOLLIES**

SIMPLE VANILLA

300ml milk (see note)

300ml yoghurt (see note)

3 tablespoons runny honey
or maple syrup

1 tablespoon vanilla paste

COFFEE AND MAPLE

300ml milk (see note)

300ml yoghurt (see note)

4 shots of espresso or
60ml strong coffee

3 tablespoons maple syrup

MATCHA AND HONEY

300ml milk (see note)

300ml yoghurt (see note)

1 tablespoon matcha powder

3 tablespoons runny honey

MANGO, CARDAMOM
AND VANILLA

300ml milk (see note)

1 ripe mango, peeled and
roughly chopped

½ teaspoon ground cardamom

1 teaspoon vanilla paste

2 tablespoons coconut sugar

STRAWBERRY

300ml milk (see note)

300g strawberries, washed,
hulled and roughly chopped

1 teaspoon vanilla paste

2 tablespoons unrefined
cane sugar

As a little girl I loved only one ice lolly. I didn't choose the run-of-the-mill orange or the ice-cream van favourites apple cider or cola, or even the fancy twisted one from the corner shop. For me it was always the mini milk – vanilla, chocolate or strawberry, I didn't mind – I just loved its cooling, calming milky sweetness.

These are some more grown-up versions, though the vanilla and the strawberry go down very well with little people too. I use 75ml moulds here, the long round ones that mimic the shape of my beloved mini milks.

I tend to use a creamy oat milk, good organic whole milk or a home-made nut milk here and for the yoghurt I use good Greek or coconut yoghurt. Low-fat milk and yoghurt will not work here. You could use shop-bought nut milks but I have found that the lollies end up a little icy, as ready-made nut milks aren't as creamy as home-made; my recipe for how to make your own is on page 458.

For each mini milk recipe, blitz all of the ingredients in a blender (or use a stick blender) and taste it. Remember that things don't taste as strong when they are very cold, so if your mixture tastes perfect pre-freezing you may like to add a little more flavour or sweetness so that this remains the case when they're frozen. Pour into your ice-lolly moulds and freeze for a minimum of 4 hours.

Autumn

Best of the season
    Pumpkins and squashes
    Roots
    Leeks
    Kale
    Cavolo nero
    Chard
    Beetroot
    Mushrooms
    Borlotti beans
    Blackberries
    Cobnuts
    Plums
    Damsons
    Apples
    Pears
    Quince
    Elderberries
    Crab apples
    Chestnuts

Flowers
    Cosmos
    Tuberose
    Hypericum

Vanilla and blackberry drop scones

These were a Saturday favourite growing up. We used to make them with blueberries or strawberries on the top of the Aga at home, topping them with too much butter and far too much maple syrup. We'd make a triple batch of batter as my sister Laura and I would eat 8 or 10 on the trot.

These are a more grown-up version made with blackberries and vanilla and finished with a saffron-spiked yoghurt. Warm from the saffron, sharp and sweet from the blackberries and comforting from the childhood association. The 8-year-old in me could eat these all day.

MAKES ABOUT 10

175g white spelt flour

2 teaspoons baking powder

1 tablespoon golden caster sugar

a pinch of fine sea salt

1 medium organic egg

1 teaspoon vanilla extract or paste

150ml milk (I use unsweetened almond or oat)

150g ripe blackberries

a knob of unsalted butter

TO SERVE

a small pinch of saffron strands

100g plain yoghurt

2 tablespoons runny honey, plus extra for the table

blackberries (optional)

To make the batter put the flour, baking powder, sugar and salt into a large mixing bowl. Use a balloon whisk to stir the dry ingredients and get rid of any lumps of baking powder. Crack in the egg, then add the vanilla and the milk and use the whisk to stir everything into a thick batter. Crush the blackberries slightly, then ripple these through the mixture with a wooden spoon, so you get lovely stains of deep purple as they cook.

Next soak the saffron in a tablespoon of boiling water. Mix the yoghurt with the honey in a separate small bowl.

You can fry the drop scones on a hot flat griddle or in a frying pan. Put your oven on at its lowest setting. Heat the butter in a non-stick frying pan on a medium heat and allow it to melt and froth. Use a small ladle to scoop 4 small rounds of batter into the pan – you want each one to be about 5cm wide. Cook for a couple of minutes, until bubbles rise to the top and the bottom looks set and golden. Carefully and quickly flip the rounds over and cook for another minute or so until golden and cooked through; keep these warm on a plate in the oven while you cook the rest, adding more butter to the pan as you go if you need to.

Mix the saffron liquid into the yoghurt and mix until it's buttercup yellow. Serve the drop scones with the yoghurt, some more blackberries if you like, and a little more honey for drizzling over.

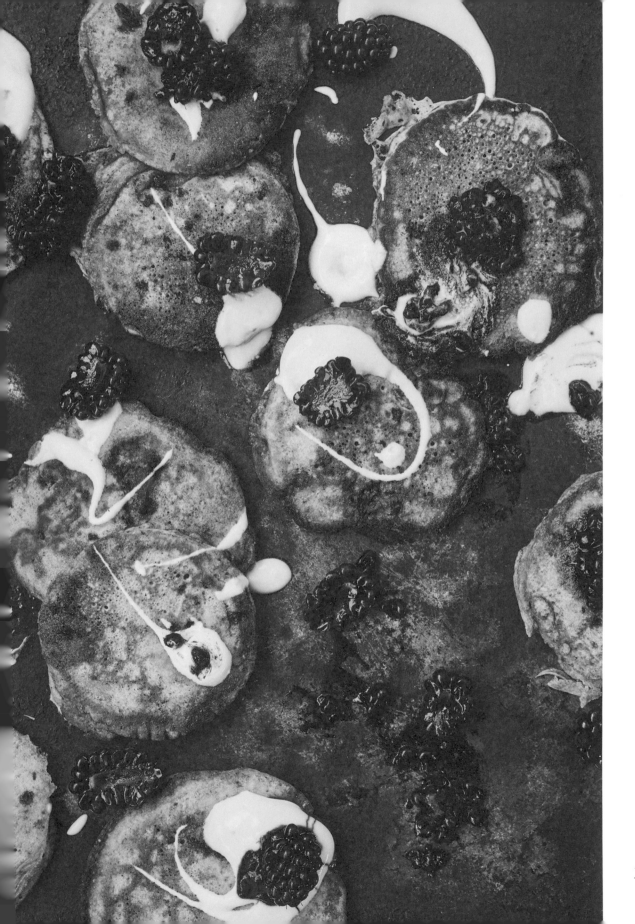

Dhal-baked eggs

Like many of my recipes, this was an attempt to partner up two of my favourite things. I love this for brunch and whilst dhal may seem a stretch for some in the morning anyone who's been to India will know that dhal and breakfast go hand in hand.

This is a friendly thing to cook on a weekend morning but it works well for lunch or dinner too. I use split red lentils, so that they cook quickly and I only have to use one pan. You could up the chilli here if that's your thing – in the morning I like to keep it gentle.

SERVES 4

1 tablespoon olive oil

a thumb-sized piece of ginger, peeled and finely chopped

2 cloves of garlic, finely chopped

a small bunch of coriander, leaves picked, stalks finely chopped

1 teaspoon cumin seeds

1 teaspoon ground coriander

1 teaspoon ground turmeric, or a small thumb-sized piece of fresh root, grated

300g split red lentils

200g spinach, washed

the juice of 1 lemon

4 organic eggs

1 green chilli, finely sliced

plain yoghurt, to serve

Fill and boil the kettle. Heat the oil in a large wide pan with a lid. Add the ginger and garlic, then the coriander stalks, stirring frequently until the edges of the garlic pick up a little colour.

Add the spices and cook for a minute or so to let them toast and release their oils. Add the lentils and stir to coat in the oil. Add 1 litre of water from the kettle and a good pinch of salt, then stir well. Cook on a low heat for 20–30 minutes, or until the lentils are well cooked and the mixture has thickened. You want it to be thick enough so that it just about holds its shape when you make a little well for your eggs.

Add the spinach and put the lid on for 2 minutes, or until the leaves have wilted, then stir well.

When you are almost ready to eat, add the lemon juice and taste the lentils, adding a little more salt and pepper if you need to.

Make four wells in the lentils, then crack an egg into each one and pop the lid back on until the egg whites are firm and the yolks are still runny – this should take about 5 minutes.

To serve, scatter the eggs with the chilli, coriander leaves and have the yoghurt on the side for everyone to help themselves.

Mustardy mushrooms on toast

Autumn on a piece of bread. This is what we eat for a quick dinner, sometimes topped with a poached egg. I am very particular about how I cook mushrooms: in a large pan with lots of space for any moisture to escape and a very high heat so the mushrooms crisp and brown around the edges. If you are making this for more than two people I would suggest cooking them in two batches.

I have been lucky enough to go on lots of mushroom-picking trips with one of my mentors and food heroes, Gennaro Contaldo; the mushrooms I tasted with him, cooked on a simple fire in the woods, are unmatched. My autumnal favourites are girolles, and porcini (or ceps) as well as black trompette and lamb's foot. Use a mixture of what you can get, even some Portobellos would work if wild ones are hard to find.

Set your griddle or grill to the highest heat possible and leave to warm up while you prepare the mushrooms. Use a pastry brush or a piece of damp kitchen paper to wipe away any dirt from the mushrooms, gently brushing the underside too. If you are lucky enough to have girolle mushrooms you can use a small knife to peel away the outer layer of the stalk to clean them. Tear the mushrooms into bite-sized pieces.

Heat your largest frying pan on a high heat and arrange the mushrooms in the pan – you don't want any oil or butter in the pan at this stage. Sprinkle a pinch of salt over the mushrooms and fry them in the dry pan for about 8 minutes, stirring regularly, until the mushrooms have reduced in size by half and any water has evaporated.

Put the bread on the griddle or under the grill to char on each side. Next, add the knob of butter to the pan and allow it to melt and sizzle. Add the garlic and thyme and stir them through the mushrooms. Continue to cook for 2 minutes, then add a splash of vinegar and the mustard and stir everything well.

Taste and take off the heat when the sharpness from the vinegar has evaporated. Serve on the charred slices of toast.

SERVES 2

200g mushrooms (see above)

2 slices of good bread

a knob of butter

1 clove of garlic, finely chopped

a couple of sprigs of thyme

a splash of cider vinegar

1 heaped teaspoon Dijon mustard

Quick squash piadinas

If you haven't come across them before, piadinas are filled Italian flatbreads. These are filled with squash, black olives, chilli and white beans, which add creaminess and substance, and I make a quick basil and tomato salsa to sit next to them. They make a perfect quick lunch or dinner with some salad on the side. They're a great way to use up a leftover bit of squash, though sweet potatoes would work just as well if those are what you have. The Parmesan is optional – I often make these without any cheese at all.

SERVES 2 AS A MEAL, 4 AS A SNACK

olive oil

¼ of a butternut squash (about 200g), peeled, seeds removed and grated

10 black olives, pitted and roughly chopped

1 red chilli, finely chopped

1 x 400g tin of white beans, drained (or 250g home-cooked, see page 461)

50g Parmesan (I use a vegetarian one; optional)

the zest and juice of 1 unwaxed lemon

4 medium piadina flatbreads or flour tortillas

FOR THE TOMATO SALSA

200g ripe vine or cherry tomatoes

a small bunch of basil

1 teaspoon balsamic vinegar

1 tablespoon extra virgin olive oil

Heat a dash of olive oil in a large frying pan over a medium heat, add the squash and season with salt and pepper. Add the olives and chilli, then cook for 8–10 minutes, until the squash has softened and lost its rawness.

Transfer to a bowl and add the beans, then gently mash everything – you still want to have some flecks of unmashed squash. Grate in the Parmesan, if using, add the lemon zest and juice, then taste and season if needed. Set aside.

Chop the tomatoes into a salsa consistency, add the basil and chop again, then transfer to a bowl, add the balsamic and olive oil and season with salt and pepper.

Warm a frying pan big enough for your flatbreads over a medium heat. Lay a flatbread flat in the pan, quickly spoon half the squash mixture over it and even it out. Put another flatbread on top and dry-fry until it is blistered and golden brown, then use a spatula to flip it over and do the same on the other side. Keep the piadina warm while you make the next one.

Serve straight from the pan with the tomato salsa and a little salad, if you are making a meal of it.

Butter bean, roast lemon and caramelised onion hummus

This really is much more than hummus. I use plump butter beans instead of chickpeas and pan-roasted lemons to bring a spike of mellow acidity, which is nicely balanced out by sweet, slow-cooked onions. I happily eat this with some cooked grains and some steamed veg on the side for a simple dinner.

Heat a medium frying pan with a little olive oil. Once hot, add the sliced onions and cook on a medium heat for 10–15 minutes until browned and beginning to crisp a little. Push to one side of the pan. Put the lemons, cut-side down, into one half of the pan. Cook for 4–5 minutes until softened, sticky and brown on the underneath, all the while stirring the onions. Transfer the onions and lemons to a bowl to cool a little.

Put the coriander seeds into the pan and toast for a few minutes until they are starting to brown and smell toasty. Scrape them into a pestle and mortar with all the goodness from the bottom of the pan and bash until quite fine.

Put the beans into a food processor with the tahini, a good pinch of salt and 1 tablespoon of extra virgin olive oil. Blitz well, until cloudy and creamy. Squeeze in the juice from all the lemon halves and scrape in some of the roasted middles, taking care to pick out any seeds. Add half the onions and pulse a couple of times – try to keep a bit of texture here.

Serve with the rest of the onions scattered on top and a drizzle more extra virgin olive oil. Serve piled on to flatbreads, with baby vegetables or next to some warm cooked grains and veg.

SERVES 4

olive oil

4 onions, finely sliced

2 unwaxed lemons, halved

1 teaspoon coriander seeds

2 x 400g tins or 1 x 660g jar of cooked butter beans, drained

1 tablespoon light tahini

a pinch of flaky sea salt

extra virgin olive oil

yoghurt flatbreads (see page 456), to serve

Roast cauliflower, mustard and Cheddar soup

This soup is based on the flavours of piccalilli, though it's mellower and less fiery than the stuff you might spoon out of a jar. It's a perky bowl of soup with a subtle kick from a bit of cider vinegar and some mellow spice. I use the brassicas that are starting to show up as the leaves begin to turn.

This is great served with cheese on toast, with a good dash of Worcestershire sauce.

Preheat your oven to 220°C/200°C fan/gas 7. Heat a little oil in a heavy-based soup-sized saucepan. Once hot, add the onion and fennel and a pinch of salt and cook for 10–15 minutes until soft and sweet.

Meanwhile, cut the cauliflower into little florets and do the same with the broccoli. Put them on a baking tray with some salt, pepper, half the cumin seeds and a good drizzle of olive oil and roast for 20–30 minutes, until crisp and golden.

Back to the onions and fennel. Once they are soft and sweet, turn the heat up a little and add the rest of the cumin seeds, the mustard seeds, turmeric and mustard powder. Allow the mustard seeds to pop as you stir the spices for a couple of minutes to toast them. Next add the apples, chillies, bay leaves, vinegar and the bread and cook for another minute, then add the vegetable stock. Bring to the boil and simmer for 15 minutes.

Ladle the soup into a high-speed blender and blitz for a minute until smooth. Taste and add more salt and pepper if you like.

Once the soup is ready and the brassicas are nicely golden and roasted, ladle the soup into bowls, top with the roasted cauliflower and broccoli and add a good grating of Cheddar.

SERVES 4

olive oil

1 onion, finely chopped

1 bulb of fennel, finely sliced

1 medium cauliflower (about 800g)

200g broccoli

1 tablespoon cumin seeds

1 tablespoon black mustard seeds

1 teaspoon ground turmeric

1 heaped teaspoon English mustard powder

2 good eating apples, grated

2 green chillies, roughly chopped

2 bay leaves

1 tablespoon cider vinegar

2 slices of good bread

1 litre hot vegetable stock

50g Cheddar, grated or crumbled, to serve

319

Smoky corn chowder

I eat this on early autumn days, when the cold starts to set in, when the jumpers come down from the loft and the fire gets lit for the first time, but there is still some papery husked sweet corn around. This is a dish that feels filling and warming while still having crunch and freshness. The first time I made it, John ate three bowls.

If you can get your hands on it, smoked water is an amazing ingredient; you can buy it from Halen Môn, the Welsh sea salt makers. It's also great in risottos and stews if you invest in a bottle.

Bring a small pan of water to the boil, add the eggs and cook for 6 minutes so the yolk is still soft but not runny. Once they are cooked, crack their shells on the work surface so they are easy to peel, then run them under cold water for a minute.

Next put a drizzle of the oil into a large heavy-based saucepan. Once it's hot, add the leek and garlic and cook for 10–12 minutes, until the leeks are soft and sweet but not browned.

Meanwhile, chop the potatoes into rough 1cm pieces. Cut the corn from its cobs; I do this by resting the base of the corn in a bowl so it catches the kernels as they are cut. Once the leeks have had their time, add the potatoes and corn to the pan with the stock and smoked water, if you are using it, then bring to a simmer and cook for 15 minutes or until the potatoes are cooked through, and their edges are almost collapsing.

Use this time to peel your eggs and cut them in half, and pick the coriander leaves from their stalks. Roughly chop the coriander leaves.

Once the potatoes are cooked, stir in the crème fraîche and lemon juice and half of the coriander and stir to warm them through, then take the pan off the heat.

Serve the chowder in bowls, with the halved egg on top and more coriander scattered over.

SERVES 4

4 organic eggs

olive oil

1 large leek, finely sliced

2 cloves of garlic, finely sliced

2 large floury potatoes, peeled

3 ears of corn

400ml vegetable stock

2 tablespoons smoked water (optional; see intro)

a large bunch of coriander

150ml crème fraîche

the juice of ½ a lemon

Simple yellow split pea soup with green olives

A comforting buttery bowl topped with a quick punch of flavour. This soup celebrates split peas, which seem to have fallen off our cooking radar somewhat, but are such good value and cook down to a satisfying yellow, creamy mess. It's simple and quick and mostly made with store-cupboard staples, topped and finished with a flurry of flavours. This is a soup that will sustain.

The protein we get from beans is not a complete protein like those found in eggs, dairy or quinoa. Pulses have only eight of the nine essential amino acids that make up protein, but the missing piece of the jigsaw can be filled with grains or sesame seeds, which contain the ninth. So eating your pulses with a little bread, or hummus made with tahini, will form a complete protein, providing more energy and nourishment.

SERVES 4–6

450g dried yellow split peas

2 tablespoons sesame seeds, toasted

1 tablespoon extra virgin olive oil, plus extra to finish

2 onions, finely chopped

the zest and juice of 2 unwaxed lemons (use the zest for topping)

FOR THE TOPPING

½ a cucumber

1 clove of garlic, finely chopped

200g Greek yoghurt

a handful of green olives, pitted and chopped

a small bunch of mint leaves, chopped

Soak the split peas in cold water overnight. This isn't essential, but will halve the cooking time.

Put the drained peas in a large saucepan and cover with cold water. Bring to a rapid boil for 10 minutes, then reduce the heat and simmer for 20–30 minutes or until tender. Drain, season, then stir through the toasted sesame seeds and set aside.

Put a large pot on a medium heat. Add the oil, onions and a large pinch of salt. Cook for 5 minutes or so, until soft. Add the cooked split peas and 350ml of cold water. Bring to a simmer for a few minutes, then remove from the heat. Ladle half the soup into a bowl and set aside. Use a stick blender to purée the rest of the soup in the pan. Stir the chunky soup back into the purée. You can thin the soup with more water (or stock) a bit at a time. Add the lemon juice. Taste and adjust the seasoning.

While the soup is cooking, prepare the toppings. Slice the cucumber lengthways, then scoop out and discard the seeds. Coarsely grate it into a bowl. Add the lemon zest and garlic, and season with a big pinch of salt.

Ladle the soup into bowls. Top each with a generous dollop of the yoghurt, a spoonful of the chopped olives, some mint, a spoonful of cucumber and a drizzle of olive oil.

Squash and pink peppercorn salad

This is a salad for bridging the gap between the warm late summer days and the abundance of autumn. I use a speed peeler to peel the squash into thin ribbons – they aren't cooked but they soften and mellow once dressed with the lime juice. The simple dressing is made with lime and pink peppercorns, with no oil, to keep it fresh.

I serve this with tofu, crisped in the frying pan with honey and soy and some steamed brown rice if I want to make a meal of it.

Peel the squash into thin ribbons with a speed peeler or mandoline. Use quite a light touch here, as you want the squash to be delicate and thin; applying too much force will give you thicker pieces.

SERVES 2 AS MAIN, 4 AS A SIDE

Place the squash in a large bowl with the lime zest, juice and some salt then toss to coat.

500g piece of butternut squash, peeled and deseeded

1 unwaxed limes

1 tablespoon pink peppercorns

½ a bunch of mint, leaves picked

Roughly bash the pink peppercorns in a pestle and mortar and add them to the bowl. Toss again to mix the peppercorns through. Next, roughly chop the mint leaves and toss them through the squash. Taste and add more salt, pepper or lime if you think it needs it.

Serve just on its own for a refreshing salad or with rice and tofu (see above) for a more substantial supper.

324

Chard, leek and walnut crostata

This forgiving tart comes together pretty quickly. The star here is the flaky walnut-spiked pastry. It sits around a centre of sweet buttery leeks, chard and some verdant green herbs. It's quite a crumbly pastry, thanks to the walnuts, but they make it so toasty and flaky it's worth it. The tart is free form, so if the pastry cracks you can pinch it back together with your finger easily — just be sure to do a final check around the outside of the pastry once it's filled to make sure all holes are pinched and no filling can escape. I serve this with some simple boiled potatoes and a lemon dressed salad.

SERVES 4–6

olive oil

2 leeks, outer leaves removed, washed and finely shredded

a bunch of chard (about 200g)

2 cloves of garlic, chopped

a pinch of dried chilli flakes

1 teaspoon fennel seeds

1 tablespoon red wine vinegar

a large mixed bunch of soft herbs, leaves picked

25g Parmesan (I use a vegetarian one)

3 medium organic eggs

FOR THE PASTRY

50g walnuts

200g white spelt flour

½ teaspoon flaky sea salt

100g very cold butter, cut into cubes

2 tablespoons ice-cold water

First, make the pastry. Put the walnuts into a food processor and blitz until you have fine, uniform crumbs, but keep an eye on it — if you go too far, they will start to come together as a nut butter. Add the flour and salt and pulse a few times to mix everything evenly.

Next, add the butter and pulse a few times until you have a rough looking dough. With the motor running, add a tablespoon of the very cold water and pulse again for four turns of the blade. Take the lid off and pinch the dough with your fingers. Add a little more water if it feels dry and keep blitzing until the dough comes together in a ball; it should be a buttery pastry and not feel crumbly. Wrap the dough in cling film or greaseproof paper and put it into the fridge.

Next, warm a frying pan over a medium heat, pour in a drizzle of olive oil and add the leeks and a pinch of salt. Fry for 5–7 minutes, until the leeks are soft and sweet.

While this is happening, wash the chard and strip the leaves from their stalks. Slice the stalks into 2cm lengths, then roll up the leaves and slice across the middle into 1cm-wide ribbons.

Back to the leeks. Add the garlic, dried chilli and fennel seeds and fry in the pan for a couple of minutes to toast the spices. When the pan is smelling aromatic, add the chard stalks and stir. Cook for 5 minutes until the stalks lose their rawness, then stir in the leaves and add the vinegar. Cook until the leaves have wilted — about 4 minutes. →

Put the vegetables on to a plate to cool and preheat your oven to 220°C/200°C fan/gas 7.

Finely chop the herbs and place them in a large mixing bowl. Grate in the Parmesan and whisk in the eggs with a fork. Season with salt and pepper.

Take the walnut pastry out of the fridge and line a large baking sheet with baking paper. Drizzle some olive oil into the centre of the paper. If your baking sheet is quite flat, you should be able to roll the pastry out to a round about 30cm across and 1cm deep. If you have a standard deep roasting tray, flip it over and place the paper on the underside instead.

Mix the cooled vegetables with the egg mixture. Arrange the vegetables in the centre of the pastry, leaving about 3cm around the edge. Gently fold the pastry border back over the vegetables, pleating a little as you go. It will be crumbly and more difficult to handle than other doughs and may break at its edges, but it will be worth it for the flaky short pastry at the end.

Place the crostata in the centre of the hot oven and bake for 35 minutes, until the edges are deep golden and the filling is starting to bubble, then turn the heat down to 200°C/180°C fan/gas 6 and bake for a further 15 minutes, until the pastry is cooked through.

Cool on the baking sheet for 10 minutes, then slide on to a wire rack to cool and let the pastry crisp up.

Turmeric and quinoa bowl with quick pickled cabbage

A meal in a bowl, this is quick enough to put together any night of the week and is bright, filling autumn eating. If you have a jar of sauerkraut in your fridge (a recipe for my favourite is on page 381), you could skip the quick pickled cabbage and use a couple of tablespoons in its place.

I love the subtle curry tones of shiso leaves, which are available in most Asian supermarkets, but if you can't get them, coriander — though a different flavour — will also work well.

Finely shred the white cabbage, then put it into a bowl with a good pinch of sea salt, the vinegar, honey, coriander, caraway seeds, ginger and green chilli. Scrunch it all together with your hands in the bowl to get the pickling process happening.

I like to start by dry-toasting my quinoa in the saucepan until it makes a popping sound — this adds a deeper, toasty flavour to the dish. Add 500ml of water, a good pinch of sea salt, the turmeric and lemon halves, and cook for about 10–15 minutes, or until all the water has been absorbed and the little curly grain has popped out. I keep the pan on the heat until all the water has gone and I can hear the popping again. Drain any excess water, then squeeze the lemon juice into the pan, reserving a little, add a little olive oil, and more salt, if needed, and a little twist of black pepper.

Meanwhile, bring a saucepan of water to the boil, lower in your eggs and boil them for 6 minutes. Drain, crack the shells and run under cold water until they are cool.

Peel and destone the avocado, slice and squeeze over a little lemon juice. Once the eggs are cool enough to handle, peel them, then roll them in the sesame seeds and cut in half — your yolks should be just set, but still soft.

Put your quinoa into a bowl, top with the pickled cabbage, avocado, egg, herbs and some more sesame seeds.

SERVES 2

FOR THE PICKLED CABBAGE

½ a small white cabbage

2 tablespoons white wine vinegar

1 teaspoon runny honey

1 teaspoon coriander seeds

a pinch of caraway seeds

a 1cm piece of ginger, peeled and finely grated

1 green chilli, finely sliced

200g quinoa (a mugful)

½ teaspoon ground turmeric or a small thumb of fresh turmeric, grated

1 lemon, cut in half

olive oil

2 organic eggs

1 ripe avocado

2 tablespoons black sesame seeds, plus more for sprinkling

a handful of shiso or coriander leaves

Figs, pistachios and labneh

This is a simple thing to make on an autumn day. Its success relies purely on the figs you use – they need to be ripe, soft and jammy, as they are the star of the show. I use fenugreek here to add some spice – the seeds have a subtle but pleasantly bitter note and taste a little like burnt sugar or maple syrup. Fenugreek is not as well used as lots of other spices but I would urge you to buy some if you don't have it already; it's a great spice to add to curries – toasted and bashed, or to sprinkle over yoghurt or hummus. It's widely used in Middle Eastern cooking, so goes very well here with figs.

To make the labneh yourself turn to the recipe on page 456. I find it incredibly satisfying to make: a little cradle of muslin with pure sheet-white yoghurt hanging, getting thicker and more delicious. If you don't want to make it, use a very thick Greek yoghurt.

If you want to make your labneh, you'll need to start the night before, following the recipe on page 456.

Toast the sesame seeds, pistachios and fenugreek in a dry pan over a medium heat until the sesame seeds are beginning to brown, the fenugreek begins to smell sugary and toasty and the pistachios are warmed and their oils have released – they won't pick up any colour. Transfer to a bowl and, once cool, bash in a pestle and mortar – not too much, just enough so the fenugreek is cracked and the pistachios have broken up a little.

Mix a pinch of salt through the labneh or yoghurt, then spoon it into the middle of a big serving plate and use the back of a spoon to spread it out a bit, creating undulating waves and ups and downs for everything to fall into.

Make a cross in the top of the figs, then tear them into halves and quarters and scatter them over the yoghurt. Scatter over the nuts, leaves and lemon zest, season with a good pinch of salt and pepper and drizzle with a slick of olive oil.

SERVES 4

200g labneh (see page 456) or thick Greek yoghurt

25g sesame seeds

50g shelled pistachios, roughly chopped

1 teaspoon fenugreek seeds

8 ripe figs

a couple of handfuls of peppery leaves (mizuna, rocket, watercress)

the zest of 1 unwaxed lemon

extra virgin olive oil

Sri Lankan squash dhal

This is often on our table in autumn. It's warming and is the sort of thing you can sit on your lap on the sofa and eat with a spoon. I roast butternut squash to pile on top, along with some crispy, minerally kale, which add a bit more interest to the usually one-textured dhal. I eat this with some roti or chapatis and yoghurt.

Here I use a Sri Lankan curry powder, one of my new obsessions. My recipe is on page 189 but you could use the same amount of a good shop-bought garam masala plus a ¼ teaspoon of ground cloves.

SERVES 6

200g red lentils

1 medium butternut squash (about 750g), peeled

coconut or rapeseed oil

3 tablespoons Sri Lankan curry powder (see note)

1 onion, finely chopped

2 cloves of garlic, finely sliced

2 green chillies, chopped (deseeded if you like)

1 cinnamon stick

1 heaped teaspoon ground turmeric or a small thumb of fresh turmeric, grated

1 x 400g tin of coconut milk

1 teaspoon vegetable stock powder or ½ a stock cube

FOR THE KALE

200g kale, leaves stripped, stalks reserved

the zest and juice of 1 unwaxed lime

TO SERVE

rotis or chapatis

plain yoghurt

Preheat the oven to 220°C/200°C fan/gas 7. Wash the lentils in cold running water until the water runs clear, then put them into a bowl of cold water to soak while you get on with everything else.

Cut the squash into rough 1cm pieces, then place on a baking tray with a little oil, salt, pepper and a teaspoon of curry powder and toss so everything is coated in the spices and oil. Cover with foil and roast in the hot oven for 20 minutes, then another 10 with the foil off.

Heat a splash of oil in a deep, lidded saucepan and, once hot, add the onion, garlic, chillies and the cinnamon stick and cook for 10 minutes, until soft and sweet. Fill and boil the kettle.

Add the rest of the curry powder with the turmeric to the pan, then take out 1 tablespoon of the mixture and keep in a bowl for later. Drain and add the lentils, the coconut milk, stock powder and 200ml of hot water and bring to the boil, then turn the heat down and simmer for 10 minutes until it has thickened and most of the water has evaporated.

Tear the kale leaves into bite-sized pieces, discard any particularly tough stalks and finely chop the rest. Heat a little oil in a frying pan over a medium heat, and add the reserved spiced onions and the kale stalks. Cook for 3–4 minutes, until the stalks soften a bit, then add the leaves and stir for a couple of minutes. Once wilted, take the pan off the heat and add the lime zest and juice and a pinch of salt.

Once the squash is cooked, take it out of the oven and stir three quarters of it through the dhal. Serve in deep bowls with the last of the squash and the kale, the chapatis and the yoghurt.

Smoky mushroom and roast kale lasagne

This is based on the delicious Vincisgrassi, a mushroom lasagne that hails from the Le Marche region in Italy. The authentic Vincisgrassi uses the smokiness of Parma ham. I didn't want to stop eating this dish, one of my most craved, when I stopped eating meat, so this is topped with some oven-roasted kale instead and an optional dash of smoked water (see page 320). If you like it you can also add truffle oil; personally I am not a fan, but I know it is well loved so I will leave that decision up to you. I use a mixture of wild mushrooms like girolles and porcini, along with some more substantial ones like chestnut or portobellos.

Vegans can make this using dried pasta sheets, which are usually made without eggs, and almond milk, a dairy-free butter and vegan Parmesan. This may sound like a lot of changes but it works well, and I make it this way for the vegans in my family often.

Cover the porcini with 200ml of boiling water. Clean your mushrooms, using a brush or damp kitchen paper to dust off any dirt, then tear or slice them into bite-sized pieces.

For the béchamel, heat the milk in a pan with the onion, bay and peppercorns until boiling. Remove from the heat and leave to infuse for 30 minutes. Strain through a fine sieve into a jug and set aside for later.

Next cook your mushrooms – you will need to do this in a couple of batches. Melt half the butter in a large frying pan over a very high heat and add a splash of olive oil. Let the pan get nice and hot, then add half the fresh mushrooms and cook, moving them around the pan, until they are browned and crisp (about 5–7 minutes). Season with a pinch of salt and remove the first batch to a large bowl. Put the pan back on the heat, add the rest of the butter and a bit more oil, and cook the rest of the mushrooms.

Once the second batch is golden, drain the porcini, keeping the soaking liquid, then roughly chop them and add them to the pan of mushrooms along with the parsley. Stir together and tip into the bowl with the rest of the mushrooms. →

SERVES 4–6

30g dried porcini

450g mushrooms (see note)

25g butter, plus more
for greasing

olive oil

2 tablespoons chopped
flat-leaf parsley

150g kale, stalks removed,
leaves torn into bite-
sized pieces

300g fresh lasagne sheets

150g Parmesan (I use a
vegetarian one), grated
plus a little extra

truffle oil (optional)

FOR THE BÉCHAMEL

1 litre whole milk or
almond milk

½ small onion

2 bay leaves

8 black peppercorns

50g butter

75g plain flour

1 tablespoon smoked water
(optional; see page 320)

Now back to your sauce. Melt the butter in a heavy-bottomed pan, add the flour and mix well, allowing it to cook for a couple of minutes so the flour loses its rawness. Take the pan off the heat and add the milk bit by bit, starting with small drops and stirring well with a balloon whisk to prevent lumps forming. Once you have mixed in all the milk, stir in the porcini soaking liquid and put the pan back on the heat. Bring to the boil, stirring constantly – the mixture will thicken. Simmer for 3 minutes, then stir in the smoked water (if using) and the parsley and mushroom mixture and heat gently. Taste and season with more salt and pepper if it's needed.

In a bowl, scrunch the kale with a tablespoon of olive oil and some salt and pepper and mix through the sauce too.

Preheat the oven to 220°C/200°C fan/gas 7. Butter an ovenproof dish (about 20 x 30cm). If you are using dried pasta sheets, boil the pasta in salted water according to the packet instructions. If you are using fresh, cook the sheets in boiling water for 2 minutes, cooking 4 squares at a time and assembling the dish as you go.

Start with a layer of pasta, then sauce, then a sprinkling of Parmesan and keep going, building up the layers until you have used all the pasta sheets, and finishing with a layer of sauce and Parmesan. Bake in the oven for 25–30 minutes, until golden brown on top and bubbling. Drizzle with truffle oil if you like, and serve with more Parmesan and some green salad.

Roast cauliflower steaks with Taleggio and pickled peppers

I have a difficult relationship with cauliflower. Despite its recent renaissance it's not something I get excited about often. But roasted to within an inch of its life, soft and buttery in the centre, I think it can be a thing of beauty. These cauliflower steaks are now the only way I want to eat cauliflower. Topped with capers, pickled red chilli, olives and some Taleggio, these steaks are elevated to the main event. When I first came up with the recipe I made it three times in one week as we all loved it so much. I eat the steaks with some lemon-dressed greens or salad and not much else. Preheating the baking tray makes sure that the steaks brown and cook evenly on both sides.

SERVES 4–6

2 large cauliflowers
    (about 800g each)

2 tablespoons olive oil

6 small pickled red chilli
    peppers (about 30g),
    roughly chopped

100g breadcrumbs

50g black olives, pitted
    and roughly chopped

4 tablespoons baby capers

a small bunch of flat-leaf
    parsley, chopped

1 unwaxed lemon

150g Taleggio cheese,
    fridge cold

TO SERVE

green salad

boiled new potatoes

Preheat your oven to 220°C/200°C fan/gas 7 and place a baking tray in the oven to heat up for 10 minutes (you may need two if your tray is small); this is so the bottom of the steaks browns nicely.

Cut the root off the bottom of the cauliflower so it sits flat on the board, then cut 1cm off all sides of the cauliflower heads. Cut the cauliflowers into 2cm-thick steaks (how many steaks you get depends on the size and shape of your cauliflowers). Season each side of the steak with salt and pepper and drizzle with the oil. Put on to the hot baking tray and place in the oven for about 20 minutes, until golden on both sides.

While the steaks are in the oven, make your topping. Roughly chop 150g of the remaining cauliflower offcuts (any left over can be blitzed up and used for the cauliflower rice on page 36) and place in a bowl with the chillies, breadcrumbs, olives, capers and parsley. Finely grate in the zest of the lemon, then coarsely grate in the cheese and mix well.

Once the cauliflower steaks have had their time in the oven, take them out and divide the topping between them. Gently press the topping down so it sticks to the steaks. Put back into the oven for 10 minutes, until the cheese is melting and golden.

Serve with a bright green salad and perhaps a few boiled new potatoes if you are hungry. Any leftovers are great chopped up and tossed through some pasta.

Pumpkin and red lentil kofte with smoky tomato sauce

SERVES 4 (MAKES ABOUT 18 LITTLE KOFTE)

550g pumpkin or butternut squash, cut into small cubes

olive oil

1 red onion, finely chopped

150g red lentils

a good pinch of dried chilli flakes

1 teaspoon ground cinnamon

the seeds from 2 cardamom pods, ground to a powder

1 teaspoon ground turmeric

1 tablespoon tomato purée

100g dried apricots (I use the unsulphured ones), roughly chopped

100g unsalted shelled pistachios, or almonds, roughly chopped

1 organic egg

olive oil

mint and parsley leaves, to serve

FOR THE SMOKY TOMATO SAUCE

2 red onions

1kg ripe vine tomatoes, halved

1 teaspoon smoked hot paprika

olive oil

1 green chilli

1 teaspoon runny honey

This is an outrageously good combination of gently spiced squash and lentil kofte and a smoky green-chilli-spiked tomato sauce. It's one of the dishes I often make when I have a mixed table of diners, some sold on eating mostly vegetables, and others still sceptical – it shouts with deliciousness.

This is quite satisfying as it is, but if you wanted something to sit beside it, some giant couscous, orzo or quinoa dressed with lemon and oil would be great.

Preheat your oven to 220°C/200°C fan/gas 7.

Put the chopped pumpkin into a baking tray, drizzle over some olive oil, season with salt and pepper and cover the tray with foil. Roast in the hot oven for 20 minutes with the foil on, then remove the foil and roast for a further 10 minutes.

For your sauce, put the onions and tomatoes into a roasting tin, add the smoked paprika and a little olive oil and season well with salt and pepper. Toss to make sure everything is coated, then roast in the hot oven for about 45 minutes, or until the tomatoes have shrivelled and lost a lot of their moisture. Fill and boil your kettle.

Meanwhile, get a large frying pan on a medium heat, add a drizzle of olive oil, the onion and cook for 10 minutes until soft and sweet.

At the same time, put the lentils into plenty of boiling water and cook for about 12 minutes until they are tender, then drain and allow to sit in the sieve to steam dry.

Once the onion in the pan is soft and sweet, add the spices and cook for a couple of minutes to toast them, then take the pan off the heat, scoop the onions into a large mixing bowl and leave to cool.

Once cool, add the tomato purée and the chopped dried fruit and nuts. Once the lentils are cool, add those too along with the egg. →

Once the squash is ready, allow it to cool a little, then use a fork to mash it up on the baking tray and scoop into the kofte mixture. Mash everything together until you have a rough mixture that will come together in a ball when you squeeze it in your hand. Season with salt and pepper and put into the fridge for 20 minutes to rest.

Line a baking tray with baking paper. Take the bowl out of the oven and shape the mixture into little golf-ball-sized rounds. You may need a bowl of warm water nearby to dip your fingers in as you go, as the kofte mixture can become sticky. Place the shaped kofte on a lined tray and put them back into the fridge for another 15 minutes to firm up.

Meanwhile, take the tomatoes out of the oven and roughly chop the chilli. Blitz the tomatoes in a food processor with the chopped chilli and taste. Add a little more salt, pepper and the teaspoon of honey if your tomatoes aren't that sweet, remembering that the dried fruit in the kofte will bring some sweetness to the dish. When you're happy, set aside until you're ready to eat.

Heat a large frying pan over a medium heat, add a drizzle of olive oil and fry the kofte in batches, gingerly rolling them over to brown and crisp on all sides for about 5–7 minutes. Meanwhile, gently warm the sauce through.

Serve the kofte with the tomato sauce, the herb leaves and a grain (see note in intro) if you are hungry.

Toasted quinoa, kale and lemon bake

This bake gets full points for wholesome ingredients: kale, quinoa and almond milk; it tastes anything but wholesome, though; it is generous and sustaining. This works best with a fresh head of kale, which I often find is more delicate, softer and more full-flavoured than the pre-chopped stuff you buy in bags, but either will work.

Vegans can use coconut oil and replace the cheese with vegan Parmesan or a teaspoon of nutritional yeast. Gluten-free flour works well here too. Leftovers can be sliced once the bake has cooled and set and quickly warmed in a pan with a little olive oil, which yields very good crispy sides.

Preheat the oven to 210°C/190°C fan/gas 6. Butter a medium ovenproof gratin dish or baking dish. Fill and boil your kettle.

Rinse the quinoa under running water, put it into a pan and toast it for a couple of minutes with no oil until it smells nutty, stirring all the time to stop it burning. Next, add a good pinch of salt and 1 litre of hot water from the kettle, bring to the boil, then simmer for 15 minutes until tender. When the quinoa is cooked, drain it in a sieve, but use a bowl underneath to catch the liquid; you will use this later.

Half fill a large saucepan with boiling water and bring back to the boil. Add a pinch of salt, then add the kale leaves – you may need to press down to immerse it all – and cook until tender; this will take about 3 minutes. Drain the kale well and blend to a purée with 4 tablespoons of its cooking water.

Melt the butter in a saucepan until bubbling, add the flour and cook for a minute or so, so it loses its raw flour flavour, then add 200ml of the quinoa cooking water and the milk. Stir or whisk over a medium heat until the sauce has thickened; this will take a few minutes. Add the spices, the lemon zest and some salt and pepper.

Add the puréed kale, lemon juice, thyme and cooked quinoa and grate in half the cheese. Pour into the greased baking dish and grate over the remaining cheese. Bake for 35 minutes, until crisp on top.

SERVES 4

200g quinoa

1kg head of kale, leaves stripped (about 400g without the stalks)

2 tablespoons butter or coconut oil, plus extra for greasing

2 tablespoons white spelt flour

170ml milk (I use unsweetened almond)

½ teaspoon ground allspice

⅛ a fresh nutmeg, grated

the zest and juice of 1 unwaxed lemon

a few sprigs of thyme, leaves picked

100g Gruyère (I use a vegetarian one)

341

Making friends with your freezer

Most evenings I like to cook something fresh from scratch. Having a pan in my hands and hearing the rock of a knife on the board is when I feel at my happiest. But, like anyone, some nights I don't have time for an hour at the stove yet still want to eat something nourishing and full of flavour. Sometimes that's a sourdough pizza from around the corner, or a quick omelette and a couple of rounds of toast, but most often when I don't feel the urge or have the time to cook I turn to my freezer.

My freezer is stacked with bags and containers of food that are ready to go. A meal can be made in the time it takes to defrost some dhal and prepare a quick shock of lime, coriander and green chilli to go on top. In the days after my son was born I was deeply smug about the few days I had spent cooking and filling my freezer. We relied on it for the first three weeks. And with him still so little it's great to know we have back-up dinners if it's been a long day. A freezer full of food for me is like insurance for your taste buds, well-being and sanity. It's also a great way to cook if you live on your own or in a couple as most recipes cater for four and it's always cheaper and easier to cook for more. Who wants to be left with half an onion?

Batch cooking

I make a big batch of a soup, stew or dhal every couple of weeks; even little falafels or polpette (see page 366) can be frozen. Every so often I'll make a big lasagne or lentil shepherd's pie and freeze half. Below is a list of recipes that you could freeze. Make the base recipe and leave off any fresh garnishes if you plan to freeze the lot. If your pans and freezer are big enough you could even double or triple the recipe.

Finishing touches

One thing I love about making a big batch for the freezer is the opportunity to use a recipe in lots of different ways. As you take each portion out you can be guided by what you feel like that day, adding final flourishes, texture and even some quickly chopped fresh elements. These will bring your once frozen dinner back to life. Here are a few ideas for freezer staples:

Soup

— Add a swirl of yoghurt mixed with a little tahini and some toasted seeds.

— Top with chopped herbs, oil and chopped toasted almonds (see page 459).

— Swirl in a good spoonful of pesto and some quick olive oil, salt and pepper croutons.

— Top with crispy kale and a grating of cheese.

Dhal

— Serve with a boiled egg, chopped toasted cashews, chilli and coriander.

— With a quick chop of coriander, mint, green chilli and lime.

— With mango chutney, crushed poppadoms and lots of mint.

— With wilted greens, yoghurt and grated cucumber and lots of lemon.

Polpette

— Have with spaghetti, chopped cherry tomatoes, oil and basil.

— Rolled into a flatbread with hummus, pickles and leaves.

— Squashed into a burger bun or good bread with avocado, gherkins, mayo and hot sauce.

— With a quick tomato sauce, quinoa, fresh herbs and lemon zest.

Vegetable stew

— Use as a base for baked eggs.

— Add some cooked chickpeas and a poached egg and top with torn basil.

— Stir in some lentils, top with some mashed veg and bake for a 'shepherds pie'.

— With creamy polenta, greens and some Parmesan (I use a vegetarian one).

Here are a list of recipes from this book most suited to batch cooking and freezing:

— Turmeric and lime-leaf broth with roasted roots (page 402)

— Squash polpette (page 366)

— Gentle potato chowder with toasted chilli oil (page 22)

— Green peppercorn and lemongrass coconut broth (page 27)

— Little pea and white bean polpette (page 43)

— Quick carrot dhal (page 46)

— Butter bean stew with kale and sticky blood oranges (page 50)

— Sri Lankan green bean and tomato curry (page 189)

— Pistachio and ricotta dumplings with peas and herbs (page 208)

— Pumpkin and red lentil kofte with smoky tomato sauce (page 338)

— Boston beans for a crowd (page 354)

— Sri Lankan squash dhal (page 332)

— Cauliflower-topped Puy lentil pie (page 422)

— Smoky mushroom and roast kale lasagne (page 333)

Extending the seasons

Autumn is an abundant time of year so as well as being a means of having ready-to-eat food, freezing is a great way of preserving without having to worry about sterilising jars and getting out the jam pan. It is also a great way to hold on to some of the things we love to eat in summer for a bit longer, the chillies and tomatoes, the blackberries and sloes of autumn. A freezer is a magical kitchen time machine.

Making the most of your freezer

— Portioning: I like to freeze things I will use in small portions in ice cube trays or silicone moulds and once frozen pop them out into a freezer bag (which I wash and reuse). This is great for baby food, herb garnishes, pestos etc.

— Maximising space: freeze anything like cooked beans or berries flat on a tray first and then tip them into a bag; that way they will freeze individually and you can use as much as you need rather than having to defrost a whole block.

Herbs

— Juice your herbs (see page 86): they can then be frozen and used in a multitude of dishes.

— Freeze woody herbs whole and use from the freezer.

— Chop leftover soft herbs and pile into ice cube trays; cover with water or olive oil and push down to submerge them.

Fruit

— Avocados: these freeze well; I mash mine with lime first and freeze in ice cube trays.

— Bananas: peel and chop bananas so that they can be broken down by a food processor or blender for smoothies.

— Berries: freeze flat on a tray first, then scoop into bags.

— Citrus: freeze the juice or slices which can be added to drinks like ice cubes.

Grains and pulses

— Make a double batch of hummus; it freezes well.

— Cook a big batch of dried beans or lentils (see page 461) and freeze in portions; they will taste so much better than tinned ones.

— Cooked grains freeze well.

Other things I keep in the freezer

— Corn tortillas from The Cool Chile company: you can cook them from frozen.

— Seeded flour tortillas.

— Good sourdough – sliced – for toast.

— Pizza dough: rolled out into bases after its first prove and frozen between greaseproof paper.

Kale and butter bean pie

Sometimes I crave crunch and texture from a pie. This one is crisp, with a buttery, rösti-like grated celeriac roof. The flavours beneath are warm and satisfying: the round sweetness of nutmeg, custardy butter beans, toasted walnuts, the minerals of kale and a sharp punch of cider vinegar. If you are after a really hearty meal, you could even serve this with some mashed potato. Use parsnips instead of swede here if you like – they will roast in the same time.

Preheat the oven to 220°C/200°C fan/gas 7. Spread the swede out on a baking tray, drizzle with olive oil, season with salt and pepper and roast for about 30 minutes, or until golden-edged and tender. Spread the walnuts on a tray and toast in the oven alongside the swede for 6 minutes, or until golden. Roughly chop and set aside.

Heat a little olive oil in a large pan and add the red onion, cook for about 10 minutes or until soft, then add the garlic and cook until it just begins to colour at the edges. Quickly add the flour and stir for a minute to cook out its rawness, then add the stock little by little, stirring after each ladleful so the sauce doesn't become lumpy.

Strip the kale leaves from the stalks, slice the stalks really finely and tear any big leaves in half. Add the kale to the pan with the vinegar, put the lid on and allow the kale to wilt for a couple of minutes. Add the butter beans and use a spoon to mash them a little. Take the pan off the heat and add the mustard, cheese, walnuts and roasted swede. Stir to combine, taste and season with salt and pepper, then pour into an ovenproof dish (about 20 x 25cm).

To make the topping, grate the celeriac using the coarse side of a box grater (you could also use a food processor to do this). Tip the celeriac into a sieve, sprinkle with salt and allow to sit for a few minutes to draw some moisture out. You can squeeze the celeriac with your hands to speed the process up a bit. Transfer the celeriac to a bowl, grate the nutmeg over, then add the thyme leaves. Give everything a quick mix with your hands, then scatter it over the pie filling. Dot the butter on top and bake for 20 minutes, or until the filling is bubbling and the topping is golden.

SERVES 4

- 1 small swede (about 500g), peeled and cut into 1cm chunks
- olive oil
- 100g walnuts
- 1 red onion, finely sliced
- 2 garlic cloves, peeled and finely sliced
- 2 heaped tablespoons flour (I use buckwheat flour)
- 300ml vegetable stock
- 200g kale
- 1 tablespoon cider vinegar
- 1 x 400g tin of butter beans, drained (or 250g home-cooked see page 461)
- 1 heaped tablespoon wholegrain mustard
- 100g Cheddar, crumbled into small pieces

FOR THE RÖSTI TOPPING

- 1 large celeriac, peeled
- ½ a whole nutmeg
- a small bunch of thyme, leaves picked
- 2 tablespoons butter or olive oil

Parsnip, butter bean and blackberry traybake

This is a tray full of all that is good about autumn: honey and mustard roast parsnips, cold-weather herbs, butter beans that char and crisp, and blackberries that burst and dye the pale parsnips a deep purple in the heat of the oven. It's a painting of a dish. I finish it off with some buttery toasted rye flakes and hazelnuts. Serve this in the tray in the middle of the table for maximum effect.

SERVES 4–6

750g parsnips, peeled

a small bunch of thyme

6 bay leaves

2 tablespoons wholegrain mustard

2 tablespoons cider vinegar

2 tablespoons runny honey

olive oil

1 x 400g tin of butter beans, drained (or 250g home-cooked, see page 461)

200g blackberries

30g butter or olive oil

50g rye flakes or rolled oats

25g hazelnuts, toasted and roughly chopped

TO SERVE

cooked greens dressed with lemon and olive oil

Preheat your oven to 200°C/180°C fan/gas 6. Cut your parsnips into halves and quarters and tumble them into your largest roasting tray. Add a good pinch of salt and pepper and most of the thyme and bay. Mix the mustard, vinegar, honey and 3 tablespoons of oil and pour half of it over the parsnips, saving the other half for later. Toss everything together to coat each parsnip well, then roast in the hot oven for 25 minutes, until the parsnips are beginning to turn golden.

Once the parsnips have had their time, take them out of the oven, add the beans and blackberries and gently turn the parsnips over to mix them in. Roast for another 20 minutes.

While this cooks, heat the butter in a frying pan with the remaining thyme and add the rye flakes, chopped hazelnuts and a good pinch of salt. Move them around in the pan until the flakes are golden and they smell buttery and toasty, then transfer to a bowl.

The bake is ready when the blackberries have burst and painted the golden parsnips, and the beans have crisped and popped out of their skins a little. Pour the rest of the mustard and honey dressing over the tray and turn everything over in it to coat each parsnip and bean. Sprinkle the rye and hazelnuts over the top and serve in the middle of the table with your greens.

Chermoula, carrot and chickpea fritters

SERVES 2

1 x 400g tin of chickpeas,
    drained (or 250g home-
    cooked, see page 461)

olive oil

2 carrots (about
    250g), peeled

1 clove of garlic, finely
    chopped

a small bunch of coriander,
    stalks and leaves
    finely chopped

1 small preserved lemon,
    skin only, finely chopped

2 teaspoons cumin seeds,
    toasted

2 teaspoons sweet smoked
    paprika

100g cottage cheese

4 tablespoons chickpea
    (gram) or plain flour

FOR THE HERB SALSA

40g currants or golden raisins

1 small preserved lemon,
    skin only, finely diced

a small bunch of flat-leaf
    parsley, leaves picked

a small bunch of coriander,
    finely chopped

3 tablespoons olive oil

2 teaspoons pomegranate
    molasses

TO SERVE

mashed avocado

green salad

These little carrot fritters make use of the much forgotten cottage cheese, the preserve of 1980s dieters, but if you buy a good one made with whole milk, it's a gentle, creamy cheese, with a welcome texture, which deserves more attention. Chermoula is a smoky chilli-spiked herb salsa from North Africa — this version uses preserved lemon — a big flavour that pitches in to elevate the grated carrot and chickpeas.

I use chickpea (gram) flour to bind my fritters, but plain flour will do just as well. For a vegan version, leave out the cottage cheese and up the chickpeas by 100g. If you don't have pomegranate molasses, a mixture of honey and balsamic vinegar works in its place.

Put the chickpeas into a blender with 2 tablespoons of olive oil and blitz until you have a rough, crumbly texture. Tip into a large mixing bowl.

Grate the carrots into the bowl, add the garlic, coriander, preserved lemon, spices, cottage cheese and flour, then mix together lightly. You don't want to over-mix the batter — there should still be flecks of cottage cheese visible. Lightly season with salt (as the preserved lemons are salty) and plenty of freshly ground black pepper.

Now for the salsa. If you are using raisins, chop them up a little. Mix all the ingredients, including the currants or chopped raisins, together in a small bowl, then taste and adjust to your liking, adding a little more pomegranate molasses if needed.

Divide the fritter mixture into 8 and use your hands to shape into small patties. Put a large non-stick frying pan on a medium heat, adding a couple of tablespoons of olive oil. Once hot, lower in the fritters and leave to cook for 3–4 minutes until golden brown on one side, then flip them over to cook the other side.

Serve the fritters with generous spoonfuls of the salsa, mashed avocado and a shock of green salad.

Chard, lentil and bay gratin

This gratin tastes greater and more indulgent than the sum of its parts; it's also very easy to throw together. It is one of the rare occasions I use double cream, but in this instance it is well worth it. The flavours are firmly rooted in Italy, though I use Cheddar to top it as I like the sharpness it adds. We eat this with some steamed broccoli or greens on the side and nothing more. I have made this using a thin cashew cream for vegans (see page 110 for the recipe).

Put the stock into a saucepan with the tomatoes and bay leaves and bring to a simmer. Cook for 10–15 minutes until the mixture has reduced by about a third, then pour in the cream and the lentils and cover to keep warm.

Cut the chard stalks from their leaves and shred the leaves into 1cm-wide ribbons, then cut the stems into 2cm lengths, keeping them separate.

Heat a shallow ovenproof pan with a lid on a medium heat, add a knob of butter or drizzle of oil and add the garlic, cook for a minute or two before adding the chard stalks, then cover and cook for 5 minutes until they have lost their rawness. Take the lid off and stir in the leaves, then take the pan off the heat.

Pour in the lentil mixture, add a good grating of nutmeg and use a spoon to turn everything over until it is well mixed. If you don't have an ovenproof pan you could transfer the mixture to a gratin dish at this point. Dot over the cheese, if you are using it, then bake in the hot oven for 25 minutes, until golden and bubbling.

SERVES 4

250ml vegetable stock

1 x 400g tin of chopped tomatoes

3 bay leaves

250ml double cream

1 x 400g tin of green Puy lentils, drained (or 250g home-cooked, see page 461)

400g chard (Swiss or rainbow)

butter or olive oil

2 cloves of garlic, finely chopped

a whole nutmeg

50g mature Cheddar, grated (optional)

Roasting tray dinners

The principle of the roasting tray dinner outlined below works well with almost anything. I follow a basic formula of one or two vegetables, a herb, an accent flavour, such as chilli or lemon, and then something hearty – a pulse or some torn-up bread. Bear in mind that you need a vegetable that softens when it cooks – such as sweet potato or courgette – to add a little stickiness and to stop things burning. If you are roasting something (such as potatoes) that won't do that, you might want to add a little stock or wine to make sure everything cooks evenly and so the flavours mingle in the best way possible.

Try this with whatever takes your fancy; here I've given a few suggestions. Use a deep, approximately A4-sized baking tray here. Bake for 30–55 minutes at 220°C/200°C fan/gas 7 until the vegetables are soft and golden. Each serves about 4.

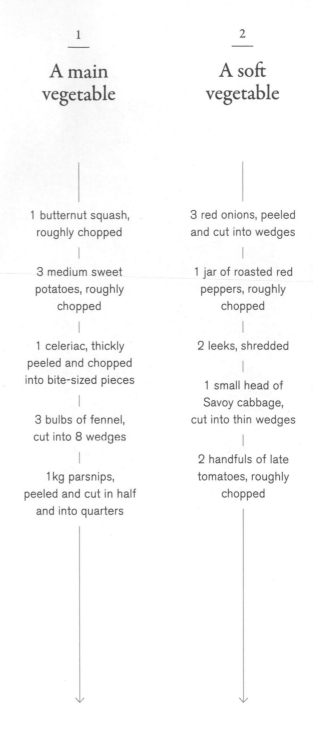

1
A main vegetable

1 butternut squash, roughly chopped

3 medium sweet potatoes, roughly chopped

1 celeriac, thickly peeled and chopped into bite-sized pieces

3 bulbs of fennel, cut into 8 wedges

1kg parsnips, peeled and cut in half and into quarters

2
A soft vegetable

3 red onions, peeled and cut into wedges

1 jar of roasted red peppers, roughly chopped

2 leeks, shredded

1 small head of Savoy cabbage, cut into thin wedges

2 handfuls of late tomatoes, roughly chopped

3	4	5	6
A hearty add-on	Liquid	A herb	A flavour boost
1 x 400g tin of butter beans, drained	100ml vegetable stock	a small bunch of any woody herb, such as thyme, rosemary, oregano, sage or bay, leaves picked	the zest of 1 lemon
1 x 400g tin of chickpeas, drained	100ml cider		a teaspoon of hot smoked paprika
1 x 200g packet of ricotta (see page 364 for method)	100ml red or white wine	a large bunch of a soft herb, mint, basil, tarragon, roughly chopped	the zest of 1 orange
1 x 200g block of feta cheese			a handful of fruit, blackberries or chopped plums or pears
2 slices of good bread, torn			a tablespoon of spice: cumin, coriander, mustard seeds

Boston beans for a crowd

I made these for Dylan's first birthday. There were about 20 of us and we put a huge pot in the middle of the table and ate them with baked potatoes and a lime-spiked red cabbage slaw (see the recipe on page 381). They seem to be popular with people of all ages and are particularly good around Bonfire Night. Indeed, you could cook them in a big cast-iron pan in the embers of the fire if that's your kind of thing. This makes a big batch of beans that will feed a crowd; leftovers can be frozen or will keep in the fridge for 4–5 days, and in my opinion the beans are best the day after they are cooked.

This is one instance where I would encourage you to cook your own beans, or to use tinned. I regularly talk about jarred beans being superior to tinned, but here they will be too soft and break down too much whilst cooking.

SERVES 8

2 red onions, peeled and halved

4 tomatoes, stalks and all

2 carrots, scrubbed

1 large leek, washed and cut into a few big pieces

2 bay leaves

1 whole chipotle chilli or 1 heaped teaspoon chipotle flakes

250g home-cooked haricot beans (see page 461), cooking water reserved, or 2 x 400g tins of haricot beans or butter beans, liquid reserved

3 tablespoons English mustard powder

4 tablespoons molasses

3 tablespoons Worcestershire sauce (I use a vegetarian one)

Put a large cast-iron pot or deep saucepan on a low heat, then add the vegetables, bay leaves and chilli to the pot, followed by the beans and their liquid. Add the mustard powder, molasses and Worcestershire sauce. Give it a good stir, using a folding rather than a mixing motion – you don't want to break up the beans.

Bring to a gentle simmer, then turn the heat down and cook uncovered on a very low heat for 1½ hours without stirring (stirring will break up the beans), until the sauce is thick and sticky. Carefully remove the onion, tomato, carrots, leek, chilli (if using a whole chilli) and bay leaves. Discard the bay leaves, then set the rest aside for a few minutes to cool slightly before spooning into a food processor and blitzing until smooth. Once smooth, stir this mixture back into the beans.

Next, add a good amount of salt to the beans, stir well and taste. Balance with a little Worcestershire sauce, molasses, mustard or salt, if needed. Serve your beans simply on toast, topped with a poached egg, on a jacket potato or with my sweet potato mash (see page 357).

Angel hair with lemon and cold-weather herbs

This pasta is as simple as they get, dressed with oil, herbs and a little garlic and lemon; it is the kind of pasta I like best. I ate this on a rare day off from the white tableclothed restaurant I worked at in a tiny village in the wilds of Tuscany. I sat and ate this in a simple trattoria in Florence, an hour's bus ride away, where there were plastic tablecloths and wine straight out of a barrel.

I still remember this as one of the best bowls of pasta I have ever eaten, and each time I have it it's like resetting my cooking clock, a reminder that simple is pretty much always best.

Bring a large pan of well-salted water to the boil; you want enough water for the pasta to really swim around in it and enough salt that the water tastes like the sea. Add the pasta and cook at a rolling boil for 4 minutes.

Meanwhile, strip the rosemary and thyme leaves from their stalks and discard the stalks.

Place a frying pan on a medium heat, add the olive oil, garlic and all the herbs and allow the oil to heat and cook the herbs gently. Be careful, you don't want the herbs to crisp, just to release their fragrance into the oil – take them off the heat before they crisp.

SERVES 4

350g angel hair pasta

4 sprigs of rosemary

4 sprigs of thyme

200ml extra virgin olive oil

2 cloves of garlic, finely sliced

12 sage leaves

2 unwaxed lemons

30g Parmesan (I use a vegetarian one), plus extra to serve

Drain your cooked pasta, keeping a mugful of the pasta water. Use tongs to scoop the pasta into the frying pan with the herbs and toss it in the oil over the heat for a minute or so, adding a little of the starchy pasta water to loosen the sauce and allow it to coat the pasta better.

Take the pan off the heat and grate in the zest of the lemons and the Parmesan. Use tongs to toss and make sure that each little angel hair is coated in the herbs, oil, cheese and zest. Taste and season with a little salt and pepper if you like, twirl on to four plates and serve with more Parmesan for grating over the top.

Sweet potato mash with coriander and chilli

This is a recipe for the most delicious sweet potato mash I can remember eating. It's not a meal in itself but it has so much flavour and depth that I find myself making it and then building meals around it, not the other way around. It's based on a recipe by one of my favourite ever cooks, Skye Gyngell.

This mash has so much going on that it can be paired with quite simple things. Try topping it with crispy halloumi, serving it with peppery greens and a poached egg or piling it into tortillas with black beans and avocados for quick tacos.

Peel the sweet potatoes and cut them roughly into 2cm cubes, then put them into a large saucepan and add the chilli. Pour in enough cold water to cover, add a good pinch of salt and bring to the boil over a medium heat.

Once they have come to the boil, lower the heat and simmer for about 15 minutes, until the potatoes are really cooked through, then drain in a colander and leave them to steam dry for 5 minutes.

Take a handful of the sweet potato and put it into the food processor. Slice the stem off the chilli, roughly chop the rest of it and add this too. Add the coriander leaves and stems, butter or coconut oil, tamari and maple syrup and blitz until very smooth. Meanwhile, mash the rest of the sweet potato with a potato masher. Mix the whizzed potato through the mash, then taste and adjust the seasoning if needs be.

MAKES ENOUGH FOR 4

1kg sweet potatoes

1 red chilli

a small bunch of coriander

50g butter or coconut oil

2 tablespoons tamari
   or soy sauce

2 tablespoons maple syrup

Chard and ricotta pasta for Dylan

Food has taken on a new meaning for me in the last couple of years. It's an everyday miracle and this is what I try to remind myself when I am inevitably reaching for a cinnamon bun or a bar of chocolate. But over the last year, when I was pregnant and beyond, the food I ate was actually helping me create another human – another total miracle.

As the son of a food writer, I imagined Dylan would be sipping spirulina smoothies by now, but that's not the case. In fact his palate is quite delicate, he's a pasta lover. What I have begun to understand even more deeply is that we each have our own journey in food, and that eating is learning. Just because I offer him food it doesn't mean he will eat it; he's surrounded by food all day long but he still wants pasta and that's okay, it's a lifelong journey and an adventure. This one is for you, my little guy.

Pull the chard leaves away from the stalks. Warm a couple of tablespoons of olive oil in a deep frying pan over a medium heat. Finely shred the chard stalks and add them to the pan with the garlic and a pinch of salt. Allow the stalks to cook like this for a couple of minutes, then grate in the zest of the lemon. Cook for a further 3 minutes, until the stalks have lost their rawness and toughness.

Put a large pan of salted water on to boil and when it's at a rolling boil, add the spaghetti and cook according to the packet instructions.

SERVES 2

150g chard

olive oil

1 clove of garlic, finely chopped

1 unwaxed lemon

200g spaghetti

100g ricotta

whole nutmeg, for grating

Back to the chard. Finely shred the leaves and add them to the pan of stalks. Spoon in a dash of pasta water (no more than about 3 tablespoons) to help the leaves steam and wilt as they cook.

Mix the ricotta with the juice of half the lemon, and season well with salt and pepper.

Drain the pasta, reserving a mugful of pasta water. Add the pasta, ricotta and reserved pasta water to the pan of chard and mix well. Finish with a good grating of nutmeg and serve in warm bowls.

Autumn bowl

I love how gentle and nurturing eating from a bowl feels. A reminder, perhaps, of childhood meals spooned from a bowl – but it's also unfussy, quick and adaptable. It requires food that's sufficiently soft to tackle without a knife. Bowl food, as I see it, is a meal that's built around a subtly flavoured grain or pulse. Food that is simultaneously soothing, bolstering, undemanding and sustaining. And it's easy to tweak favourite combinations as the seasons change.

This is my version of a bowl I ate in California. Autumn is peppered with warmer days that feel like the end of summer, and this is what I eat on those days. Filling and warming but punchy and fresh, thanks to a quick chilli sauce. This makes more than you need and will keep in the fridge for a week or so.

SERVES 2

150g brown rice (about a mugful)

1 teaspoon coconut oil

1 head of spring greens

olive oil

200g mushrooms

butter, for frying

the juice and zest of 1 unwaxed lemon

2 organic eggs

a small bunch of basil, leaves picked

FOR THE SAUCE

6 red chillies

2 jarred roasted red peppers, roughly chopped

1 clove of garlic, chopped

1 tablespoon white wine vinegar

1 tablespoon runny honey

2 teaspoons light olive oil

Preheat the oven to 200°C/180°C fan/gas 6. First, cook your brown rice – put it into a saucepan with twice its volume of cold water, a good pinch of salt and the coconut oil. Turn the heat on to high, bring to the boil and boil for 20–25 minutes. Keep an eye on it to make sure it doesn't boil dry. You can add a bit more boiling water, if needed.

Cut your head of spring greens into slim wedges (how many will depend on the size and shape of your cabbage), place on a baking tray and toss them in a little olive oil. Season the greens with salt and pepper, then put in the oven to roast for around 25 minutes.

Meanwhile, make your chilli sauce. If you like things hot, keep the seeds in; otherwise deseed the chillies. Put the chillies, red peppers and a pinch of salt into a pestle and mortar or a blender and bash or blitz until you have a coarsely-textured paste. Add the other ingredients and mix well.

Sauté the mushrooms in a large, hot pan with a little butter until starting to crisp and caramelise around the edges. Once they are cooked, season, add the juice of half the lemon and keep warm.

Fry your eggs to your liking; dress the rice with the lemon zest and juice from the other half of the lemon and a little olive oil. Add salt and pepper and pile all the elements into the bowl in the order you prefer – I like to keep things separate so I can make up each forkful as I choose – and finish with a scattering of basil.

Orzo with spiced tomato sauce and feta

This is our new weeknight staple. It's much more than it looks; the toasted spices give the tomato sauce another dimension, and while I love simple *pasta pomodoro* it's nice to have something else that's easily on hand to mix up a quick weeknight pasta. I keep all these spices at home and most of the fresh things can be bought at my (in fairness, pretty good) corner shop. Dried oregano will stand in for fresh if you don't have it.

If you are using fresh tomatoes, roughly chop them, discarding the cores. Heat a frying pan on a medium heat and add the cumin, coriander and nigella seeds. Toast for a minute or so until they release their fragrance.

Add a splash of oil to the pan, then add the onion, garlic and chilli powder and cook on a low heat for 10 minutes, until the onions are soft and sweet. Then add the tomatoes and a good pinch of salt and pepper, stir and cook for about 20 minutes until they have broken down and formed a sweet soupy tomato sauce; you can add a little water here to loosen the sauce if necessary. Pick the oregano leaves from their stems and add them to the pan. Season well with salt and pepper, remembering that you will be adding salty feta at the end.

Meanwhile cook the orzo in boiling salted water for about 10 minutes, or a couple of minutes less than the packet instructions – you'll cook the pasta for a minute or two in the sauce, so you want it to be just less than al dente. Once the orzo is ready, drain it, keeping a mugful of the pasta water.

Add the orzo to the tomato sauce and let everything cook for a minute or two, adding a little of the pasta water to loosen everything – you are looking for a gentle, thick, soup-like consistency.

Serve the pasta with lots of good olive oil (be generous here) and crumble over the feta. Eat right away.

SERVES 4

800g fresh tomatoes
or 2 x 400g tins of
chopped tomatoes

1 teaspoon cumin seeds

1 teaspoon coriander seeds

1 tablespoon nigella seeds

olive oil

1 onion, finely chopped

2 cloves of garlic, finely sliced

a pinch of chilli powder

a small bunch of oregano or
a good pinch of dried

200g orzo

good extra virgin olive
oil, to finish

200g feta cheese

Figs, ricotta, radicchio, almonds

This last year or so, since my son Dylan arrived, I've been learning a new way to cook. No more long evenings in the kitchen: for now, my cooking is sandwiched into a neat window of time before baths and stories so I've rediscovered the joy of one-tray or one-pot meals. While I love the feeling of a pan over a flame, there is something very pleasing about knowing your dinner is cooking while you sit down and do something else.

Though the method may be simple, I still want flavours and textures that excite me, as well as bringing some balance. Here figs, almonds, radicchio and plump cannellini make a complete meal.

If your ricotta is very wet, put it in a small sieve lined with muslin set over a bowl in the fridge for a few hours. You will probably get a couple of tablespoons of liquid in the bowl, which you can discard.

Preheat the oven to 220°C/200°C fan/gas 7 and get a large, lipped roasting tray. Scatter the beans into the tray, making a little space in the middle for the ricotta, then turn the cheese out into it.

Scatter the quartered figs on top of the beans. Grate the zest of the lemon all over the tray, focusing particularly on the ricotta. Sprinkle over some of the thyme leaves and dried chilli flakes and season. Drizzle a little olive oil over then roast for 45 minutes, or until the ricotta has shrunk a little and is beginning to brown, and the beans have softened and their skins crisped.

Meanwhile, make the herb oil: bash the rest of the thyme leaves until you have a deep green paste, add 4 tablespoons of olive oil, the chopped fresh chilli and season.

When your traybake has had 35 minutes, put the almonds on to a separate tray, season and roast for the last 10 minutes of the time.

Remove the traybake and the almonds from the oven, roughly chop the almonds and sprinkle over the bake with the radicchio. Drizzle over the herb oil and serve in the middle of the table for everyone to dig in.

SERVES 4

200g ricotta

1 x 400g tin or jar of cannellini beans, drained

4 figs, tough stems removed, quartered

1 unwaxed lemon

a small bunch of thyme or oregano, leaves picked

a pinch of dried chilli flakes

extra virgin olive oil

1 red chilli, finely chopped

100g almonds, skin on

1 head of radicchio, shredded

Spaghetti with squash polpette

This is my comfort food. Little polpette made from squash and fennel, speckled with lentils and light from the ricotta, tossed with spaghetti that's had the bright green kiss of some pistachio pesto.

Once rolled, the polpette freeze well and can be slowly fried from frozen in some olive oil. Here, I bake them for ease and to make their load a little lighter.

SERVES 4

350g spaghetti

a few basil leaves, to serve

FOR THE POLPETTE

olive oil

1 small fennel bulb,
    finely chopped

½ red onion, thinly sliced

1 clove of garlic, crushed

100g butternut squash,
    peeled and grated

150g cooked Puy lentils
    (about half a drained tin)

50g breadcrumbs (I use
    wholemeal)

100g ricotta cheese

the zest of 1 unwaxed lemon

25g pecorino or Parmesan
    cheese (I use a vegetarian
    one), finely grated,
    plus extra to serve

1 red chilli, chopped, or a
    pinch of dried chilli flakes

a few sprigs of parsley,
    leaves picked and
    roughly chopped

FOR THE PISTACHIO PESTO

a small handful of shelled
    pistachio nuts (about 25g)

a small bunch of basil,
    leaves picked

4 tablespoons olive oil

juice of ½ lemon

a handful of grated pecorino
    or Parmesan cheese

Put a pan over a medium heat, add a drizzle of olive oil, then the fennel and onion. Fry for 10 minutes, until soft and sweet, then add the garlic and cook for a few more minutes. Take the pan off the heat and allow to cool.

Put the fried vegetables into a mixing bowl, add the grated squash with the other polpette ingredients and mix well. Season generously and leave to sit for 20 minutes. Meanwhile, preheat the oven to 240°C/220°C fan/gas 9.

Divide the mixture into 12 and roll into little balls. Place them on a baking tray and drizzle well with olive oil, or, if you want to be precise, brush them all over for a perfectly crisp outside. Bake for 20 minutes, until they have a golden crust. You can also fry them in a little olive oil for 3–4 minutes on each side until golden brown.

While the polpette are baking, pop all the pesto ingredients into a food processor with a little salt and pepper. Add 2 tablespoons of water and blitz to a chunky paste. If you prefer a little more oil in your pesto, add some more here, but I like the freshness of it the way it is. Taste and adjust the amount of lemon, cheese and seasoning if you need to.

When the polpette have had 10 minutes in the oven, fill a large saucepan with boiling water, add salt and once at a rolling boil, add the spaghetti and cook according to the packet instructions.

Drain the spaghetti, reserving some of the cooking water. Add the pesto and mix it in well, adding a little of the reserved pasta water to loosen if needed. Put the spaghetti on to a big platter then top with the polpette, a bit more cheese and some basil leaves.

Plum, sloe gin and hazelnut cobbler

Plums and sloe gin are such a great pairing; add a crumbly hazelnut cobbler topping and you know it's going to taste pretty good, but when this came out of the oven, the plums deep magenta and the cobbler golden and puffed up, it looked and tasted even better than I had imagined. It's taken over from crumble as my go-to autumn pudding. The plums are great too just stewed with the sloe gin and eaten with yoghurt.

SERVES 4

900g plums

60ml sloe gin

the seeds from 1 vanilla pod or 1 teaspoon vanilla paste

2–4 tablespoons honey, to taste

FOR THE TOPPING

50g hazelnuts (skin on or off)

100g white spelt flour

1 teaspoon baking powder

50g raw cane sugar (rapadura, see page 293)

100g unsalted butter, chilled

a few sprigs of thyme, leaves picked

a pinch of flaky sea salt

TO SERVE

crème fraîche, yoghurt or ice cream

Preheat the oven to 240°C/220°C fan/gas 9. Cut the plums in half and remove their stones. Put the plums into a saucepan with the sloe gin and vanilla and cover with a lid. Cook over a low heat for 20–30 minutes, until the plums are soft and the liquid has thickened.

Meanwhile, make the cobbler topping. Blitz the hazelnuts in the food processor until they resemble fine breadcrumbs, then add the flour, baking powder and sugar and pulse a couple of times to combine everything. Cut the butter into cubes and add to the food processor with the thyme and salt. Blitz again until the mixture resembles rough breadcrumbs. Add a tablespoon of water and pulse again until it comes together as a firm dough.

Butter a 20cm baking dish and spoon the plums into the bottom. Drizzle over the honey and use a tablespoon to dollop the dough on top, leaving a few gaps in the topping so the juices can bubble through.

Bake in the hot oven for 15 minutes, until the cobbler topping has risen and is deep golden. Top with a few more hazelnuts if you like, and serve with crème fraîche and a swirl of honey or some ice cream.

Honey cake with lemon and coriander seeds

I would put coriander seeds in everything I made if I could get away with it. I love their clean citrus notes backed up by a heady spiced floral back note. I add them to gin and tonics, to soups and stews, to top dips and to scatter over tomato salads. In my mind they are good wherever you might think to use lemon. So here one of my favourite cakes has had a reinvention. For the picture, I poured a syrup made with the juice of ½ a lemon, half a tablespoon of honey and a tablespoon of coriander seeds over the top. It's sweet, heady and not at all savoury. Give it a try.

Preheat your oven to 190°C/170°C fan/gas 5. Grease a 24cm cake tin and line with greaseproof paper.

SERVES 8–10

200g unsalted butter, at room temperature

200g golden caster sugar

4 medium organic eggs

150g white spelt flour

the zest and juice of 2 unwaxed lemons

6 tablespoons runny honey

1 tablespoon coriander seeds, toasted and crushed to a fine powder

1½ teaspoons baking powder

150g ground almonds

First, beat the butter and sugar in a large mixing bowl until light and fluffy – you can do this in a stand mixer or with a hand-held whisk if you like. Crack in one egg, add a tablespoon of flour and beat until mixed in, then do the same with the other 3 eggs. Add the lemon zest and juice and the honey and mix.

In a bowl mix the ground coriander seeds, remaining flour, baking powder and almonds and whisk so that there are no lumps.

Mix the dry ingredients into the honey mixture until everything is combined. Spoon into the lined tin and smooth out the top. Bake in the hot oven for 50 minutes, until golden brown on top. The honey will make it brown quicker than a normal cake, so if need be cover the tin with foil to stop it browning any further. Remove from the oven and leave to cool in the tin.

Malt loaf with prunes and black tea

Malt loaf is pure nostalgia to me. I remember eating it in my grandma's flat – high up in a 1970s tower block. Inside it was perfect and spotless, well turned out like her. I'd eat this after sitting at her dressing table and putting on all her make-up, the smell of pressed powder and lipstick wafting around the bedroom. The one we ate was from the shop, spread with margarine, though this home-made one deserves some good salted butter.

Malt extract is easy enough to buy, though you may have to go to a large supermarket or wholefood shop for it. If the surface of the loaf browns more quickly than you'd like it to, cover with foil for the last few minutes of cooking. Vegans can replace the eggs with aquafaba (see page 459).

I brush the outside of the loaf with a little extra malt extract, which gives it that telltale tackiness. I then wrap it up and let it sit for a few days, as it is much better with age: the crumb softens, the fruit mellows and the shiny malty exterior soaks in. A gentle recipe, for my grandma; how I wish we could still share a slice.

MAKES A GOOD LOAF

125g prunes, pitted

125g raisins

150ml hot strong black tea

butter or oil, for greasing

150g malt extract, plus 2 tablespoons to finish

100g light muscovado sugar

125g wholemeal spelt flour

125g white spelt flour

1 teaspoon baking powder

a pinch of fine salt

2 medium organic eggs

Put the prunes and raisins into a shallow bowl, cover with the hot tea and leave to soak overnight (or as long as you can manage). Preheat the oven to 180°C/160°C fan/gas 4. Butter a deep loaf tin measuring 20 x 9cm and line it with baking paper.

Put the malt extract and muscovado sugar in a small saucepan and warm, without stirring, over a medium heat, until the sugar has dissolved, then take off the heat.

Put the flours, baking powder and salt into a large mixing bowl and use a whisk to get rid of any lumps.

Using a stick blender, purée 2 tablespoons of the soaked fruit so that you have a chunky paste. Pour the warm malt and sugar mixture into the flour, and add the fruit paste and whole fruits. Break the eggs into a small bowl, beat lightly with a fork and fold into the mixture.

Scoop the mixture – it is quite soft – into the lined loaf tin and gently smooth the surface. Bake for 50 minutes to 1 hour, until lightly springy, then remove from the oven and leave to cool in the tin. While the cake cools, brush the surface with a little more malt extract.

Blackberry, bay and honey tart

Here an easy almond and spelt pastry hugs honey-sweetened almond frangipane, a generous layer of quick blackberry compote and a scattering of blackberries. If your blackberries are particularly tart you can toss them in a little sugar or honey to sweeten.

The bay here is subtle and unlike when it cooks in stews it imparts a gentle flavour so you can be quite bold with the amount of leaves you use. Damsons would work really well here too.

SERVES 8

FOR THE PASTRY

200g light spelt flour, plus extra for dusting

a pinch of flaky sea salt

50g ground almonds

2 teaspoons runny honey

125g cold unsalted butter, cut into small pieces

1 large organic egg yolk, beaten

150g unsalted butter, at room temperature, plus extra for greasing

6 tablespoons runny honey

3 medium organic eggs

150g ground almonds

3 tablespoons plain flour (I use white spelt)

the zest of 1 unwaxed lemon

the zest of 1 unwaxed clementine

the seeds from 1 vanilla pod

350g blackberries

4–6 bay leaves

TO SERVE

4 heaped tablespoons Greek yoghurt

1 unwaxed lime

a squeeze of runny honey

You can make your pastry by hand or in a food processor. Put the flour, salt, almonds and honey into a large mixing bowl. Using your fingertips, rub the butter into the flour until the mixture looks like coarse breadcrumbs. Add the egg and gently work everything together using your hands until you have a ball of dough. Remember not to work the pastry too much at this stage or it will be chewy. Wrap the dough in cling film and pop it into the fridge to rest for at least 30 minutes.

Butter a 22cm non-stick loose-bottomed tart tin. On a lightly floured surface roll out your pastry, turning it every so often, until it's about ½cm thick. Carefully roll your pastry around the rolling pin, then unroll it carefully over the tin. Ease the pastry into the tin, making sure you push it into all the sides. Trim off any excess, then prick the base of the pastry case all over with a fork and pop it into the freezer for 30 minutes.

Preheat your oven to 200°C/180°C fan/gas 6. Get yourself a large square piece of greaseproof paper, scrunch it up, then unwrap it and use it to line your pastry case. Fill the case right up to the top with uncooked rice or ceramic baking beans, and bake blind for 10 minutes in the hot oven. Take the case out, carefully remove the rice and greaseproof paper (you can save the rice to use for blind baking another time), then return the case to the oven to cook for a further 5–10 minutes, until it's firm and almost biscuit-like. Leave to cool.

While the pastry case is cooling, make your frangipane. Mix the butter and honey until soft, then add the eggs one by one and stir well. Mix in the almonds, flour, citrus zests and vanilla and mix until you have a smooth thick paste. →

Purée half the blackberries with a stick blender and pour over the cooled tart base, then top with the frangipane. Scatter over the remaining blackberries and push them into the frangipane a little, then lay the bay leaves on top and push these in too. Bake in the oven for 30–40 minutes, until the frangipane is set and golden brown. If the edges of the pastry or the top of the tart look as if they are browning too fast you can cover them with foil.

Mix the yoghurt with the zest of the lime, a little of its juice and the honey and keep in the fridge until needed.

Allow the baked tart to cool before taking it out of the tin and removing the bay leaves. Serve just warm in generous slices, with spoonfuls of the lime yoghurt.

Maple toffee apple and pear crisp

This is everything I want in an autumn pudding. Melting orchard fruits spiked with ginger and cardamom and a topping that's half crisp and half crumble, which reminds me of oatmeal cookies eaten as a child. I eat this with thick Greek yoghurt mixed with a little honey and vanilla or, if it's really cold, good hot vanilla custard.

Preheat your oven to 200°C/180°C fan/gas 6.

Peel the apples and pears and roughly slice them. Toss them with the maple syrup in a roasting tray and cover the tray with foil. Roast for 15 minutes in the hot oven, then remove the foil and roast for a further 10 minutes until the edges catch and caramelise.

Meanwhile, roughly chop 50g of the prunes and all the figs, finely chop the ginger, and place the whole lot into the bottom of a 24cm round baking dish. Grate over the zest and add the juice of ½ the lemon, add the vanilla and spices and mix everything together. Cover the dish with a clean tea towel and leave to one side.

Make the topping by rubbing the oats, almonds, butter, sugar, flour and salt together with your fingers. It will feel wetter than a crumble topping and you'll be left with larger pieces of butter, but you should have a very rough crumbly dough after about 4 minutes. Chop the remaining prunes roughly and mix them through too.

When your apples are ready, mix them with the fruit and spices in the baking dish, then sprinkle over the topping. Bake in the oven for 25 minutes, until deep golden.

I serve mine with some Greek or coconut yogurt, whipped with a little vanilla and honey.

SERVES 4–6

3 apples

3 pears

2 tablespoons maple syrup

75g prunes

50g dried figs

2 pieces of candied ginger, finely chopped

1 unwaxed lemon

the seeds from 1 vanilla pod or 1 teaspoon vanilla paste

½ teaspoon ground cinnamon

½ teaspoon ground cardamom

FOR THE TOPPING

100g rolled oats

50g ground almonds

100g butter or coconut oil

75g light brown sugar

100g white spelt flour

a small pinch of salt

TO SERVE

Greek or coconut yoghurt, whipped with a little vanilla and honey

Flavoured spirits

Pretty much my favourite ever holiday was one spent with John on a small deserted island off the coast of north Wales only accessible by boat if the seas are on your side. We were there for a week and there was very little to do apart from watch the birds and the sea, climb the hill and jump from the rocks into the crashing waves. Every night we watched the sun set and sipped our own sloe whisky. That was the first year I made it and it's a ritual I've kept up, so we now have sloe gin, whisky and brandy for Christmas. I've begun experimenting with other flavours too. This is a rough guide but if you'd like something more exact try the Bergamot gin on page 452.

Flavours

Fruit

You can use a huge range to flavour your spirit. I like to extend the life of autumn berries and fruits; try damsons, blackberries and sloes. Rhubarb, late cherries, cranberries and blackcurrants also work well, and citrus is amazing — see page 452 for more on that.

Use 200–400g of fruit per litre of spirit depending on how strong the flavour of the fruit is.

Herbs

Adding a few sprigs of a herb will help infuse your spirit with a botanical note but go easy as they can be strong. Use 1–2 sprigs or leaves depending on how strong the herb is. I love rosemary, thyme, basil, sage and bay. Mint and elderflower work well in the early summer too.

Spices

Spice will add depth and warmth to your spirit. I prefer to use fresher-tasting spices like cardamom, vanilla and coriander but cloves, nutmeg, fresh ginger and juniper work well too. Use anything from a pinch to a heaped teaspoon depending on the potency of the spice and how spiced you want it to be.

Sweetness

I like to add some sugar to all my flavoured spirits (I do have quite a sweet tooth). How much will depend on the sweetness of the fruit I'm adding, sloes for instance need a lot of sugar — I add about 6 tablespoons to each litre bottle; less for sweeter fruits. Once it's been infusing for a couple of days, taste your spirit and if it is too tart you can always add a little extra.

Choose your spirit

White spirits such as white rum, vodka or gin are more neutral. Whisky or brandy work too but you might need to think more carefully about the flavours you add to them as it's harder to complement the deeper flavours of dark spirits; autumn fruits and spices work well. The better the quality of the spirit the nicer your finished drink will taste; you don't need to buy the very best but equally you'll taste it if you use fire water.

To make your spirit

Put your flavourings into a wide-topped bottle or kilner jar with a lid and pour over your spirit.

How long to infuse

Different flavourings will take varying amounts of time to infuse. You need to trust your taste buds here and taste every day or so until it tastes good to you. Here is a rough guide:

— Leave strong flavourings, such as chilli, vanilla and citrus for about a day.

— Woody herbs and spices need 5–7 days.

— Berries and strong-flavoured fruit can take around 3–4 weeks to fully impart their flavour.

— Milder fruits and florals will take up to a month.

When it's ready, pass it through a sieve to remove all the flavourings and then through a sieve lined with muslin to get rid of any leftover bits that might make it turn sour. The spirit will keep in a cool dark place for about a year.

To serve

Serve mixed with tonic, fruit juice or seltzer over ice with lots of citrus slices and/or cucumber. I like a tiny sloe whisky or sloe brandy around the fire on a camping trip.

Honey and tahini halva

Growing up we always had little boxes of halva at home, tucked away in a corner of the bread bin. My mum adores it; she'd buy it by the ounce from our local deli. It was one of the things I could never make my mind up about, loving the buttery sweetness of each mouthful but being slightly disarmed by the gentle but present back note of tahini. Now, I love the stuff, but I find it hard to find any that's good and not packed with glucose syrup, so I have taken to making it myself. I am definitely becoming more and more like my mum and I couldn't be happier about it.

Grease a small container, roughly 12 x 5cm, and line it with greaseproof paper.

In a heavy-bottomed saucepan, heat the honey over a medium heat and keep an eye on the pan – as soon as bubbles start to form around the sides, set your timer for 5 minutes.

Fill a small bowl with very cold water. At the end of the 5 minutes, use a clean spoon to drop a small amount of the honey (about half a teaspoon) into the bowl; do not touch it while it is hot. The honey will drop to the bottom and once it has sat there and cooled for 30 seconds or so you can test it – it should come together as a tacky ball between your fingers. If it's too soft, put the pan back on the heat but for no more than a minute, as the honey changes very quickly once hot and you don't want it to go past the tacky ball stage.

MAKES 20 SMALL PIECES

flavourless oil, for greasing
200g runny honey
150g light tahini

Set the honey aside for 3 minutes to cool, then add the tahini and beat with a wooden spoon to combine.

Pour the mixture into the lined tin and chill for at least 36 hours, then cut into small squares. It will keep in the fridge for up to a month.

Red cabbage and juniper sauerkraut

You can eat this two ways, either raw as a quick slaw, or you can leave it for a few weeks to ferment into a bright fuchsia sauerkraut.

It makes a clean-tasting autumnal slaw; but a little time and fermentation sharpens the flavours and turns it into a different offering altogether. If you want to eat it in its crunchy, slaw stage, you'll only need to add a good pinch of salt.

There are so many virtues to sauerkraut. We have been making and eating ferments – kombucha (see page 56) – for the last few years and I have to say that as well as being good to eat I do think they have had a positive overall effect on how I feel. I am not a fan of the super fermented style, so I keep my fermentation times quite short (up to one week in the summer, perhaps two in the winter) but I'll leave that up to you and your taste buds.

While there are a lot of great things about fermented foods, filling your house with wonderful smells is not one, so find a nice cool spot where this can sit and leave it be until you are ready to jar it up and put it in the fridge.

If you are planning to ferment your cabbage you will need 1–3 weeks and a large bowl, a ceramic crock or a large, deep Tupperware with a lid, a plate that fits inside the crock, a heavy weight (a jar with water in it, a heavy stone, a pestle) and a tea towel.

Put the cabbage and fennel into a large bowl as you prepare it and sprinkle with the 2 tablespoons of salt as you go, layer by layer (if you plan to eat this as a slaw, just sprinkle the whole lot with the pinch). Bash the juniper and fennel seeds in a pestle and mortar to a coarse powder. Add the apple and spices to the vegetables and massage together for a few minutes. The cabbage should start letting out water, helped along by the salt.

If you are eating this as a slaw, stop at this stage and serve. →

MAKES ABOUT 4 JARS OR SERVES 8

1kg red cabbage, finely chopped or sliced on a mandoline

800g fennel, finely chopped or sliced on a mandoline

a good pinch of flaky sea salt or 2 tablespoons fine sea salt

1 tablespoon juniper berries

1 tablespoon fennel seeds

200g crisp eating apples, grated

To ferment, pack the whole lot, including all the juices, into your crock or Tupperware and press down firmly so that it is covered by the liquid. Place a plate on top of this and use the weight to add pressure. Cover with the tea towel. You may not have much liquid at this point, but check it every few hours for the first day, removing the cloth, weight and plate and applying pressure with clean hands – this will help extract more liquid. By the end of the day you should have about a centimetre or two of liquid above the top of the cabbage. Replace the plate, weight and cloth each time. You want the natural yeasts in the atmosphere to get into the container while keeping out flies and dust. Keep in a cool, darkish part of your kitchen.

The sauerkraut will start to taste good within a few days but improves greatly by the second week. Check it every couple of days to make sure it is still submerged, pressing down if not. If a little surface growth appears, simply scrape it off – it is not a problem. When your kraut is ready, press it into sterilised jars with some of the liquid and a tight-fitting lid. Store in the fridge for up to 3 weeks.

Winter

Best of the season
- Turnips
- Jerusalem artichoke
- Savoy cabbage
- Red cabbage
- Carrots
- Beetroot
- Parsnips
- Kale
- Leeks
- Potatoes
- Celeriac
- Red cabbage
- Brussels sprouts
- Cauliflower
- Swede
- Blood oranges
- Bergamots
- Medlars
- Sloes
- Quince
- Chestnuts
- Apples
- Clementines
- Tangerines
- Pomegranate

Flowers
- Winter jasmine
- Dogwood
- Honeysuckle
- Poinsetta

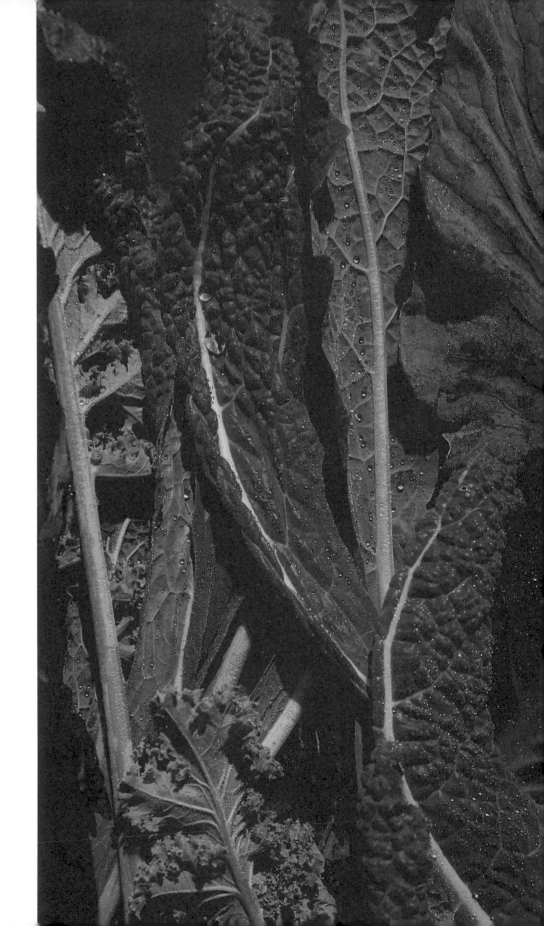

Chocolate rye porridge with quick honey pears

I have had an up-and-down relationship with porridge my whole life. The ups: its warmth on a cold day, a bowl in my hands like a morning hot-water bottle. The downside: the monotonous texture – I want each spoonful to be different and interesting. I know for some this reliable consistency is the appeal, but not for me.

For me, porridge is as much of an opportunity to get interesting flavour and texture into my day as any other. I know the traditionalists out there might be rolling their eyes, but porridge is personal. Round at mine, my winter morning staples are oats flecked with poppy seeds, cooked in almond milk with lemon zest and vanilla. Another favourite is coconut milk with pinhead oatmeal, a good pinch of cardamom and a little honey, topped with toasted coconut and ripe vanilla-scented persimmon.

This, though, seems to be my very favourite of winter breakfasts: chocolate, a malty back note from the rye flakes and a very quick honeyed pear compote. I use 50/50 rye flakes to oats, but it can be made with oats alone if that is what you have. Barley malt works well on top too, if you want an extra hit of sweetness.

_____

SERVES 2

FOR THE QUICK
   HONEY PEARS

2 pears, cored and sliced

1 tablespoon runny honey

50g rolled rye flakes

50g rolled oats

300ml unsweetened almond
   milk or cow's milk

a pinch of flaky sea salt

2 teaspoons raw cacao
   or unsweetened
   cocoa powder

a pinch of ground cinnamon

2 teaspoons runny honey

TO SERVE

2 tablespoons almond butter

a handful of chopped almonds

First, make the pear topping. Heat the pears and honey in a small pan over a medium heat for 5 minutes, or until just warmed through and beginning to soften, adding a tiny splash of water if it's looking too dry.

Meanwhile, put all the porridge ingredients into a pan with 100ml of hot water and cook for 5–8 minutes until the oats come together; add more water if it looks too thick.

Spoon the porridge into bowls and top with the pears, almond butter and almonds.

Greens, coconut sambal and mustard seed fried eggs

I most often eat this for breakfast but it would sit happily on the table at any time of day. This kind of breakfast is on every brunch menu when I go to visit my sister in LA, and is popping up more and more around where I live too. It's really simple to make at home and the gentle Indian flavours make for an enlivening start to the day. I use a few cherry tomatoes here but I know they are far from their best in winter, so if you'd prefer you could use a few tinned cherry tomatoes.

First, make the sambal. Put the chilli, garlic, tomatoes and shallots into a mortar with a big pinch of salt and the zest of the lime; bash with the pestle until you have a rough paste.

Heat a frying pan with the coconut oil and fry the paste for a few minutes until it smells really fragrant and has turned a deep red colour. Scrape out into a bowl to cool and set aside while you get on with the greens.

Tear the leaves of the greens from their stalks and roughly chop the stalks, discarding any particularly tough ones. Put the pan back on the heat, add the coconut oil, then the stalks and the chilli, and fry for a couple of minutes to soften a little.

Once the stalks have softened, add the leaves and fry, stirring regularly for 4–5 minutes, until they wilt and turn a deep green. Squeeze over the lemon juice, stir, put on two plates and keep warm, then put the pan back on the heat for the eggs.

Grate the creamed coconut into a bowl and mix through the cooled sambal paste. Add the lime juice, stir and taste to adjust the seasoning, adding more salt, lime and even a bit more chilli if needed.

To fry the eggs, melt the teaspoon of coconut oil in the pan over a medium heat and add the mustard seeds. Leave until they start to pop. Crack in the eggs and cook until the whites are completely set and the mustard seeds gather around the edges. Place the eggs on top of the greens and serve everything with a couple of charred chapatis and the sambal.

SERVES 2

FOR THE SAMBAL

1 red chilli, roughly chopped

1 clove of garlic, bashed

4 cherry tomatoes, roughly chopped

3 shallots, finely chopped

the zest and juice of 1 unwaxed lime

1 tablespoon coconut oil

50g creamed coconut

FOR THE GREENS

1 small head of cavolo nero, kale or winter greens

1 teaspoon coconut oil

1 red chilli, finely chopped

the juice of ½ a lemon

FOR THE EGGS

1 teaspoon coconut oil

1 teaspoon mustard seeds

2 organic eggs

toasted chapatis, to serve

Potato and mustard seed masala omelette

I ate this on repeat on a trip to Kerala a few years ago and it has become one of those recipes that makes its way into my kitchen so often that it feels like a good friend. It makes an amazing quick supper, without compromising on interest and flavour. In the summer I make this with tomatoes in place of the roots – most other vegetables that blend well with a bit of spice would be welcome, too. We also eat it for a weekend brunch, paired with a spoonful of avocado and a cup of coffee or milky chai. Use any cooked roots here; this is a great way to use up leftovers.

SERVES 2

1 teaspoon black
  mustard seeds

a pinch of cumin seeds

a pinch of ground turmeric

a pinch of garam masala

2 handfuls of leftover
  cooked root veg, cut
  into 1cm slices

a bunch of spring onions,
  finely chopped

a small bunch of coriander,
  stalks finely chopped,
  leaves roughly chopped

1 green chilli, finely chopped

4 organic eggs

a knob of butter

1 unwaxed lemon

Heat a non-stick pan on a medium heat and add the mustard and cumin seeds. Keep moving them around the pan until they start smelling toasty and the mustard seeds begin to pop. Next, add the turmeric and garam masala and take the pan off the heat.

Tip the spices into a bowl and add the potatoes or other roots, spring onions, coriander and chilli. Mix well, then scoop out a third of the mixture and put to one side.

Break the eggs into the bowl, add a good pinch of salt and mix everything together with a fork. You can either cook one large omelette or two small ones. Either way, heat a suitably sized non-stick frying pan over a medium heat and add the butter. Swirl it around to make sure the pan is well covered with butter, add all or half the mixture, swirling the eggs around for 30 seconds or so, then use a spatula to pull the eggs away from the side of the pan, tipping the pan to let the still-runny egg fill the gap. Leave it to set for a minute.

Slide the omelette on to a plate and top with the rest of the potato mixture. Finish with a little lemon zest and a squeeze of lemon juice.

Winter root and seaweed fritters

Fritters have become one of the things I cook the most and these are crisp and moreish as well as being packed with goodness. There are lots more fritter ideas on page 126. If seaweed is a bridge too far, you can leave it out, but it's a subtle note, not a mouthful of sea. If you are finding seaweed hard to come by, sheets of toasted nori (sushi seaweed) are usually easy to get your hands on and can be crumbled into the mixture. Clearspring is a favourite brand for seaweed.

Yuzu is a Japanese citrus fruit that adds a bright zippy note. It's hard to come by fresh in the UK but bottles of juice are now widely available. A mix of lime and clementine would work well too.

────────────────────

Start by making the sauce. Put the lemon and orange zest into a mortar with the chilli, yuzu juice and a good pinch of salt. Use the pestle to grind the mixture into a thick dipping sauce, then transfer to a bowl and set aside.

Roughly chop the pumpkin seeds then grate the root veg, using the coarse side of a box grater or the coarse grater attachment of your food processor (this will be much quicker).

Put the onion into a large mixing bowl with a big pinch of salt and the zest of the lemon. Squeeze in a few drops of juice and use your hands to scrunch the onion together until it has broken down a bit and is lightly pickled.

Next add the grated veg, seaweed, flour, chilli, ginger and the pumpkin seeds. Season the mix well with a little more salt and a good bit of black pepper, then mix in the eggs.

Pour a little oil into a heavy frying pan and spoon heaped tablespoons of the batter into the pan – you should be able to get about 16 fritters out of the mixture. Press down gently with a spatula to flatten. Cook for 2–3 minutes on each side, not moving them much, so a lovely golden crust develops. Keep the fritters warm in a low oven as you cook the next batch. Serve with the yuzukosho and some peppery leaves.

SERVES 4 (MAKES 16 LITTLE FRITTERS)

FOR THE YUZUKOSHO SAUCE

the zest of 1 unwaxed lemon

the zest of 1 unwaxed orange or mandarin

1 red chilli, finely chopped

1 tablespoon yuzu juice (see note above)

2 tablespoons pumpkin seeds, toasted

500g root vegetables, peeled

1 red onion, finely sliced

1 unwaxed lemon

2 tablespoons dried seaweed flakes (e.g. dulse, wakame)

1 tablespoon flour (I use chickpea or gram flour)

1 red chilli, finely chopped

a small thumb-sized piece of ginger, peeled and grated

4 organic or free-range eggs, lightly beaten

olive oil or coconut oil

peppery leaves, to serve

Fennel and lemon Scotch eggs with tomato chutney

MAKES 4

6 medium organic eggs

1 tablepoon sweet
   smoked paprika

olive oil

1 red onion, finely chopped

2 cloves of garlic, finely sliced

1 tablespoon fennel seeds

1 x 400g tin of butter beans,
   drained

1 small sweet potato (about
   120g), grated

50g grated cheese
   (I usually use Cheddar)

the zest of 1 unwaxed lemon

1 red chilli, finely chopped
   (or a good pinch of
   dried chilli flakes)

a small bunch of flat-leaf
   parsley, leaves picked
   and roughly chopped

100g mixed small seeds (e.g.
   sesame, sunflower)

Dijon mustard, to serve
   (optional)

mayonnaise, to serve
   (optional)

FOR THE TOMATO CHUTNEY

1 x 400g tin of chopped
   tomatoes

1 small stick of cinnamon

2 tablespoons capers

1 tablespoon red wine vinegar

My husband John loves Scotch eggs. I have to say I've always thought they were a little bit suspicious, but I've been persuaded that they do have an appeal. These are delicious. They are a great portable snack, the perfect size for lunch with a few leaves. They are also a great thing to make ahead, as they sit well and are good cold. I make these with a quick tomato chutney but a shop-bought one would work just as well.

The size of egg is important here, as the timing is based on medium ones. I use seeds to coat the eggs, which is much less fuss than the usual flour, egg and breadcrumbs. If you want a runny yolk you can deep-fry the eggs until golden on the outside, for 3–4 minutes, but I opt for oven baking to keep them a little lighter; it does give you a hard-boiled centre but that's okay by me.

First, put four of the eggs into a pan of cold water and bring to the boil. Once the water is boiling, start a timer and boil for 3 minutes. Crack the cooked eggs just to break the shell, then sit them in cold water until they are cool enough to handle. Carefully peel them, then roll them in the smoked paprika until they are covered in dusty bright red.

Preheat the oven to 200°C/180°C fan/gas 6.

Meanwhile, put a frying pan on a medium heat and add a little olive oil. Fry the onion and garlic for 5 minutes until soft and sweet, then take out half of the onion and put into a bowl with the leftover smoked paprika, the fennel seeds and a good pinch of salt and pepper.

For the chutney, put the pan with the rest of the onion back onto the heat. Add the tomatoes, cinnamon, capers and the red wine vinegar, then cook for 20 minutes until reduced and thick – a chutney consistency.

In another bowl mash the beans with a potato masher until pretty smooth. Add the sweet potato, cheese, lemon zest, chilli and parsley, along with the onion and garlic mixture, and crack in one of the remaining eggs. Mix well, season with salt and pepper and divide into four equal portions. →

In the palm of one hand, flatten one quarter of the bean mixture into an oval-shaped pattie. Pop a paprika-dusted egg into the middle of the pattie. Gently and quickly shape the mixture around the egg evenly, moulding it with your hands (almost like you're handling a hot potato), making sure the egg is snugly wrapped with no air gaps.

Crack the remaining egg into a shallow dish and beat well. Put the seeds on a plate with a good pinch of salt.

Roll the wrapped eggs in the beaten egg, then in the seeds, and place on a baking tray lined with baking paper. Repeat with the other three eggs.

Put into the hot oven for 30–40 minutes, until golden. Rest for a few minutes before eating with the cooled chutney, as well as some Dijon mustard and mayonnaise, if that's your thing.

Mini squash and chive dumplings

I make these dumplings year round but I find them especially pleasing in the winter when the party season hits, as they are the perfect thing to have with a glass of something sparkling. Or I make a batch for dinner and freeze the rest; they are a brilliant travel or plane snack as they hold up to being carried around.

These do take time to put together; I enlist a couple of helpers for the dumpling folding. The finished dumplings will be more than worth the effort and the process is social if done with friends, meditative if done on your own. They can be made ahead and frozen if you like.

You can make gyoza pastry yourself, but I always buy it. You'll find packets of fresh or frozen in most Asian supermarkets and they are readily available online and in bigger supermarkets. If you are using frozen gyoza wrappers, make sure they are defrosted before you use them: it will take 30 minutes. Cover them with a slightly damp piece of kitchen paper to stop them drying out and be gentle when pulling them apart. You will find lots of videos online, if you are struggling to work out exactly how to fold your gyozas.

To make the filling, put the chilli, garlic, ginger and spring onions into a food processor and blitz until finely chopped (or pound by hand in a pestle and mortar, if you like).

Add the cabbage and squash to the food processor, along with the sesame oil and soy sauce, and blitz again until you have a coarse paste (you can finely chop the cabbage and grate the squash if you don't have a food processor). Scrape the mixture into a bowl and mix in the chives.

To assemble the dumplings, you'll need the filling, the gyoza wrappers, a bowl of cold water and a clean tray. Take one of the wrappers from the pile and put it in the palm of your hand: you will need to do this slowly and carefully. Keep the rest of the wrappers covered with damp kitchen paper to stop them drying out. Spoon a heaped teaspoon of the filling into the middle of the wrapper – don't be tempted to overfill it or it will be hard to seal. Use your finger to dampen the edge of the wrapper with a little water. →

MAKES ABOUT 30

½ a red chilli, deseeded and roughly chopped

2 cloves of garlic, peeled

a 3cm piece of ginger, peeled and chopped

2 spring onions, trimmed and chopped

200g white cabbage, roughly chopped

200g butternut squash, peeled, deseeded and roughly chopped

1 teaspoon sesame oil

½ tablespoon soy sauce

a small bunch of chives, chopped

30 gyoza wrappers, defrosted if frozen

groundnut or vegetable oil

FOR THE DIPPING SAUCE

8 tablespoons soy sauce or tamari

8 tablespoons brown rice vinegar

4 tablespoons runny honey

2 tablespoons chilli sauce

1 tablespoon toasted sesame seeds

Fold the wrapper in half, then fold the edge into little pleats, working from one side to the other until the whole open edge is sealed. Press down firmly along the edge to seal completely. Keep going until you've used up all the filling. The dumplings can be stored in the fridge for a couple of days or in the freezer for a few months.

When you are ready to cook the dumplings, make your dipping sauce by whisking all the ingredients together in a small bowl. Fill and boil the kettle.

Pour a little oil into a non-stick frying pan (for which you have a lid) big enough to hold at least 8 dumplings and put it on a medium heat, remembering that you need to cook them in a single layer. As the pan starts to warm, put the dumplings in, with their flat bottoms in contact with the pan. Fry them until they are golden underneath. →

As soon as the bottoms are crisp, pour in hot water from the kettle to come halfway up the side of the dumplings. Turn the heat up, bring the water to the boil and cover with a lid. Once boiling, reduce the heat to medium and cook for 8 minutes.

When the dumplings are cooked, remove the lid and turn the heat up to high. The water should almost have evaporated. You now want to cook them for a final minute or so until the bottoms get nice and crisp. Serve warm with the dipping sauce.

Roasted onion and miso soup with a rarebit top

This is one of the most comforting things that I can remember cooking. The slow sweet onions and miso make a deeply-flavoured soup with just the right blend of mellow sweetness and savoury punch. The soup is good on its own but it's taken to a new level of comfort and deliciousness with a quick rarebit top. Cheese, mustard and crème fraîche (though you could use good thick Greek yoghurt too) melt on to toasted bread for a burnished golden roof, the top stays crisp and the bottom soaks up the soup, like a good dumpling. Here I cook the onions without oil, as the salt encourages them to release their liquid and cook to a pleasing butteriness.

I've not tried a vegan version but I'm guessing that swapping the cheese for a tablespoon of nutritional yeast and the crème fraîche for some non-dairy yoghurt might work well, though you'd only need to grill it for a minute or two.

SERVES 4

4 medium onions, finely sliced

1 tablespoon rapeseed oil

2 tablespoons flour (I use spelt)

a 250ml glass of white wine

1.5 litres good vegetable stock

a few sprigs of thyme

1 tablespoon dark miso

FOR THE RAREBIT TOPPING

100g Cheddar cheese

1 teaspoon wholegrain mustard

a good dash of Worcestershire sauce (I use a vegetarian one)

6 tablespoons crème fraîche

4 slices of good sourdough bread

Put the onions into a pan over a low heat and sprinkle with a generous pinch of salt. Stir and cover, leaving the pan on the heat until the onions are totally soft and have reduced in size by about half – you don't want too much colour here. You may need to add a splash of water occasionally if the onions look like they're catching. This will take about 20 minutes.

Next, add the oil and the flour and stir constantly for about 3 minutes to help the flour cook out, then add the wine and let it bubble for a minute. Add the veg stock and the thyme sprigs and cook for 1 hour, until deep, rich and golden.

Once the soup has had its time simmering, add the miso and stir through. Taste for seasoning, adding some black pepper; you shouldn't need more salt as the miso is quite salty. Remove the thyme sprigs.

Preheat your overhead grill. Mix the cheese, mustard, Worcestershire sauce and crème fraîche and spread liberally over the 4 pieces of bread. Ladle the soup into heatproof bowls, top each with a slice of the bread and put under the grill until the cheese is bubbling.

Velvet squash broth with miso and soba

A blanket of a soup for a cold day. I first made this on a bitterly cold morning, mist creeping up the garden, and every breath visible as I walked to the shop for a hand of ginger. This soup is loosely rooted in Japan – I use sake here, but white wine would work too.

The miso stirred into a paste with bashed toasted walnuts is a great addition to noodle soups, to a sandwich, and I just spoon it out of the bowl too. I use 100 per cent buckwheat soba noodles, but any soba or thin rice noodles would work.

First, heat a large pan on a medium heat and add a good drizzle of oil, then add the leeks with a pinch of salt. Cook for 10–15 minutes, until soft and sweet, adding a little water if they stick.

Next, peel the butternut squash (I do this for a really velvety soup but you can leave the skin on, it just might not be quite as smooth) and cut into small pieces (about 2cm). Once the leeks are cooked, add the sesame seeds and ginger to the pan, turn up the heat and cook until the sesame seeds are starting to brown and toast.

Now add the squash, sake or wine, and stock and allow to simmer for about 20–25 minutes or until the squash is well cooked through. Squeeze in the juice of the lime. Blend the soup until velvety smooth, then put it back in the pan.

While the soup is cooking, toast the walnuts in a dry pan over a low heat, then bash them in a pestle and mortar until they look like rough breadcrumbs and mix with the miso, honey, tamari and vinegar.

Cook the soba noodles according to their instructions, refresh them under cold water until cold, then leave them to one side.

Taste the soup and add more salt and lime if it needs it, remembering it is quite neutral and flavour will be added by the walnut miso.

To serve, put the noodles into four deep bowls and ladle over the broth. Finish with a spoonful of the miso, and some sesame seeds and herbs if you want.

SERVES 4

groundnut or rapeseed oil

2 leeks, trimmed and shredded

1 butternut squash (about 800g)

2 tablespoons sesame seeds

a small piece of ginger, peeled and chopped

200ml sake or white wine

1.5 litres good veg stock

1 lime

100g walnuts

2 tablespoons white miso

2 tablespoons runny honey

1 tablespoon tamari or soy sauce

a tablespoon of rice wine vinegar

300g soba noodles

TO SERVE

toasted sesame seeds

Asian herbs (I use coriander and shiso)

Turmeric and lime leaf broth with roasted roots

A combination of lifting aromatics and wintry earthy roots, roasted until crisp around the edges and sweet. A broth for cold days and especially good if you are feeling the chill of the day or need some perking up from feeling under the weather. You could use whatever roots you have to hand; potatoes and beetroots work well too, but I like the flavour of the sweeter roots against the heady turmeric and lime leaves. I particularly love using swede here; it's an underrated root that should, in my opinion, be used as much as in-vogue sweet potatoes or the ever-present parsnip.

Preheat the oven to 220°C/200°C fan/gas 7.

Place the chopped roots on a baking tray with a big pinch of salt and a tablespoon of coconut oil. Put into the oven and remove after 5 minutes to toss everything in the oil. Return to the oven for about 35 minutes until everything is golden, tossing from time to time.

Grate the ginger and turmeric, pick the coriander leaves from the stalks, roughly chop the stalks and set the leaves aside.

Put another tablespoon of oil into a small saucepan, add half the shallots and cook for about 5 minutes over a medium heat until beginning to brown. Next add the coriander stalks, garlic, coriander seeds, red chilli, turmeric and ginger and cook for a few minutes before adding the coconut milk and lime leaves. Fill the emptied coconut milk tin with water and pour it into the pan. Season well with salt and pepper and simmer for 10 minutes.

Meanwhile, heat a pan over a high heat with another tablespoon of coconut oil and once it's melted and really hot, add the remaining shallots and cook until crisp and golden, taking care not to let them get too dark – there is a sweet spot when they are just brown but they will darken quickly, so be ready to scoop them out with a slotted spoon, then drain on kitchen paper to keep their crispness.

Once the roots are ready, spoon the cooked quinoa or rice into four bowls, top with the roots, ladle over the soup and top with the coriander leaves and crispy shallots. Serve with the lime or lemon wedges.

SERVES 4

8 small carrots (200g), halved if big

4 small parsnips (350g), quartered or halved

1 small swede (500g), peeled and roughly chopped

coconut oil

a small thumb-sized piece of ginger, peeled

a small thumb-sized piece of turmeric, peeled

a bunch of coriander

2 banana shallots, finely sliced

1 clove of garlic, finely sliced

1 tablespoon coriander seeds, bashed

1 red chilli, finely chopped

1 x 400g tin of coconut milk

4 lime leaves

TO SERVE

200g cooked quinoa or wild rice (about 75g uncooked)

1 lemon or lime, cut into wedges

Kale and Brussels sprouts Caesar slaw

This is a staple winter salad, fresh but generous in flavour all at once. The dressing is based on the rich flavours of a Caesar salad dressing but using soaked nuts and seeds as a base, which adds creaminess without adding too much oil and is a filling addition to the salad. I am sure a few more toasted seeds or nuts scattered over the top would be good.

You can use pretty much any winter greens or cabbage, but be sure to shred them quite thinly. The cheese can be left out or swapped for whatever you have (any blue or hard cheese) and any soft herbs you have (a mixture of a couple works best).

The slaw is better after sitting for a couple of hours, as the dressing softens the greens a little, and the flavours will come together. Seed and nut butters work instead of the soaked seeds and nuts if that's easier, but choose a gentle, ideally untoasted one. This is a great way to use up leftover Christmas greens and cheese.

SERVES 6–8

FOR THE DRESSING

50g sunflower seeds

50g nuts (I use blanched almonds)

1 clove of garlic, peeled

1 tablespoon Dijon mustard

the juice of ½ a lemon

about 400g greens, stalks removed

350g raw Brussels sprouts

a small bunch of soft herbs

about 150g blue cheese or hard cheese (optional)

First, soak your seeds and nuts for the dressing in cold water: 15 minutes will do, but you could leave them as long as overnight – this helps the dressing become creamier.

Once soaked, drain the seeds and nuts and put them into a blender (a high-speed blender works best here) with all the other dressing ingredients, then blend until smooth. Add 200ml of water and blend again to a creamy dressing (how long you need to blitz it for will depend on the speed of your blender). Keep in the fridge until you are ready to dress the salad.

Slice the greens and sprouts as finely as you can, then put them all into a big bowl. Roughly chop the herbs and add these to the bowl, then pour over the dressing and mix well. I do this with clean hands to make sure that the dressing coats every little bit of green. When you are ready to serve, crumble over some leftover cheese, if using.

Miso roast squash and potatoes with almonds and kale

A centrepiece of a dish; squash, potatoes and greens cooked together in one tray. The harissa, miso and lemon combo is a great foil for some of the richer dishes which show up at this time of year. I eat this on its own; sometimes we cut some tofu into little pieces and add it to the tray, tossing it in the dressing for the last 10 minutes of cooking too.

I have served this on Christmas Day for the last few years; the ease of cooking vegetables together helps with time and oven space.

Preheat the oven to 220°C/200°C fan/gas 7.

Cut the potatoes into halves or quarters no larger than your thumb. Cut the squash in half lengthways (no need to peel), use a spoon to scoop out the seeds, then cut it into 2cm slices.

SERVES 8

500g small waxy potatoes, scrubbed clean,

700g butternut or other squash

4 tablespoons olive oil

3 tablespoons white miso

2 tablespoons harissa

the juice of 1 lemon

100g kale, stalks removed, leaves shredded

100g almonds, skin on, toasted

In a small bowl mix together the olive oil, miso, harissa and lemon juice.

Put the potatoes and squash on to a baking tray with half the harissa mixture. Toss well, using your hands, to make sure everything is coated. Roast for 40–45 minutes until everything is cooked through and browning at the edges. Turn everything once or twice to make sure it browns evenly, and keep a close eye on it as it can burn in a flash.

Add the shredded kale and roast for a final 10 minutes. It should crisp up a little. Transfer to a serving dish, spoon over the remaining dressing and scatter with the toasted almonds.

Homemade curry pastes

	Malaysian rendang	Lemon and harissa tagine
Spices	a few gratings of nutmeg the seeds from 3 cardamom pods 1 small cinnamon stick white peppercorns	1 tablespoon coriander seeds a small cinnamon stick a good pinch of saffron threads
Aromatics	4 lime leaves or the zest of 1 unwaxed lime 2 shallots, roughly chopped 2 stalks of lemongrass, bashed and roughly chopped a thumb-sized piece of ginger, peeled	4 preserved lemons, flesh discarded, pith finely sliced 2 small red onions and 4 cloves of garlic, roughly chopped and cooked until soft and sweet
Base	1 × 400ml tin of coconut milk	1 × 400g tin of chopped tomatoes
Chilli	4 dried red chillies, soaked in warm water to soften	2 tablespoons harissa
Oil	1 tablespoon groundnut oil	1 tablespoon olive oil
Top note	a small bunch of coriander	a small bunch of mint

South Indian curry leaf	Smoky Thai massaman	Method
		1
a small handful of curry leaves	½ teaspoon cloves	Toast the spices (for smoky Thai massaman, toast the aromatics too).
1 tablespoon mustard seeds	2 tablespoons cumin seeds	
1 tablespoon cumin seeds	1 teaspoon coriander seeds	
1 teaspoon coriander seeds	a small cinnamon stick	
a thumb-sized piece of ginger	3 shallots, roughly chopped	
2 cloves of garlic, peeled	5 cloves of garlic, peeled	
a 2cm piece of turmeric (or ½ teaspoon dried)	2 stalks of lemongrass, bashed and roughly chopped	
	a thumb-sized piece of ginger, peeled	**2**
1 × 200g block of creamed coconut	1 × 400ml tin of coconut milk	Blend the spices and aromatics to a paste.
	2 tablespoons tamarind paste	
2 fresh green chillies	5 dried red chillies	
2 tablespoons coconut oil	2 tablespoons groundnut oil	
		3
a small bunch of coriander	1 tablespoon runny honey	Add the base, chilli, oil and top note to the mixture and blend again to form a loose paste.

Party bao with sweet potato and pickled cucumber

MAKES 20

FOR THE BAO

120g unsalted butter

2 x 7g sachets of dried yeast

1kg strong white bread flour, plus extra for rolling

1 teaspoon baking powder

¾ teaspoon bicarbonate of soda

2 tablespoons flaky sea salt

olive oil

FOR THE FILLING

1.5kg sweet potatoes, sliced lengthways and chopped into 2cm slices

4 tablespoons tamari or dark soy sauce

2 tablespoons runny honey

2 tablespoons finely grated ginger

1 tablespoon five-spice powder

2 good pinches of chilli flakes

6 tablespoons toasted sesame oil

1 large cucumber

2 tablespoons mirin

1 tablespoon honey or maple syrup

3 tablespoons rice wine vinegar

a pinch of freshly ground white pepper →

I love bao. If you've not come across them, they are light but pleasingly chewy little steamed buns stuffed with flavourful fillings. Not so long ago, while I was pregnant, I got into a habit of buying them and every Saturday, without fail, I walked to the little bao stand at Broadway Market, a short stroll from my house, to get one of their daikon bao. There is something so pleasing about the cloud-like little dumplings, always packed with flavourful stuffings and piquant lime and chilli.

These are a bit of an undertaking. I tend to make them when I am having a few people round. I think they suit being eaten with a drink. As a snack I'd suggest two; three to make a meal of them. I double this for a party. Leftover buns make a great vehicle for some scrambled egg the next morning too, with the leftover sauce and some spring onions and chilli — an idea stolen from my lovely friend Georgie.

This recipe makes 20 bao, perfect for a party. You can easily halve the recipe if you're just cooking for a few friends.

You can make the bao a day in advance (re-steaming them before serving).

Melt the butter in a saucepan over a low heat. Put the yeast into a large bowl with 450ml of warm water and leave for a few minutes until tiny bubbles begin to form.

Now mix in the flour, baking powder, bicarbonate of soda, sea salt and the melted butter until it all comes together, then knead for 10 minutes to a silky dough. Place in an oiled bowl, cover and leave in a warm place to prove for a couple of hours.

Once the dough has doubled in size, knock it back by kneading it for a few seconds on a floured surface. Split it in half, then, using your hands, roll each half into equal-sized logs.

Cut each log into 20 small, equal pieces (I find it easiest to cut each into 4, then cut those smaller pieces into 5). Roll each piece of dough into a ball and place on baking sheets lined with greaseproof paper. Cover and leave to prove again for 30–45 minutes. →

Knock each risen bun back with the palm of your hand, then, using a rolling pin, roll into oval shapes about 12cm long and 9cm wide. Coat a chopstick with a little oil, place it across the width of each bun and fold the dough over, then gently remove the chopstick.

Set a large steamer (preferably with two tiers) over a medium heat, and get the water boiling. Place a layer of baking parchment in each steamer basket, then arrange the buns on top, spaced at least 3cm apart, then leave them to steam, not too fiercely, for 10–12 minutes until they have puffed up and are light and fluffy and cooked through. Leave to cool, then cover and chill overnight if you are preparing them in advance. You could make them even further in advance and freeze them until needed.

Preheat the oven to 240°C/220°C fan/gas 9.

FOR THE DIPPING SAUCE

3 tablespoons white miso

3 tablespoons runny honey

1 tablespoon brown rice vinegar

1 green chilli, finely chopped

a large piece of ginger

TO FINISH

a bunch of spring onions, finely sliced

a large handful of coriander, leaves picked

250g salted roasted cashews, crushed

For the filling, toss the sweet potatoes into a roasting tin with the tamari, honey, ginger, five-spice, half the chilli flakes and 4 tablespoons of the sesame oil. Roast for 20–30 minutes, turning halfway, until glazed and soft.

Shred or slice the cucumber into a bowl with the other pinch of chilli flakes, the mirin, honey, rice vinegar, white pepper and the remaining sesame oil. Toss to coat and set aside for 10 minutes before eating, or chill for up to 5 days.

Make the dipping sauce by whisking all the ingredients together until you have a thick, rich sauce.

Split the buns open and fill with the roasted sweet potato, drained cucumber, spring onions, coriander and lots of crushed cashews for texture.

Creamy polenta with radicchio and charred mushrooms

The earthiness of the mushrooms and bitter notes of the radicchio make this recipe the perfect thing to eat with naturally sweet polenta.

Fill and boil the kettle. Cut the radicchio or chicory into quarters, then put the pieces into a large, shallow dish. Chop or tear your mushrooms in half and add them to the dish.

In a small bowl, combine the red wine vinegar, garlic, marjoram, olive oil and a big pinch of salt. Mix well, then pour over the radicchio and mushrooms and leave to marinate for at least 40 minutes.

Get on with your polenta. Pour 1 litre of boiling water from the kettle into a large pan over a medium heat. Slowly add the polenta in a steady stream, whisking as you go. Cook for 5 minutes or until the polenta thickens a little, then turn the heat down and simmer for 10 minutes, until cooked, stirring frequently (at least every 5 minutes) to make sure that it doesn't stick or go lumpy. The polenta is cooked when it has lost its grainy texture and feels smooth.

Add the butter and Parmesan to the cooked polenta, then season to taste with salt and black pepper. Set aside until the mushrooms have had their marinating time.

Heat a griddle over a medium heat. Remove the mushrooms and radicchio from the marinade, allowing any excess to drip off back into the shallow dish. Reserve the marinade.

Griddle the mushrooms and radicchio until they have become charred and soft throughout – about 3–4 minutes on each side. Once cooked, chop them very roughly and put them back into the marinade. Meanwhile, gently heat the polenta over a low heat to warm it through.

When everything is ready, ladle the polenta into bowls and top with the radicchio and mushrooms, another grating of Parmesan and a small pile of watercress.

SERVES 4

2 heads of radicchio or 4 of chicory

6 large portobello mushrooms

4 tablespoons red wine vinegar

4 cloves of garlic, finely sliced

a small bunch of marjoram or oregano, leaves picked

6 tablespoons olive oil

FOR THE POLENTA

150g (about a mugful) of polenta or cornmeal

25g good butter

50–75g freshly grated Parmesan, plus extra to serve

a big handful of watercress

413

Roast celeriac, fennel, clementine and almond aïoli

I made this on a bleak winter's day, a wash of grey with little going for it other than that it encouraged me to stay inside, light a fire and cook. I decided to use the celeriac that had arrived in our veg bag that week, but I wanted something filling and warming and bright too. I decided to fry the celeriac in butter until it was just brown, adding a deep caramel toastiness to the gentle veg. I did the same with a couple of heads of fennel and then boosted its freshness with some charred clementine. It was all topped off with an easy almond aïoli.

You could make a traditional aïoli if you like, but this one, made with deeply toasted almonds, backs up the brown butter. It is best made in a good high-speed blender — that way it will be super creamy and smooth; a little texture won't be the end of the world, though. I make a larger quantity than I need, as it will keep in the fridge for up to a week. I use it for sandwiches or as a dip, but if you'd prefer to keep a tight ship you can halve the ingredients.

I serve this with some spelt or quinoa and a peppery salad, dressed with a little clementine juice and good olive oil with a generous grating of black pepper.

SERVES 4

1 celeriac (about 600g)

butter or olive oil

2 heads of fennel, cut into 1cm wedges

2 clementines, peel on and cut in half

a good pinch of dried chilli flakes

the zest of 1 unwaxed lemon

flaky sea salt and freshly ground black pepper

FOR THE ALMOND AÏOLI

150g blanched almonds

1 lemon

60ml extra virgin olive oil

1 teaspoon Dijon mustard

1 small clove of garlic

Start by soaking 100g of the almonds for the aïoli in 125ml of cold water. Preheat the oven to 220°C/200°C fan/gas 7.

Thickly peel the celeriac with a knife, then cut it into irregular medium pieces about the size of a 50p coin.

Meanwhile, make the aïoli. Put the remaining 50g of almonds on to a baking tray and toast in the oven for 8 minutes. You want them to be deeply toasted and dark golden but in a matter of minutes they can go from well toasted to burned, so keep an eye on them. Once toasted, tip into a bowl and leave to cool.

Drain the soaked almonds and put them into a high-speed blender with 125ml of fresh cold water, the juice of half the lemon, the oil and mustard. Blitz on a high speed until you have a very smooth mayonnaise-like paste. Add the garlic and toasted nuts and blitz in the blender until it's smooth again. Season with salt and pepper and taste, adding a little more lemon, oil or salt if needed. →

Heat a large frying pan on a medium heat and add a good knob of butter and the celeriac. Season well and cook until browned all over, then scoop the celeriac on to a baking tray and put the pan back on the heat.

Add the fennel wedges and cook in the same manner until well browned – you may need to add some more butter as you go if anything looks like it's sticking – then add the clementines, cut-side down, and cook for 5 minutes until charred. Transfer the clementines and the fennel to the tray, and sprinkle with the dried chilli and lemon zest. Roast in the oven for 10 minutes until cooked through and charring at the edges.

Once all the veg is cooked, carefully peel the clementines from their peel, scatter over the tray, then serve the lot with generous spoonfuls of the aïoli.

Golden saffron mash with winter greens and poached eggs

This is as sunny as winter food gets. Cloud-like, buttery mash with the warm glow of saffron in the background. I top this with a poached egg, which bathes the mash thanks to its runny yolk. Greens add some minerally depth and toasted almonds some crunch. This feels sophisticated, thanks to the saffron, but it's an easy dinner and as soothing as a meal can be.

In a large saucepan, cover the potatoes with cold water, add a pinch of salt and bring to the boil over a medium heat. Allow to bubble away for 20–30 minutes, until the potatoes are tender.

Meanwhile, melt the butter in a frying pan over a medium–low heat and when it starts to bubble add half the garlic, the soaked saffron and its water. Allow to cook for 1–2 minutes until the garlic starts to look golden. Take off the heat.

Once the potatoes are ready, drain them, then return to the saucepan. Mash well, then add the saffron butter and mash again. Taste and season with salt and pepper.

De-stalk the cavolo nero, then chop the stalks into 1cm pieces and roughly tear the leaves. In the frying pan you used for the garlic and saffron butter, heat a glug of olive oil and add the remaining garlic. Allow the garlic to cook in the oil for a minute, then add the chopped cavolo nero stalks and the nutmeg. Cook over a medium heat for 3–4 minutes until the stalks start to soften.

Half-fill a large saucepan with boiling water, add 2 tablespoons of vinegar, then bring to a simmer. Break each egg into a cup and drop it gently into the simmering water. Set a timer for 3 minutes.

While the eggs are poaching, add the cavolo nero leaves to the stalks in the frying pan and sauté with the remaining tablespoon of cider vinegar. Add a pinch of salt and stir until the leaves wilt.

Carefully lift the eggs out of the water with a slotted spoon and drain on kitchen paper. Spoon the mash onto warm plates, top with the eggs, sprinkle over the almonds and serve the greens on the side.

SERVES 4

1kg floury potatoes, peeled and cut into even-sized chunks

50g butter

2 cloves of garlic, finely chopped

2 pinches of saffron, soaked in 250ml boiling water

300g cavolo nero, kale or spinach

olive oil

¼ teaspoon grated nutmeg

3 tablespoons cider vinegar

4 organic eggs, at room temperature

100g almonds, skin on, toasted

Whole roast squash

Roast squash is something that I have returned to after a few years of avoiding it. Along with the other vegetarian stalwarts of mushroom risotto and stuffed peppers, there was a time when roast squash was the offering of choice and it got a bit boring. This recipe has me welcoming roast squash back with open arms, thanks to two things: firstly its very British flavours – there's not a pomegranate in sight; and secondly how it's cooked. I roast the squash until it's completely cooked before stuffing it, making sure that it is crisp inside and out and the filling is well seasoned and light.

This is a wonderful way to use some of the more unusual varieties of squash. I use onion and kabocha squash here, filled with plump grains and sweet roast fennel, some good sharp Cheddar, and topped with toasted buttery oats. A butternut would work too, though you won't get quite as much of a hollow for stuffing. If you are using a butternut, cut it in half lengthways before roasting to make it easier to fill. Most squashes will roast in roughly the same time, with the exception of the thick-walled pumpkins; I'd avoid those.

SERVES 4

a mixture of round whole squashes, about 750g squash per person

4 bulbs of fennel

1 bulb of garlic

olive oil

250g freekeh or pearl barley

125g sharp Cheddar or other cheese

the zest of 1 unwaxed lemon

a bunch of fennel tops or dill

1 red chilli, deseeded if you like

a knob of butter

50g rolled oats or barley flakes

1 teaspoon fennel seeds

Preheat the oven to 200°C/180°C fan/gas 6.

Use a big, heavy knife to cut off the base of each squash, so they sit upright on a tray. Cleanly cut about 3–4cm off the top of each one in a single piece (you are going to put the tops back on). Use a metal spoon to scoop out the seeds and the fibres until you have a neat hollow.

Trim the fennel, removing any tough outer leaves, then cut the bulbs into a few big wedges.

Put the squash into a large roasting tray or two. Scatter the fennel wedges around and put the bulb of garlic in too. Drizzle the lot with olive oil, making sure you get inside the squash, and season with salt and pepper. Pop the tops back on the squash. Roast for 45–60 minutes, or until the squash are tender and the fennel has started to soften and brown. If your squash take a little longer, you can remove the fennel once it's nicely soft and brown, as you don't want it to overcook. →

Meanwhile, put the freekeh or pearl barley in a medium pan and cover with cold water. Add a big pinch of salt, then bring to the boil and simmer until al dente (about 12 minutes for freekeh and 25 minutes for pearl barley). Drain and transfer to a large bowl.

Remove the garlic and fennel from the roasting dish. When cool enough to handle, squeeze the roasted garlic from its papery skins into the freekeh. Roughly chop the fennel and add it to the bowl along with the cheese, lemon zest and some salt and pepper. Chop the fennel tops and chilli and add these too. Taste the mixture and adjust the seasoning, if you like. Divide the mixture between the squash and return them to the oven for 10 minutes.

Meanwhile, heat the butter in a small pan, and add the oats, fennel seeds and a little salt and pepper. Stir to coat in the butter, then toast the flakes until golden (this will take about 5 minutes). Drain on a plate lined with kitchen paper.

Once the squash and freekeh are out of the oven, take the tops off the squash and sprinkle over the toasted oats. Place in the middle of the table for everyone to dig in.

Baked celeriac macaroni with a crispy olive top

This is a take on a classic mac and cheese, but the sauce comes from some sweet roasted celeriac and plump butter beans. It's lighter and way less cloying than a straight-up mac and cheese, but still creamy, satisfying and full of flavour. I top it off with some cavolo nero (or kale), a few walnuts and black olives, which crisps to form a colourful textured crown that elevates this to another level. I add a little Parmesan to the sauce, but nutritional yeast works really well here if you'd prefer to keep it completely free of cheese.

Preheat the oven to 220°C/200°C fan/gas 7.

Thickly peel and cube the celeriac and place it on a baking tray along with the garlic, a little olive oil and a pinch of salt. Toss everything together, then roast for 20 minutes, until blistered and tender. Turn the oven down to 200°C/180°C fan/gas 6.

Transfer the roasted celeriac and garlic to a food processor with all the remaining ingredients except for the milk and pasta and blitz until you have a completely smooth, thick sauce. With the motor running, add the milk until you have a smooth and creamy sauce – the consistency of a thick béchamel – adding a little more if you need to.

Put a large pot of water on to boil with plenty of salt. Once boiling, cook the pasta for 4 minutes less than the packet instructions. Drain and return to the pot, drizzle with a little olive oil and toss to coat.

Next pour the celeriac sauce over the pasta bit by bit and keep stirring so that it folds into all the tubes. You should be able to use up all the sauce, but if you have any left over it will keep in the fridge for up to 3 days.

Transfer the pasta to an ovenproof pan or baking dish. Tumble the topping ingredients into a bowl and toss so that everything is mixed evenly, then scatter over the top of the creamy pasta. Bake for about 20–25 minutes until the pasta and sauce are warmed through, the kale is crispy and the olives blistering.

SERVES 6

- 1 celeriac (about 600g)
- 3 cloves of garlic, peeled
- 1 tablespoon olive oil
- 1 x 400g tin of butter beans, drained (or 250g home-cooked, see page 461)
- 50g freshly grated Parmesan or nutritional yeast
- 1 teaspoon wholegrain mustard
- a good pinch of cayenne pepper
- 2 tablespoons olive oil
- 1 teaspoon cider vinegar
- 400ml milk, or as needed
- 350g wholewheat macaroni or rigatoni

FOR THE TOPPING

- 250g cavolo nero or kale, leaves stripped and roughly torn
- 75g walnuts, roughly chopped
- 100g pitted black olives, such as Kalamata
- 25g grated Parmesan

Cauliflower-topped Puy lentil pie

I made this pie after a bracing walk on a wintry Welsh beach, a long stretch of sand lined with pines on one side and tempting glistening sea on the other. Icy cold, we dipped our toes in then ran to the car. On the drive home I became fixated on pie and an hour or so later we were eating a comforting crust of mashed cauliflower on top of a rich lentil ragu, cooked until the lentils were almost soft. Its warmth spread all the way to our feet. I use cauliflower but you could also use potato or a mix of roots.

SERVES 4

olive oil

2 tablespoons mustard seeds

about 20 curry leaves, fresh if possible

2 carrots, peeled and finely chopped

1 onion, finely chopped

1 tablespoon cumin seeds, bashed

1 tablespoon coriander seeds

2 cloves of garlic, peeled and finely sliced

a thumb-sized piece of ginger, peeled and finely chopped

1 x 400g tin of Puy lentils, drained (or 250g home-cooked, see page 461)

1 x 400g tin of tomatoes

1 teaspoon vegetable stock powder or ½ a stock cube

2 pitted dates (I use Medjool)

1 red chilli, deseeded and chopped

juice of 1 unwaxed lemon

2 medium cauliflowers (about 1kg with leaves removed)

1 tablespoon coconut or olive oil

Preheat the oven to 220°C/200°C fan/gas 7.

Put a good glug of oil into a large, heavy pan. Get it nice and hot, add the mustard seeds and curry leaves and cook until the seeds pop. Take the pan off the heat, reserve half the seeds and leaves, then put the pan with the remaining mixture back on the heat.

Add the carrots and onion to the pan and cook for another 10–15 minutes, or until soft, sweet and nicely browned. Add the cumin, coriander, garlic and ginger and cook for 3–4 minutes, to toast the spices and allow the garlic and ginger to release their oils. Take care that the garlic doesn't burn.

Add the lentils, tomatoes, stock and half a tin of boiling water. Roughly chop the dates and add them to the pan with the chilli and the zest of half the lemon. Season with salt and simmer on a medium heat for 15–20 minutes, or until thick, rich and flavourful.

Meanwhile, make the mash. Break the cauliflower into florets, slice the stalk and put the lot into a lidded pan with about 2cm of boiling water. Put on a high heat and steam until tender. Drain, put back in the pan and put over the heat for a minute to dry out the cauliflower.

Allow it to cool a little, then blitz in a food processor with the coconut oil and a big pinch of salt. When you have a silky smooth mash, fold in the reserved mustard seeds and curry leaves.

Once the lentils are ready, add the lemon juice and mix well. Spoon into an ovenproof dish, top with the mash and bake for 20 minutes, or until golden and bubbling.

Antique markets and shopping

I make a twice-yearly trip to my favourite antiques market. We get up at about 4.30am, fill a flask with tea, drive our camper-van down south and get to the gates as they open. That way we get the pick of the bunch, and if we're lucky we'll get to the good stuff before the buyers from posh shops and department stores do.

At Christmas it is particularly important to me to make the few gifts I buy things that have already had a life; to repurpose something or to buy something hand-crafted by someone nearby. Something that will, I hope, be held, used and passed on, or something incredible to eat and enjoy. With all the waste we create I love giving things that have been in someone else's hands and have a story or support a local artist. I can guarantee that the process of shopping for something like this will be much more enjoyable as you meet characters and hear stories and do a bit of haggling.

Antique shopping

Arthur Swallow Antiques markets in the East Midlands. Amazing for picking up unusual bargains throughout the year. Lovely Eastern European Enamelware. www.asfairs.com

International Antiques and Collectors Fairs (IACF) at Ardingly, Newark and Alexandra Palace. Ardingly is my pick. Arrive early. www.iacf.co.uk

Kempton Antiques Fair every month midweek, again arrive early. www.sunburyantiques.com

Further afield: the antiques market in Lucca, Italy is really great, and in such a glorious setting. The third weekend of every month. www.comune.lucca.it

Artisans I love

Turning Earth: an open-access ceramics studio in East London that holds regular sales for work by all their makers. www.e2.turningearth.uk

David Mellor: a institution of British design; I love their pottery. www.davidmellordesign.com

Sue Pryke: for amazing modern fine ceramics. www.suepryke.com

Quitokeeto: a wonderfully well-curated collection of home wares and antiques from the ever amazing Heidi (101cookbooks) and Wayne. www.quitokeeto.com

Blooms

Many of the florists I love are London-based but do look to them for inspiration.

The British Flower Collective: amazing British florists all looking to produce beautiful bouquets whilst reducing flower miles and making the most of seasonal blooms in the UK. Their members' list has lots of amazing florists up and down the country. www.thebritishflowercollective.com

Botany: for plants and green, east London. www.botanyshop.co.uk

Electric Daisy Flower Farm: an eccentric and different flower farm in Bradford where all the flowers are grown organically and then made into the most inventive and beautiful things. www.electricdaisyflowerfarm.co.uk

New Covent Garden flower market is where florists buy flowers. There is a charge to get in and you have to buy in larger amounts than at a florist, but it's a wonderful thing to do and the flowers are much cheaper. Arrive early for the best stuff. www.newcoventgardenmarket.com

Rebel Rebel: for amazing rainbow colour. www.rebelrebel.co.uk

Worm London: for whimsical trailing beauty and offbeat arrangements. www.wormlondon.com

Further afield: the Cours Saleya flower market in Nice; one of my favourite places ever. The mimosa there is to die for. It also does amazing fruit and veg. en.nicetourisme.com/markets

Online inspiration: Floret flowers, a stunning US flower farm www.floretflowers.com and **Saipua,** wild and wonderful New York florists http://journal.saipua.com

Food

Gloucester Services: it sounds strange recommending a service station, but this is worth going out of your way for. www.gloucesterservices.com

Harp Lane Deli: the sweetest little deli in Ludlow – great coffee and even greater Portuguese custard tarts. harplane.com

High St Delicatessen in Powys is a shop about being at the centre of a community. thehighstreetdelicatessen.com

Leila's shop: this shop in London feels like stepping back in time. A carefully chosen selection of the very best groceries, with amazing produce from the UK and Italy. Calvert Avenue, Shoreditch.

London Borough of Jam, a jam shop close to where I live. Filled with curiosities, books and tableware. Chatsworth Road, London. www.londonboroughofjam.com

Pump Street Bakery: a bakery as famous for its cinnamon buns as for its chocolate cake with sourdough crumb. www.pumpstreetbakery.com

Stroud Farmer's Market: one of the busiest markets in the UK. There's always something new to discover. fresh-n-local.co.uk/trader/stroud/

Spa Terminus Market: my favourite London food market, less well known, filled with serious producers and the best ice cream you will ever eat. www.spa-terminus.co.uk

Worton Organic Garden: 5 miles north-west of Oxford, the Blakes run a 7-acre market garden providing the local community with an amazing diversity of seasonal fresh vegetables, herbs, fruit, eggs and flowers. I've yet to make it but have heard such amazing things about their farm shop, open every weekend. www.wortonorganicgarden.com

Apple, rye and walnut Bundt

It's rare that I eat a cake without icing, but this cake has everything going for it just as it is. It's light and generous due to the grated apple; the back note of the rye adds depth and the walnuts a buttery crunch. It's the kind of cake that is just the right wintry side of stodgy. You can use aquafaba (see page 459), to make it vegan.

This cake is also good with a little Greek or coconut yoghurt whisked with some vanilla seeds or paste and a touch of honey.

Preheat the oven to 190°C/170°C fan/gas 5. Grease a Bundt tin (roughly 26cm, 9cm deep) with rapeseed oil or butter, then lightly dust the inside with flour and tap out any excess.

Put the apples into a bowl, add the lemon zest and squeeze over a few drops of the lemon juice and toss well, then add the ginger and a tablespoon of the sugar. Toss to coat, then leave to one side to allow the flavours to mix and meld.

In another bowl combine the flours, baking powder and salt and whisk to get rid of any lumps, then stir in the chopped walnuts.

Put the oil or butter into a jug with the rest of the sugar, the vanilla, eggs and the lemon juice and mix to combine.

Stir the butter and sugar mixture into the dry mixture and mix well. Then stir in the apples and pour into the mould. Bake in the hot oven for 1 hour and 15 minutes or until a skewer inserted in the centre comes out clean.

Pull the cake out of the oven and leave the tin on a baking rack to cool for at least 30 minutes or until the tin feels cool. Turn the cake out on to a plate.

SERVES 8–10

190g rapeseed oil or melted butter, plus extra for greasing

200g wholegrain spelt flour, plus extra for the tin

400g apples, peeled, cored and roughly chopped (I use Cox's)

the zest and juice of 1 unwaxed lemon

½ teaspoon ground ginger

200g unrefined brown sugar

50g rye flour

2 teaspoons baking powder

a good pinch of flaky salt

100g walnuts, roughly chopped

2 teaspoons vanilla paste

3 medium organic eggs

Almond and smoked salt blondies

These blondies are somewhat bottle blonde. Though they don't have the cocoa or hefty amount of chocolate that a brownie would (which makes them a blondie), I do use muscovado sugar, which turns them a deep dark brunette. If you like you could use a lighter sugar, though the deep maltiness of muscovado works so well. The topping is blonde, however – it's a quick, fudgy meringue-like almond topping which keeps them looking a bit blonder.

Sometimes I make these with a blend of spelt and rye flour, as I like the deep rich back note that the rye brings. The smoked salt adds something and works so well with the almonds and chocolate, but if you can't get hold of it, normal flaky salt will work just fine. These can also be made with coconut sugar and aquafaba (see page 459) which would make them vegan.

Preheat the oven to 200°C/180°C fan/gas 6. Grease a 20cm square baking tin and line with greaseproof paper.

Place the baking powder, salt and flour in a bowl and mix together with a whisk to get rid of any lumps.

Place the coconut oil or butter in a pan and melt it. Add the sugars and whisk until it has mostly dissolved, then pour into a bowl. Set aside to cool for 15 minutes.

Separate one of the eggs and keep back about 1 tablespoon of the white, then put the rest into the bowl with the yolk and the rest of the eggs. Beat the eggs, coconut oil and vanilla extract together with a whisk. Fold in the flour mixture and chocolate. Once everything is incorporated, pour the mixture into the lined tin.

Whisk the tablespoon of egg white until fluffy, then add the almonds, the extra 50g of caster sugar and a pinch of salt. Spread over the top of the blondie mixture with a spatula. Bake in the oven for 30 minutes, until crisp on top and still a little gooey inside.

Leave to cool for 10 minutes, then remove from the tin, slice into squares and try not to eat them all.

SERVES 8–10

- 2 teaspoons baking powder
- ½ teaspoon flaky smoked sea salt, plus a pinch
- 250g white spelt flour
- 180g coconut oil or unsalted butter
- 125g dark muscovado sugar
- 125g golden caster sugar, plus an extra 50g
- 3 medium organic eggs
- 2 teaspoons good vanilla extract or paste
- 125g dark chocolate (at least 70% cocoa solids), chopped into large pieces
- 100g almonds, skin on, roughly chopped
- 50g golden caster sugar

Toasted coconut rice pudding with sticky prunes

I make my own toasted coconut milk here, which is a genius idea that I pinched from my friend Heidi Swanson. I make a bigger batch than you will need, but it is a brilliant thing to have on hand for curries and soups, as well as to pour on cereal or add to porridge. You could also just use tinned coconut milk and perhaps top the pudding with some toasted coconut. I toast the coconut for the milk so that it's deep golden but not burnt – this makes the milk very different in flavour to the calmer, more neutral flavour of regular coconut milk.

I make a quick topping with Pedro Ximénez sherry, which is gloriously thick and raisiny, but you could also use some dark sherry with a couple of tablespoons of dark brown sugar. These prunes sit well with vanilla ice cream, whipped coconut yoghurt or cream, or on the side of a simple tart.

SERVES 6

FOR THE TOASTED COCONUT MILK (MAKES 1 LITRE)

200g coconut flakes
a pinch of flaky sea salt

FOR THE RICE PUDDING

butter or coconut oil, for greasing
100g short-grain rice
70g coconut sugar
1 teaspoon vanilla paste or the seeds of 1 vanilla pod

FOR THE PRUNES

150g prunes, pitted
90ml Pedro Ximénez sherry
50ml water

Preheat the oven to 220°C/200°C fan/gas 7.

Spread out the coconut in a large roasting tray and place in the centre of the oven. Toast for 5–10 minutes, until deeply golden all over, really brown but not burnt.

Put 1 litre of cold water (preferably filtered) into your blender. Add the toasted coconut and salt and blitz on the highest setting for a couple of minutes, until as smooth as possible. Strain through a nut milk bag or a muslin cloth set over a bowl.

Turn the oven temperature down to 170°C/150°C fan/gas 3 and lightly grease a 20 x 20cm brownie or cake tin with butter or coconut oil. Mix the rice, sugar, vanilla, 500ml of the coconut milk (the rest can go into a jar in the fridge to use when you like) and 300ml of water and stir well. Tip the rice into the tin and bake for 90 minutes, stirring it three or four times to ensure it cooks evenly.

About 20 minutes before the rice is due to come out of the oven, place the prunes in a small, lidded saucepan with the sherry and water over a low heat. Stew gently until the rice is done, and serve with 3–4 prunes per person.

Sea salted chocolate and lemon mousse

This is a pretty maverick way of making a chocolate mousse, which was brought to my attention by a great chef friend. It's based on a technique by the French chemist Hervé This. Don't worry, it's really quite easy, though you do have to follow the recipe to the tee. It uses water, not cream, and the mousse is whipped over a bowl of ice, which chills the chocolate. The result is a cleaner, less cloying mousse that is unadulterated chocolate, backed up by a little lemon, salt and vanilla. Lemon is rarely paired with chocolate but I think it works incredibly well. If you'd prefer, orange or even lime could be added too.

Half-fill a large mixing bowl (or saucepan) with water and ice, then sit another mixing bowl inside it.

Put the chocolate, salt, honey, vanilla and lemon zest into a saucepan with 175ml of cold water. Place on a low heat and stir until it all comes together and the chocolate has just melted.

Use a spatula to scrape the mixture into the mixing bowl set over the ice bath and whisk with a balloon whisk (an electric one will be too powerful). Keep whisking until it looks shiny but isn't yet set (like a thick chocolate sauce) – the whisk will make little ribbons of chocolate on the mousse when lifted. You will be whisking for about 3 minutes, but keep an eye on it, as the mousse will thicken really quickly, and will set in the fridge as it cools. Have a taste and check you're happy with the flavour. If the mousse tastes a little grainy, it is probably because it has been over-whisked. Don't panic, just scrape the mixture back into the original saucepan, melt and start again.

Once ready, spoon into ramekins and place in the fridge. Chill for at least 3 hours before serving.

To make the brittle, have a plate lined with greaseproof paper ready. Toast the sesame seeds in a pan on a medium heat until well browned, then add the maple syrup and take off the heat. Scoop the seed mixture onto the greaseproof paper and leave to cool completely.

Serve the mousse topped with sesame seeds and the brittle.

SERVES 4

200g dark chocolate (at
    least 70% cocoa solids)

a good pinch of flaky sea salt

2 tablespoons runny honey

the seeds from 1 vanilla pod

the zest of ½ unwaxed lemon

FOR THE QUICK BRITTLE

50g sesame seeds, plus
    extra to finish

2 tablespoons maple syrup

Fig, banana and dark chocolate cake

This is the cake I baked for Dylan's first birthday. I wanted a cake with no sugar and filled with good stuff. Dylan ate very little of his piece; instead he rubbed it all over his face and threw it on the floor, which he really enjoyed, so I guess that's the point. The rest of us loved it and I have made it for almost every celebration since. This cake has got more stages than I would usually go for, but it means you get a light cake with a good crumb and some serious depth of flavour. This is loosely based on a recipe from my friend Henrietta Inman. The recipe makes enough for an iced four-tier cake, but if you want a smaller cake just halve the quantities.

SERVES 10–12

60g coconut oil, melted, plus extra for greasing

2 tablespoons milled flax seeds

200ml hazelnut or almond milk (I use unsweetened)

2 teaspoons cider vinegar

400g dried figs, stalks removed

2½ teaspoons bicarbonate of soda

360g wholegrain spelt flour

½ teaspoon baking powder

1 teaspoon coarse sea salt, finely ground

½ teaspoon ground cinnamon

400g peeled banana (about 4 large bananas)

100g apple purée (I use one by Clearspring)

1 teaspoon vanilla extract

200g dark chocolate (85% cocoa solids), chopped

FOR THE ICING

190ml maple syrup

120g raw cacao powder

180g almond milk (I use unsweetened)

1½ teaspoons vanilla paste

120g coconut oil, melted

a pinch of flaky sea salt

Preheat the oven to 190°C/170°C fan/gas 5 and line the base of two 18–20cm round loose-bottomed cake tins with baking paper. Grease the sides with coconut oil.

Mix the flax seeds with 3 tablespoons of water and leave for about 15 minutes to form a gel. Combine your chosen nut milk with the cider vinegar and set aside.

Roughly chop the figs, then put them in a medium saucepan with 400ml of cold water and bring to the boil. Turn down to a medium boil and boil until all the water has evaporated and the figs are soft. Remove from the heat and immediately add 1 teaspoon of the bicarbonate of soda; the figs will fizz a little. Set aside to cool slightly.

Mix the spelt flour, the rest of the bicarbonate of soda, baking powder, sea salt and cinnamon and whisk to get rid of any lumps.

Mash together the bananas, apple purée, coconut oil and vanilla extract and add the flax seed gel and nut milk mix.

Blitz the figs with a stick blender to make a figgy paste, leaving a good amount of lumps, and add to the banana, flax and milk mix. Finally fold in all the dry ingredients and the chocolate until just combined. Transfer to your prepared tin.

Bake for 30 minutes, then reduce the oven temperature to 180°C/160°C fan/gas 4 and bake for a further 15–20 minutes, or until a skewer inserted in the centre comes out almost clean. Leave the cakes to cool in their tins until completely cold. →

To make the icing, put all the ingredients into a blender and whizz until smooth. If it is very runny you may want to put it in the fridge for 10–15 minutes to firm up a little, then take it out and leave at room temperature until you are ready to use it.

Cut each cake in half horizontally so you have four layers in total. Dab a little icing on the plate you're going to serve the cake on, to keep it still. Place the first layer on top, add a quarter of the icing and spread it over the top. Repeat with the following layers, finishing with the last quarter of icing on the top.

The cake will last a good 3–4 days in the fridge in a sealed container.

Mozzarella and citrus with toasted coriander seeds

This is a very lovely thing to eat at any time but I find it particularly good around Christmas – the citrus is at its best and the freshness it brings really punctuates the rest of the richness in our kitchen at this time of the year. I love the addition of coriander seeds, toasted to within an inch of their life to bring out a buttery citrus note that makes this little plate sing. Use the best olive oil you can get your hands on.

Toast the coriander seeds in a dry pan until they smell really fragrant and have turned a deeper brown. Bash them in a pestle and mortar or grind in a spice grinder until you have a fine powder.

SERVES 4

1 tablespoon coriander seeds

4 clementines or blood oranges

2 balls of buffalo mozzarella (about 250g)

2 tablespoons crème fraîche

seeds from ½ pomegranate

4 handfuls of peppery leaves

2 tablespoons good extra virgin olive oil

Next, using a very sharp knife, slice one end off a clementine so that it sits flat against your chopping board, then cut away the peel and any pith in strips from top to bottom so that no pithy white is visible. Turn the clementine on to its side and slice into thin rounds. Repeat with the other three.

Tear the mozzarella into large pieces, divide between four plates, then spoon the crème fraîche on top. Season well, then add a good pinch of the toasted coriander. Put the clementine slices on to the plates and add the pomegranate seeds. Drizzle over the oil and serve with good bread and lemon and oil dressed leaves.

Christmas Eve orecchiette

This pasta is a little more indulgent than my usual weeknight pasta, as sometimes when we are all gathered I veer towards a bit more decadence. I often make this on Christmas Eve; the warming blanket of cheesy pasta in a bowl can be eaten from laps while last presents are wrapped. It suits pretty much any winter evening, though. You can use almost any good melting cheese you have to hand or a mixture – fontina is my favourite but Cheddar or soft goat's cheese would work too. You could also use kale or greens instead of broccoli.

Bring a large pan of salted water to the boil; meanwhile, chop the stalks of the broccoli into 1cm pieces, leaving the florets intact.

Put the broccoli into the water and cook for 3 minutes, until tender and still bright green. Remove with a slotted spoon (don't drain it – you need the hot water) and leave in a colander to steam dry.

Reduce the heat to low and place a large heatproof bowl on top of the pan, making sure it doesn't touch the water. Add the crème fraîche to the bowl along with the fontina and lemon zest, then stir. Once the cheese has melted, carefully remove the bowl from the heat and set aside, then turn the heat up to high.

Add the pasta to the water and cook according to the packet instructions. Meanwhile, mix the hazelnuts with the thyme, lemon zest, olive oil and a good pinch of salt. Heat a frying pan over a medium heat, then add the nut mixture and cook for 3–4 minutes until crisp and starting to brown.

Once the pasta is ready, put the broccoli back into the pan, leave for 30 seconds just to warm it through, then drain the lot, reserving a mugful of the cooking water for later.

Put the pasta and broccoli into the bowl of melted cheese and toss to coat, adding a splash of the reserved cooking water to loosen the cheese to a smooth silky sauce.

Transfer to a serving bowl, sprinkle the nuts on top and serve.

SERVE 6

FOR THE PASTA

400g purple sprouting broccoli, trimmed

4 tablespoons crème fraîche

250g fontina (see note above), rind removed

the zest of 1 unwaxed lemon

450g orecchiette

FOR THE CRISPY HAZELNUTS

100g hazelnuts, skin on, finely chopped

a few sprigs of thyme, leaves picked and finely chopped

the zest of 1 unwaxed lemon

3 tablespoons olive oil

Celebration celeriac and sweet garlic pie

This has been my Christmas centrepiece for the last couple of years. It is everything I want in a pie: a Cheddar and winter herb flaky pastry; a creamy filling, sweet with balsamic garlic and roasted celeriac; and a crisp grated celeriac roof. This high-sided pie takes a little time, but at Christmas I think that's okay.

Put the flour into a mixing bowl. Add the butter and salt. Rub gently with your fingertips until the mixture is like fine breadcrumbs. Stir through the herbs, lemon zest and Cheddar.

Beat the egg yolk with 1 tablespoon of cold water. Add to the flour and mix until it forms a dough. Add more water, a teaspoon at a time, until it comes together into a smooth dough. Wrap in cling film and chill in the fridge while you make the filling.

For the filling, put the cloves of garlic into a saucepan, cover with cold water and bring to a gentle simmer. Cook for 2–3 minutes, then drain.

Wipe the saucepan dry. Add the garlic and 1 tablespoon of olive oil and fry on a high heat for 2 minutes. Add the balsamic vinegar and 100ml water, bring to the boil and simmer gently for 10 minutes.

Add the honey, most of the rosemary and thyme (reserving the rest, with the sage) and a good pinch of salt. Continue to cook on a medium heat for a further 5 minutes, or until most of the liquid has evaporated and the garlic cloves are coated in a dark syrup.

Meanwhile, peel the celeriac and cut it into quarters. Set aside 300g and slice the rest into 2cm-thick pieces. Put them into a saucepan, cover with hot water and boil for 7–10 minutes, until they are soft and have turned slightly translucent.

Drain and tip into a big mixing bowl. Add the cheese, crème fraîche, lemon juice, mustard, parsley, a splash of Worcestershire sauce and eggs. Add a good pinch of salt and grind of pepper and gently fold in the garlic cloves. →

SERVES 8–10

FOR THE PASTRY

250g plain spelt flour, plus a little extra for dusting

125g cold unsalted butter, cubed

½ teaspoon fine sea salt

a few sprigs each of rosemary, thyme and sage, leaves picked and finely chopped

the zest of 1 unwaxed lemon

25g good Cheddar, grated

1 medium egg yolk

50–70ml cold water

FOR THE FILLING

3 heads of garlic, cloves separated and peeled

olive oil

1 teaspoon balsamic vinegar

1 tablespoon runny honey

2 sprigs each of rosemary, thyme and sage, leaves picked and finely chopped, plus extra to finish

1kg celeriac

220g Lancashire or good Cheddar cheese, crumbled

150g crème fraîche

the juice of ½ a lemon

1 tablespoon wholegrain mustard

a small bunch of parsley, chopped

Worcestershire sauce

2 organic eggs, beaten

442

Preheat the oven to 180°C/160°C fan/gas 4. Sprinkle flour onto a work surface and roll out the pastry to 3–4mm thick. Line a 20cm-diameter cake tin with the pastry, ensuring a little spills over the edges.

Pour the filling into the pastry case. Coarsely grate the reserved celeriac and pile it on top. Finish with the reserved rosemary and thyme, all the sage, and a drizzle of olive oil. Bake for 45 minutes or until the tart filling has set and the top is golden brown.

Remove from the oven, leave to cool a little, then take it out of the tin. Lay a few herbs on top and serve warm.

Laying a celebratory table

Laying a table a job I love; every task tinged with the anticipation that the table will soon be filled with friends and family. There is something so magical about leading people into a room with a set table, candles and music. With a mood set you can serve simple food but everything will feel a bit more considered.

I have a bit of an obsession with tableware; from glasses to napkins, jugs to platters, every nook of my kitchen is filled. When laying a table think about using different heights. Glassware, candles and flowers will all add to the rise and fall. Use one colour or fabric as a guide and then build everything around that. Most of all though, make it casual and achievable; use what you have for everyday with a few added touches.

Linen

A tablecloth or a linen runner is always where I start, then you can layer up fabrics creating amazing texture. You can buy linen tablecloths now pretty affordably from most homeware shops, or buy a couple of metres off the roll from a haberdashery. I like to wash mine and hang it on the washing line so it has a crumpled texture and isn't too neat. Brown paper is a good substitute if linen feels too much. You can cut place mats from fabric too; the frayed edges look nice. Muted base tones work well for lots of different occasions, then you can use other things to create accents.

Flowers and foliage

Use the season's plants and blooms as decoration. Herbs are amazing; they will make the table smell good too. I put my herbs or flowers in little bottles, jars and modern stem vases, usually only one or two stems in each vase and playing with height. Here are some ideas of what to use throughout the year.

Winter: bay leaves, rosemary, snowdrops, winter berries and twigs, little bags of home-made truffles. Eucalyptus looks great laid down the middle of the table.

Spring: bunches of primroses, narcissi, painted Easter eggs, chocolate eggs, hyacinths.

Summer: sweet peas, roses, lemons, bunches of aromatic mint, lavender, cherries, lemons.

Autumn: imperfect squashes, rosehips in little jugs, autumn leaves, skeleton leaves, seed heads, dainty pine cones.

Place settings

Menus are nice mementos for people to take away; I have a shoebox of menus that I love to look at. They can be written on simple card or paper in your best handwriting.

Place settings are a good idea if you want to choreograph who sits where, written simply on cards or even on little pebbles with a chalk pen or marker.

If it's a really special dinner you could think about a table present to take away: home-made teas, little meringues, essential oil blends, homemade truffles, small bottles of sloe gin or cordial. I did this at my wedding but haven't done it since, so I'm talking really special meals here.

Drinks

I like to keep drinks on the table or near to it if they're in small ice buckets and jugs. That way you don't have to top everyone's drink up all night. I always keep a couple of jugs of flavoured water on hand: blackberry and sage; cucumber and mint; bergamot or lemon; rosemary and thyme.

I use a mixture of different glasses: Duralex, fine glass tumblers and Champagne saucers. Charity shops and car boot sales are amazing places to pick up old glassware.

Napkins

Linen napkins are easy to find and quite reasonable but if not then use fabric offcuts. If they have a bold pattern fold them inside out, or use squares of soft denim or simple white cloth. Tie velvet ribbon, brown string or brightly coloured twine around them; you can also lay leaves, herbs or even pressed flowers on top, securing them with a nice paper clip or even some bright washi tape.

Lights and candles

Lights are so important. I go for candles: sometimes just one, other times a mixture. Church candles, classic tapered beeswax ones, tea lights in glasses are all cheap. I love to use dark candles in grey, navy and black. For something more special, festoon lights, fairy lights or even paper lanterns hanging from the ceiling would all look amazing too.

Serving your food

I don't have matching sets of everything. I do keep plates white and pretty similar but the rest is a mixture of treasured things: platters for food, bowls for dipping and snacks. My table is a tapestry of everything I love, I almost always put all the food in the middle rather than serving it plated; I love the interaction, the hand crossing and passing around. Shop around for interesting things from antiques and vintage fairs (see page 424).

Kids' tables

Colour and fun are key here. I make my kids' tables every colour of the rainbow with party hats, pom poms, coloured napkins. Once I even made biscuits with names on – admittedly that was going a bit far.

Membrillo, buttermilk and poppy seed cake

This is quite a decadent cake. It uses membrillo, the quince paste that we eat with cheese at Christmas, to make an insanely good festive cake. I bake it like brownies as a traybake but you could use a standard cake tin too. Membrillo can be quite expensive but any fruit cheese (damson, pear) would work well in its place. There isn't much other sugar in the cake batter, as most of it comes from the membrillo. I have also made a version of this swapping good marzipan for the membrillo, which is equally delicious.

SERVES 15

70ml rapeseed oil or melted butter, plus a little extra

250g white spelt flour, plus a little extra for the tin

1 tablespoon baking powder

70g golden caster sugar

½ teaspoon fine sea salt

60g poppy seeds

the zest of 2 unwaxed lemons

2 medium organic eggs

350ml yoghurt or buttermilk

250g membrillo (quince paste), cut into tiny cubes

2 tablespoons demerara sugar

20g almonds, skin on, lightly toasted and chopped

Preheat the oven to 220°C/200°C fan/gas 7. Grease and flour a 20 x 30cm baking dish.

Combine the flour, baking powder, caster sugar, salt, poppy seeds and lemon zest in a large bowl.

In a separate smaller bowl, whisk together the eggs and the yoghurt, then whisk in the oil or melted butter.

Add to the flour mixture and stir briefly, until just combined. Gently fold in two-thirds of the membrillo cubes until they are evenly distributed. Transfer the cake mixture to the prepared dish. Arrange the remaining membrillo across the top in a pleasing pattern. Sprinkle with the demerara sugar, then the almonds.

Bake for 20–25 minutes or until a toothpick inserted in the centre comes out clean. Serve warm or at room temperature.

Salted chocolate truffles

MAKES ABOUT 48

60g coconut oil, plus a
  little extra to grease

30g coconut or light
  brown sugar

200g raw almond or cashew
  or hazelnut butter

200g dark chocolate (at
  least 70% cocoa solids)

the seeds from 1 vanilla pod

2 big pinches of flaky sea salt

ADDITIONAL FLAVOURS

the zest of 1 unwaxed orange

the zest of 1 unwaxed lemon

the zest of 1 unwaxed lime

swap the salt for
  smoked sea salt

1 red chilli, finely chopped

2 cardamom pods, seeds
  removed and crushed

½ teaspoon ground cinnamon

TO COAT – USE ONE OR
MORE

50g raw cacao or
  cocoa powder

finely chopped pistachios,
  almonds, hazelnuts

finely chopped candied
  orange peel

finely chopped candied ginger

grated chocolate (dark,
  milk or white)

crushed dried rose petals

These are very easy truffles: no tempering chocolate; no rolling or filling; just some simple melting, mixing and pouring – your own little chocolate factory. This batch makes a lot, and will keep you in truffles for a couple of weeks or can be wrapped up and given as Christmas presents. If you are giving them as a present, do remember to tell whomever you are giving them to that they need to be kept in the fridge (they will be fine out of the fridge for a few hours, though). These truffles are made with coconut oil, nut butter and coconut sugar, so they don't give me the crazy sugar high of other chocolates.

I have given you a choice of flavourings and coatings so you can take the basic mixture and make it as flavourful or as colourful as you like.

Grease a 20 x 20cm square brownie tin with coconut oil. Heat the coconut oil and sugar in a saucepan on a low heat. Once the oil has melted and the sugar has dissolved into the oil, take the pan off the heat and add the nut butter, chocolate, vanilla and salt. Stir off the heat until everything has melted. If you're adding another flavour, stir it in now.

Pour the mixture into the tin. Chill for about 2 hours until set solid. While the truffle mix is cooling, get your chosen coating or coatings ready and put each in a little bowl.

Once set, turn the truffle slab out on to a cool work surface and cut into squares (mine are 1–1½cm), then gently dip each truffle in its coating to cover.

The truffles will keep in the fridge for up to 2 weeks in a sealed container.

Vanilla and lime mulled wine

This is the mulled wine I have been making for years and it's as delicious as it is offbeat. You make a quick syrup infusion to ensure you get as much flavour as possible out of the spices and aromatics, then add the rest of the wine and warm through so that all the alcohol doesn't boil away.

Strip the zest from the clementines and limes, using a potato peeler to produce large pieces. Juice the fruit.

SERVE 10

2 clementines

2 limes

100g light brown sugar
   or maple syrup

6 cloves

1 cinnamon stick

3 fresh bay leaves, crushed
   in your hands

2 star anise

1 whole nutmeg

2 vanilla pods

2 bottles of good, full-bodied
   red wine

Put the sugar in a large saucepan over a medium heat, then add the pieces of peel and the fruit juice. Add the cloves, cinnamon stick, bay leaves, star anise and about 10 gratings of nutmeg. Halve the vanilla pods lengthways and add to the pan, then stir in just enough red wine to cover the sugar.

Let this simmer until the sugar has completely dissolved into the red wine, then bring to the boil and simmer for 4–5 minutes to allow the heat to bring out the flavours.

Turn the heat down to low and add the rest of the wine. Gently heat without boiling, then cover and leave to sit for about 30 minutes. When you are ready to serve, warm the mulled wine again without boiling and ladle it into heatproof glasses.

Bergamot gin

Winter is the time for citrus in every shade, from lemon chiffon to saffron mandarins, tangerines, Moro blood oranges, kumquats and tiny key limes. To my delight, I managed to get my hands on some Meyer lemons recently, a less acidic variety, with a sherbet tangerine kick – they hail from California. Any of these citrus fruits would work well in this gin, but I've used my favourite of all, the bergamot.

The heady bergamot orange is a fragrant citrus that grows in France and Italy. It looks like a squat green lemon. Its juice is more acidic than lemon but its peel is uplifting – it has a deeper, almost woody citrus scent. I adore it. You can also buy bergamot lemons which look like a traditional lemon but taste sweeter, with a more orange skin; I like to use the greener bergamot oranges as they have more of the floral lemony notes I love, but both work. I have made a pretty pink-tinged blood orange version too.

I make this in a similar way to limoncello, with some added sugar, so it's sweeter than regular gin, meaning you can drink it straight over ice or in a gin and tonic. I made a big batch this year that I'm saving for next year's Christmas presents.

Peel long strips of rind from the bergamots using a vegetable peeler, taking care not to use too much of a heavy hand, otherwise you'll end up with a lot of bitter pith.

Place the peel in the bottom of a lidded clean glass jar or bottle and add the gin, using a funnel if it's easier. Leave in a dark place for the flavours to develop; this can take from 1–3 weeks. Generally, once the peel has turned white, all its flavour has been infused.

Once your gin has had its steeping time you are ready to mix it with the sugar syrup. Put the sugar and 300ml of cold water into a saucepan and bring to a gentle boil, allowing all the sugar to dissolve, then simmer for a further 10 minutes. Allow to cool completely.

Strain the gin into a jug, then add about the same volume of sugar syrup and taste it, adding a little more to taste – the more sugar the smoother the flavour.

Pour the gin into sterilised bottles and secure with a top. It will keep for years, although it's unlikely to last that long.

MAKES 650ML

6 bergamots
500ml good gin
300g golden caster sugar

Grapefruit and bay bitters

Last Christmas was a write-off. We all got ill – a rare occurrence in our family – and Christmas was cancelled. Once we were better we finally managed to get dressed and walk to the local pub. We sat round a table, all a bit overexcited to be outside. We ordered gin and tonics – not the traditional recovery remedy, I guess – and they arrived in huge glasses, with cucumber, elderflower and spiked with the most delicious grapefruit bitters. The bitters turned a pretty standard gin and tonic into something incredible. I don't drink that much, so when I do have a glass of wine or a gin and tonic I want it to be the best it can possibly be.

I'd never thought of making bitters before, but after a bit of research I couldn't believe how easy they were – a few flavours left in some alcohol for a few weeks. They make a great present in a nice little bottle too. You could swap in most citrus here.

MAKES 250ML

1 grapefruit

1 orange

¼ teaspoon coriander seeds

½ teaspoon black peppercorns

1 bay leaf

a 1cm piece of cinnamon stick

1 cardamom pod, just split open

1 vanilla pod, split open

1 coffee bean

250ml vodka

Preheat the oven to 140°C/120°C fan/gas 2. Very finely peel the zest from both the grapefruit and the orange, using a vegetable peeler, and spread it out on a baking tray. Bake for 20 minutes, until dry but not quite brittle, then remove and allow to cool on the tray.

Put the zest with all the other ingredients into a large jar and pour over the vodka. Leave to steep for 2–3 weeks. How quickly it steeps will depend on the warmth of the room and the potency of all the ingredients, so once you hit 2 weeks, keep tasting it and bottle it once you are happy with the flavour.

Strain the vodka through a muslin cloth, squeezing through all the last bits of liquid. Pour into a little bottle and store in a cool place; it should keep for years, as only a dash is used at a time.

To use the bitters, add half a teaspoon to a gin and tonic or to sparkling water.

Basics

Labneh

A strained yoghurt that is thicker than Greek yoghurt. Use it like ricotta in salads or mix with herbs, lemon zest and drizzle with good oil to use as a dip. You can even roll it into balls and store them under oil in the fridge if you want to keep it a little longer; it will keep for 5–6 days. This is a staple in our house and we make about a batch a week. Remember to make it the night before you want to eat it.

MAKES ABOUT 350G

1 teaspoon flaky sea salt	500g full-fat Greek yoghurt

Whisk the salt into the yoghurt. Pour into the middle of a piece of cheesecloth set in a sieve resting over a bowl, tie the corners together and suspend over the bowl in the fridge overnight. If you don't have cheesecloth you can strain it through a coffee filter.

The following day, gently remove the labneh from the cheesecloth and store it in the fridge. Bring to room temperature before using.

Yoghurt flatbreads

There is a corner shop about 100 paces from my house but I still find myself making these in a fix; they are pleasingly simple and also work brilliantly in a frying pan or on a barbecue.

MAKES 4

200g plain flour (I use spelt), plus extra for dusting	1 teaspoon baking powder
	200g Greek yoghurt, or 150ml warm water

Put all the ingredients into the bowl of your food processor and pulse until the mixture forms a ball. If you don't have a food processor, this can be done in a bowl using a fork to begin with, followed by your hands; it will just take a little longer.

Tip the dough out on to a clean work surface dusted with flour and knead for a minute or so, to bring it all together. Put the dough into a flour-dusted bowl and cover with a plate. Put to one side to rise a little for 10–15 minutes. Don't expect it to rise like normal dough but it may puff up a tiny bit.

Dust another clean work surface and rolling pin with flour, then divide the dough into four equal pieces. Using your hands, pat and flatten out the dough, then use the rolling pin to roll each piece into a disc roughly 20cm in diameter and 2–3mm thick.

To cook in a frying pan: Warm a frying pan or griddle that's a bit larger than your flatbreads over a medium heat. Once your pan is nicely hot, cook each flatbread for 1–2 minutes on each side, until nicely puffed up and golden in places, turning it with tongs.

To cook on a barbecue: once your barbecue flames have died down but it's still good and hot, cook each flatbread for 1–2 minutes on each side, turning with tongs, until nicely puffed up, and a little charred (see page 274 for some barbecue tips).

Quick, no-rise frying pan pizza dough

To get a super crisp base start your pizza in a thick-based pan on the heat; I use a 28cm cast iron one but you could use a couple of smaller ones. If you don't have a cast iron pan put your dough on to a thick baking tray on the hob instead, which will help with the crust.

MAKES TWO MEDIUM PIZZAS

300g white spelt flour, plus extra for dusting

150ml tepid water

1 teaspoon baking powder

fine sea salt

1 tablespoon olive oil, plus more for cooking

Preheat your oven to 240°C/220°C fan/ gas 9 or as hot as it will go. You'll also need a large frying pan for this recipe (it needs to be ovenproof).

Put the flour, water and baking powder into a food processor with a good pinch of salt and the tablespoon of olive oil and pulse until the dough comes together in a ball. You could also do this in a bowl using a fork to begin with, followed by your hands; it will just take a little longer. Tip it out and bring the dough together in your hands.

Get your frying pan on a medium–high heat (if you have two pans about the right size you can do both pizzas at once). Cut the dough into two equal halves and cover one half. Put the other half on to a floured work surface and roll it out into a 1cm-thick circle, about the size of your frying pan.

Get all your toppings to hand, drizzle a little oil into the hot pan, then lift the dough into the pan. Leave it on the heat for about 3 minutes, so the base is starting to cook, then quickly top your pizza (see the toppings chart below) and put it into the oven for 8–10 minutes. Be careful when taking it out as the pan handle will be very hot!

Slow sourdough pizza base

To make this recipe you will need an active sourdough starter – this is a mixture of flour and water that has been left to ferment over time. You would normally keep it in your fridge and 'feed' it with flour and water once a week. If you don't have a starter, see if you can get a friend to give you one, the best starters are ones that have been alive for years.

Assuming you are going to make the dough in the evening to make pizzas for the next day's lunch or dinner, you will need to feed your sourdough starter using your normal method that morning. Repeat this again at lunchtime, then leave the starter at room temperature (it should be nice and bubbly).

Base sauce	Cheese	Vegetable	Flourish
pesto	ricotta	blanched purple sprouting broccoli	olives and capers
romesco sauce	Parmesan (I use a vegetarian one)	griddled courgettes and their flowers	herbs – basil/rosemary/ thyme/oregano
garlic and olive oil	pecorino (I use a vegetarian one)	wilted greens	fresh red or green chilli
tomato sauce	Taleggio	radicchio	an egg cracked in the middle
roasted tomato tomato sauce	mozzarella	thinly sliced new potatoes	a sprinkling of dried chilli and fennel seeds

Your starter will be active enough to use by the evening.

You can also use this dough to make sourdough loaves (see below).

**MAKES 6 MEDIUM PIZZAS
    OR 12 SMALL PIZZETTE**

300g sourdough starter

200g wholemeal flour

300g white spelt flour,
    plus extra for dusting

300ml lukewarm water

15g fine sea salt

Combine all the ingredients except the salt in a large mixing bowl. Stir with a large wooden spoon until it comes together then use your hands to bring it together into a ball. Let the dough rest in a floured bowl for 20 minutes, then sprinkle over the salt and mix again. Turn the dough out on to a clean floured work surface and knead for 5–10 minutes, until it is no longer sticky (add additional flour if the dough is too sticky or water if it is too dry).

Split the dough into four balls and put them on a floured baking sheet. Cover with a damp kitchen towel or cling film then put them into the fridge for 12–24 hours.

Take the dough out of the fridge about 2 hours before you plan to make the pizzas.

Follow the instructions on page 457 for how to make pizza

If you don't want to use all the dough to make pizza straight away you can freeze the dough. Once the four balls have had their fridge prove, divide each ball into three again and place in the freezer on a flat tray overnight, and then pop off the tray into a freezer bag, where they will keep for 3 months. Defrost the dough fully before using it, then flour a work surface well and stretch out the dough with your hands until you're happy with the shape and size. Add your toppings and bake as usual.

To make a sourdough loaf

This dough can also be baked as a large 1kg loaf or two smaller 500g loaves. To do this don't split the dough into four before the first prove, then knock it back after the first prove and shape it into a round or place into two 500g tins. Allow it to prove overnight in the fridge, covered loosely with a clean cloth, until the dough has doubled in size and doesn't spring back when pressed with a finger. Take the loaves out of the fridge two hours before you want to bake them and let them come to room temperature. Preheat your oven to 240°C/220°C fan/gas 9 then bake small loaves for 30 minutes and a large one for 45–50 minutes until golden and it sounds hollow when tapped.

Home-made milks from nuts, oats and seeds

I have a few types of milk in my fridge at any one time, usually a small carton of organic cow's milk, almond milk and oat milk. I like to vary the kinds of milk I use, to make sure I am getting as much nutrition as possible and to make the most of their individual flavours.

It is easy, more nutritious and much cheaper to make your own non-dairy milk at home. All you need is a decent blender and a nut milk bag (a muslin bag made for draining nut milk) or failing that, a piece of muslin or a thin tea towel.

These milks can be made from most nuts and seeds and some grains. My favourites are almonds, pistachios, walnuts, hazelnuts, macadamia nuts, cashew nuts, sunflower seeds, pumpkin seeds, sesame seeds, hemp seeds and oats. Here is a universal recipe that can be used for any of these. It works on ratios rather than weight, so I use a US cup measure, but if you don't have one of these don't worry – a mug will work fine.

Take 1 cup of your chosen nut, seed or oat and place in a bowl. Cover with a cup of cold (ideally filtered) water and leave to soak for 8 hours; this will allow the nut to release all its nutrients and maximise the goodness in your milk.

Once the soaking time is up, drain the nuts and place in a blender, discarding the soaking water. Add 4 cups of fresh cold (ideally filtered) water to the blender and blitz until you have a thin, smooth, cloudy mixture.

You can add any flavourings at this point if you like: a teaspoon of vanilla paste or the seeds from a pod, a few dates or a tablespoon of runny honey to sweeten. Spices like cinnamon (about a teaspoon) and cardamom (half a teaspoon) also work well. Once added blitz again.

Put a nut milk bag or cloth over the mouth of a jug and pour the nut milk through. Allow it to sit and drip into the jug for 5–10 minutes, then use your hands to squeeze out as much moisture from the nuts as you can.

Pour the milk into a clean bottle; it will keep in the fridge for 3–4 days. The leftover nut pulp can be added to hummus or can be used in place of ground almonds in baking.

A quick note on toasting nuts

I use toasted nuts in a lot of my recipes. I have assumed that most people know how to toast nuts but if it's not something you do regularly, here is a quick guide.

To toast in the oven: Put your nuts on a baking tray in an oven preheated to 200°C/180°C fan/gas 6 for 4–8 minutes depending on the size of the nut and how much you want them toasted. Once toasted, tip into a bowl and leave to cool, they will keep cooking if you leave them on the hot baking tray.

To toast in a pan: heat a frying pan over a low heat, add the nuts then toss every 30 seconds

or so until they have subtly changed colour and smell toasty. Once toasted, tip into a bowl and leave to cool, they will keep cooking if you leave them in the hot pan.

The degree to which you toast your nuts will have a huge effect on the flavour of the finished dish. I usually toast mine to a medium toast – still buttery with a little toasty flavour – but for some dishes you might want to keep the flavour cleaner and toast them less; for richer dishes, toast them more.

Aquafaba

Aquafaba is the water left over from cooking legumes and pulses, such as chickpeas. When whipped, it miraculously transforms into a meringue-like consistency, and can be used in place of eggs in baking dishes.

How to use aquafaba in baking

To use aquafaba, first you have to make sure it's thick enough. If you're using tinned chickpeas, the chances are it will be, although note that it can vary from brand to brand. If you're cooking your pulses from scratch, make sure you discard the soaking water and always cook your beans in fresh water. Cook and cool the beans, then drain, reserving the precious liquid. If the liquid isn't gloopy, reduce it by about a quarter. If you don't want to use the pulses you've cooked straight away, you can freeze them in sandwich bags. Make sure your aquafaba is well sieved, you don't want to end up with pieces of chickpea in your meringue.

The general rule for aquafaba is 1 tablespoon for 1 yolk, 2 tablespoons for 1 white and 3 tablespoons for a whole egg. So, in a cake that calls for 3 eggs, you would use 9 tablespoons (or 135ml) of aquafaba. One 400g tin of beans will yield around 150ml of aquafaba.

If you have a stand mixer or electric whisk, now is the time to use it as however it's being used, aquafaba always needs to be whisked. Place the aquafaba in a scrupulously clean bowl, and whisk, just as you would with egg white to make meringue. The aquafaba is ready to use when it's holding its own and forming soft peaks with the whisk.

Aquafaba meringues

These are a revelation. Totally egg-free meringues that have a perfect texture and chew. Ideally this would be done in a stand mixer (because they're the most powerful) but an electric hand whisk will work too.

MAKES 10–12 LARGE MERINGUES

a flavourless oil, such as groundnut oil	1½ teaspoons cream of tartar
1 400g tin chickpeas	the seeds from 1 vanilla pod or 1 teaspoon vanilla paste
a pinch of fine sea salt	
150g golden caster sugar	

Preheat your oven to 110°C/90°C fan/gas ¼. Line 2 baking trays with non-stick baking paper and rub it with a tiny drop of oil.

Using a sieve, drain the chickpeas and measure out 150ml of chickpea water. Pop the chickpeas in the fridge or freezer to use later. Pour the chickpea water into the bowl of your stand mixer (or large mixing bowl), add the salt and whisk on a high speed until the aquafaba is white and very stiff.

In a bowl, combine the sugar and cream of tartar. Turn the mixer speed down a little, then add the sugar to the aquafaba one tablespoon at a time, making sure that each spoonful of sugar has dissolved before you add the next – you can check this by rubbing a little of the mixture between your fingers; if it's grainy keep going.

Continue until all the sugar has gone, then add the vanilla and whisk on high for another

couple of minutes. The meringue should now be looking very thick and glossy; if it's not, keep whisking.

Spoon 10–12 piles of the meringue mixture on to the baking trays, making sure they have a little space to spread and bake for 2 hours until crisp on the outside and caramel-coloured. After two hours, turn the oven off but leave the meringues inside to cool completely – it's really important that you don't open the door while the meringues are cooking or cooling. The meringues will keep for 2 days in a sealed container.

Easy vegetable stock

This recipe is one from *A Modern Way to Eat*. It's a favourite in my house and still my preferred way to make stock. You'll need two 1-litre preserving jars that will fit in your fridge. Don't feel tied to the amounts of veg below – the great thing about stock is that you can use up all the trimmings and odds and ends you have in the fridge. Just work to the same ratio, half-filling your litre jars with veg.

MAKES 2 LITRES

2 carrots, roughly chopped	2 sticks of celery, roughly chopped
1 red onion, cut into wedges	2 bay leaves, scrunched
1 leek, cut into rounds	a small bunch of thyme
	1 teaspoon flaky sea salt
	a few black peppercorns

Fill the kettle and boil it. Divide the chopped veg and other ingredients between your two 1-litre jars. Fill the jars with the just-boiled water, leaving a couple of centimetres' gap at the top – each jar should hold about 750ml. Pop the lids on and leave in a safe place to cool down.

When cool, sieve straight away for a light veg stock, or put into the fridge for 12 hours and then sieve for a more full-bodied stock.

Once sieved, pour the stock back into the jars and store in the fridge, where it will keep for up to a week.

Perfect home-cooked pulses

I have moved from using tinned pulses to cooking my own in big batches and freezing them in portions; they are much more delicious and buttery cooked at home.

The length of time it takes to cook a dried pulse will depend on how long ago it was dried. The older it is, the longer it will take to cook. I encourage you to buy pulses from places where they are less likely to have been sitting around for a long time; supermarkets and anywhere that has loose pulses that you buy by weight are good options.

A note on beans and protein. Pulses have only seven of the essential eight amino acids, which make up a complete protein. But the missing piece of the jigsaw can be filled by grains or sesame seeds, which contain the eighth. So eat your pulses with a little bread or in hummus with tahini.

Soaking
Most beans need an overnight soak in double their volume of fresh cold (ideally filtered) water. Soaking them makes them much easier to digest and reduces their famous side-effects as well as their cooking time; it also allows them to cook more evenly. If you don't have time to soak them, don't fret, as there are a couple of other options. Give them a quick soak, for as much time as you have but ideally for 2 hours, or cook them without soaking – though in my experience the time you save by not soaking them will only be replaced by the extra time they take to cook.

Cooking
Drain the soaked pulses, put them into your largest pan, and cover with cold water to about 3cm above the level of the pulses. Bring to the boil, then boil steadily for 5 minutes

(10 for kidney beans) – this is important, as it deactivates the toxins in the pulses – and after that turn down the heat to a very gentle simmer and cook until tender and creamy. Cooking on a low heat like this will make sure the skins stay intact and that your pulses cook evenly. It is better to shake your pan rather than stir with a wooden spoon, as stirring will break the skins of the pulse. A cooked pulse should remain intact but should collapse into a buttery, creamy mush when squeezed. Chickpeas will remain a little harder but should still be soft throughout. I season my pulses once they are cooked, as seasoning them while cooking is said to toughen them.

Freezing
You can freeze your cooled pulses in their cooking liquid, in portions as they would come in a tin, but I prefer to freeze them without their liquid. I season them well, then drain the liquid and allow the pulses to cool before freezing them in meal-sized bags. If I have time I freeze them on a tray first, to stop them sticking together, and bag them up once frozen.

Soaking and cooking times for dried pulses

Quick
Soak 30 minutes and cook 30–40 minutes.

lentils
moth beans
mung beans
split peas

Short
Soak 2–3 hours and cook 30–40 minutes.

aduki beans
black-eyed beans

Medium
Soak 4 hours and cook 1–1½ hours.

borlotti beans
butter beans
cannellini beans
haricot beans
kidney beans
pinto beans

Long
Soak 8 hours or overnight and cook 1½–3 hours.

chickpeas
fava beans
soya beans

Index